NAVIGATING THE STOCK MARKET

NAVIGATING THE STOCK MARKET

A Practical Guide for Buying, Selling, and AI Risk Management

ARSHAD KHAN

MERCURY LEARNING AND INFORMATION
Boston, Massachusetts

Publisher: David Pallai
MERCURY LEARNING AND INFORMATION
121 High Street, 3rd Floor
Boston, MA 02110
info@merclearning.com
www.merclearning.com
800-232-0223

A. Khan. *Navigating the Stock Market: A Practical Guide for Buying, Selling, and AI Risk Management.*
ISBN: 978-1-50152-277-2

Library of Congress Control Number: 2024930874

242526321   This book is printed on acid-free paper in the United States of America.

CONTENTS

PREFACE

Welcome to the dynamic realm of stock investing, a world brimming with both opportunities and challenges. Embark on a journey through the intricacies of the stock market with *Navigating the Stock Market: A Practical Guide for Buying, Selling, and AI Risk Management*. This book is designed to lead you through the complexities of stock investing, offering valuable insights and practical strategies to enrich your investment experience.

Our systematic approach begins with the foundational elements of "Planning, Research, and Screening," where we emphasize the significance of meticulous planning, thorough research, and effective screening processes as the cornerstone of successful investing.

As you progress, explore the art of making informed investment decisions during the buying process in the "Buying" chapter. Explore the characteristics that distinguish winning stocks and learn to identify potential investment opportunities in "Picking Winning Characteristics." Learn the intricacies of analyzing companies, industries, and sectors in "Company, Industry, and Sector Analysis" to make well-informed investment choices.

The book continues with the strategic art of selling stocks in the "Selling" chapter, where we examine factors guiding decisions to maximize returns. Uncover the mysteries of stock prices and valuation in "Stock Prices and Valuation," essential components for evaluating the true worth of your investments. Explore the significance of profitability and price performance metrics in "Profitability and Price Performance," and understand the widely used P/E ratio as a tool for assessing relative value in "Price/Earnings (P/E) Ratio."

Understand the dynamics of market behavior in "Market Behavior," and gain insights into trends and patterns that impact investment decisions. Explore technical analysis in "Technical Analysis," utilizing charts and indicators to predict future price movements. Learn to monitor economic indicators in "Monitoring the Economy" and discover effective techniques for monitoring stocks, groups, and sectors in "Monitoring Stocks, Groups, and Sectors" to stay ahead of market movements.

Further chapters discuss monitoring market indicators and psychological factors and receive a collection of miscellaneous tips and strategies to enhance your investing prowess. Learn to avoid common pitfalls during buying and selling processes in "Buying and Selling Mistakes to Avoid" and then gain insights into general mistakes investors often make in "Common Mistakes to Avoid." Take a comprehensive look at risk management strategies in "Risk Management" to safeguard your investment portfolio.

This journey not only imparts traditional investment wisdom but also navigates through the cutting-edge landscape of AI-driven stock market activities. In the chapter "AI in Stock Investing," we explore the evolving role of AI in shaping investment strategies, uncovering opportunities for enhancing decision-making processes, and maximizing returns through algorithmic trading and predictive analytics.

The subsequent chapter, "AI Risks and How to Mitigate Them," addresses the challenges posed by the integration of AI in stock market activities. Understand algorithmic bias, opacity, and potential pitfalls, and gain practical strategies to mitigate these risks. Emphasizing transparency initiatives, ethical considerations, and collaborative regulatory efforts, this chapter builds a resilient and trustworthy financial ecosystem.

Whether you are a novice investor or a seasoned veteran, this book aims to empower you with the knowledge and tools necessary to make sound investment decisions. May your stock investing journey be both rewarding and enlightening.

Happy investing!

A. Khan
February 2024

1

PLANNING, RESEARCH, AND SCREENING

BASIC REQUIREMENTS FOR STOCK MARKET INVESTING

In this section, aspiring investors will discover the fundamental principles and essential prerequisites, laying a solid foundation for navigating the complexities of the stock market with confidence and strategic insight.

Understand the Difference Between Saving and Investing

Understanding the key distinction between saving and investing is essential for making informed financial decisions. When individuals opt to save their money in a traditional savings account, they typically earn a fixed rate of return. While this approach offers the benefit of security and the assurance that the funds will not be subjected to significant risk, it comes with the drawback of very low interest rates. Over time, the saved funds do not experience any substantial growth or appreciation. In contrast, when individuals choose to invest their money, the returns they receive are contingent on the price appreciation or depreciation of their chosen investment vehicles. Investing inherently carries a degree of risk, and it is crucial to grasp the fundamental concept that higher potential rewards are often associated with higher levels of risk. This recognition is particularly pertinent when contemplating ventures into the stock market, where the potential for substantial returns comes with the inherent volatility of the market.

It is important to note that even a seemingly modest increase in the rate of return, such as 1%–2%, can have a significant impact on the growth of an investment over time in comparison to a traditional savings account. For instance, consider a $10,000 investment that yields a 2% higher return, for example 10% instead of 8%. Over a 30-year period, this seemingly small difference can translate into more than $73,000 in additional returns. This highlights the potential for investing to substantially outpace traditional savings in terms of wealth accumulation over the long term. Therefore, individuals must weigh the trade-offs between the safety of saving and the growth potential of investing when making financial decisions that align with their risk tolerance and long-term financial goals.

Being Too Conservative Can Be Risky

Over the course of history, it has become evident that an overly conservative approach to investments can entail its own set of risks. Since 1926, stocks have consistently outperformed the inflation rate, exhibiting a significant advantage over fixed-income investments. This historical data underscores a key principle: the greater the short-term volatility an investment exhibits, the more potential it has to outpace the rate of inflation over an extended period. While stock market investments may exhibit short-term fluctuations and volatility, they have demonstrated their ability to not only keep pace with inflation, but to outperform both inflation and fixed income securities in the long run. Consequently, considering the long-term implications of inflation and the uncertainty surrounding future financial needs, excessively conservative investment strategies may prove riskier than they initially appear.

In essence, an overly conservative investment approach can lead to the erosion of purchasing power over time, particularly in the face of inflation. As the cost of living gradually rises, investments that fail to yield returns that outstrip inflation can inadvertently diminish the real value of one's savings. In contrast, a judicious allocation of assets that includes a balanced exposure to stocks can serve as a hedge against inflation, ensuring that the growth of investments keeps pace with, and potentially exceeds, the rising cost of goods and services over the long term. Therefore, it is essential for investors to consider not only the short-term volatility but also the long-term potential for wealth preservation when making investment decisions, avoiding the pitfall of being excessively conservative to safeguard their financial future.

The Need to Believe in the Stock Market

Investing in the stock market is a decision that should be underpinned by a fundamental belief in its potential to generate superior returns. This belief forms the cornerstone of a successful investment strategy because it is essential to have confidence in the market's ability to deliver long-term financial growth, even in the face of inherent risks. Believing in the stock market means understanding that it can provide substantial rewards, but it requires a commitment to serious investment and a willingness to navigate the associated uncertainties. If you harbor doubts or lack the dedication to dedicate time and effort to your investments, it may be prudent to steer clear of the stock market.

In such circumstances, there are alternative avenues available. You can consider entrusting your funds to a mutual fund or a professional money management company. These entities are staffed with experienced professionals who can manage your investments on your behalf, helping you benefit from the potential of the stock market without having to actively engage in the investment process. While it is crucial to believe in the stock market to invest directly, partnering with these financial institutions can offer a more hands-off approach, providing you with the opportunity to benefit from the market's potential while leaving the intricacies of investment management to experts. Ultimately, the decision hinges on your level of conviction, commitment, and your personal financial goals.

Should You Invest in Stocks or Stay Away From Them?

Investing in stocks or staying away from them should be a decision tailored to individual financial circumstances and objectives. Two distinct groups of individuals can benefit from or should consider avoiding stock market investments. The first group comprises those individuals who are in the process of building capital. For these individuals, whose savings tend to grow slowly, the primary objectives revolve around not only facilitating the growth of their savings but also protecting their capital from the erosive effects of inflation, which can gradually erode its value over time. By venturing into the stock market, they aim to harness the potential for higher returns that can outpace inflation, thus ensuring that their accumulated wealth maintains or increases its real value over time.

Conversely, the other group of individuals who should carefully consider minimizing their exposure to stocks or even staying away from them entirely are those who cannot afford to risk their capital, require access to funds in the near term, or are closer to retirement age. This group encompasses individuals who have already accumulated capital and are primarily concerned with preserving their wealth from the corrosive impact of inflation, rather than aggressively pursuing substantial growth. Those in or nearing retirement often prioritize capital preservation and immediate liquidity to meet their financial needs and lifestyle, making them less suited for the inherent volatility of the stock market. Thus, understanding one's financial goals, risk tolerance, and stage of life is pivotal in determining whether to embrace stock market investments or opt for more conservative financial strategies.

Appreciate the Power of Compounding

Understanding and appreciating the power of compounding is a fundamental principle in the realm of finance that can have a profound impact on the accumulation of capital over time. Even a relatively small variance in the compound rate can lead to significant differences in the growth of investments. This concept becomes particularly evident when considering the performance of stocks. For instance, if an individual invests in a stock with an annual compound growth rate of 12%, that stock will double in value in just six years. In contrast, a stock growing at a more modest rate of 8% will take nine years to double in value. This simple illustration underscores the importance of selecting investments that exhibit above-average growth rates for investors seeking high returns through capital gains.

It is worth noting that while growth stocks have the potential to be more profitable than income-generating stocks, they also come with a higher degree of risk and volatility. Investors aiming for substantial returns should weigh the potential benefits of investing in growth stocks against the increased level of risk associated with them. The choice between growth and income-generating stocks should be aligned with an individual's risk tolerance, investment horizon, and financial objectives. Acknowledging the power of compounding and the relationship between growth rates and investment outcomes is crucial for making informed investment decisions that can foster the long-term accumulation of capital.

Use the Rule of 72 Tool

The "rule of 72" is a valuable tool in the world of finance that provides a quick and easy method to estimate the time it takes for an investment to double in value based on its expected rate of return. This rule is particularly helpful for investors to gauge the potential growth of their investments over time. The rule of 72 is applied by dividing the number 72 by the anticipated annual rate of return for the investment. For example, let's consider an investment that is projected to grow at a 4% annual rate. By performing the calculation of 72 divided by 4, the result is 18, which signifies that it will take eighteen years for the investment to double at the 4% rate of return. In the case of a more robust rate of return, such as 8%, the rule of 72 demonstrates that the investment would double in a mere nine years (72 divided by 8).

This rule serves as a valuable tool for investors to quickly evaluate and compare the growth potential of different investment opportunities. It offers a simplified yet effective way to understand the impact of compounding and the significance of various rates of return on wealth accumulation. By employing the rule of 72, investors can make more informed decisions about their investment strategies, helping them set realistic financial goals and plan for the future with a clearer understanding of the timeframes involved in their investment objectives.

OBJECTIVE AND METHOD

In this section, investors will gain clarity on defining their investment goals and adopting a methodical investing approach, laying the groundwork for a purposeful and systematic approach to successful stock investing.

Determine Your Objectives

Setting clear investment objectives is a critical first step when contemplating stock market investments. These objectives serve as a compass, guiding your investment strategy and helping you make informed decisions that align with your financial goals. Understanding your rate of return expectations and risk tolerance is vital in this process. For investors with conservative expectations and a low tolerance for risk, or those with a shorter time horizon, alternative investment vehicles that are less volatile may be more suitable. By defining your objectives, you can establish a foundation for making informed investment choices.

Once your objectives are well-defined, you can more accurately assess how to allocate your funds in the stock market. This includes determining the percentage of your portfolio that you are comfortable investing in stocks. The allocation decision should reflect your risk tolerance and time horizon. If you seek higher returns and can bear the associated risk, you may opt for a larger allocation to stocks. Conversely, if you prioritize capital preservation or have a shorter investment horizon, a smaller allocation to stocks might be more prudent. Your objectives also play a crucial role in guiding your stock selection. By clarifying your investment goals, you can choose stocks that align with your objectives, whether you're seeking income, capital growth, or a combination of both. Therefore, establishing your objectives is a pivotal part of the investment process, helping you tailor your investment strategy to your specific financial needs and circumstances.

Follow a Simple Investing Approach

Adopting a straightforward and uncomplicated investing approach is prudent advice, especially for those who are not professional investors. While the financial world can be rife with complex investment strategies, theories, and jargon, it is crucial not to be overwhelmed or confused by these intricacies. Instead, investors should focus on identifying and adhering to simple yet effective rules. These rules should be well-founded, time-tested, and have demonstrated their reliability in the market over the years. By choosing straightforward, proven guidelines, investors can navigate the markets with greater clarity and confidence.

Without a set of well-defined rules, investing can become a haphazard and unpredictable endeavor. It is possible to achieve success occasionally, but the likelihood of maintaining consistent success becomes considerably low. Hence, having a set of straightforward and dependable rules in place is pivotal for making informed and disciplined investment decisions. Furthermore, it is equally important to rigorously follow these rules once they have been established. A disciplined approach to investing ensures that you adhere to your pre-defined strategy and resist impulsive decisions that can be driven by emotions or short-term market fluctuations. This steadfast commitment to your rules can help you maintain a consistent and rational approach to investing, ultimately contributing to more sound and rewarding financial outcomes.

Define Your Method and Follow It

Establishing a well-defined and methodical approach to investing is a crucial prerequisite for achieving consistent success in the financial markets. Your chosen method should be a clear, systematic framework that outlines the decision-making process for both buying and selling investments. These rules can range from being simple to more intricate, depending on your individual investment approach and temperament. For instance, a well-defined buying rule might specify that you will only invest in companies with an annual earnings growth rate exceeding 20% and a price-earnings (P/E) ratio below 25. Similarly, a clear selling rule could mandate that you sell a stock if it experiences a decline of more than 10% or fails to meet its earnings expectations.

Once your method is in place, it is imperative to follow it consistently. While you may choose to adapt or refine your method over time based on the insights and experience you gain, it is essential to avoid frequent or impulsive changes. Consistency in following your defined method helps you avoid knee-jerk reactions to market fluctuations and emotional decision-making, which can be detrimental to your investment performance. By adhering to your established rules and making adjustments thoughtfully and methodically, you can maintain a structured and rational approach to investing, enhancing your ability to make informed and calculated decisions in the ever-changing world of financial markets.

Follow Your Method With Discipline

An established investment method is not a temporary or occasional guideline; rather, it is intended to serve as a long-term framework for your financial journey. It is crucial to understand that once you have defined and implemented a method, you must adhere to it consistently and with unwavering discipline. This means not altering or abandoning your method due to isolated poor trades or unique experiences. Emotional reactions to temporary setbacks or unexpected market events can lead to impulsive decisions that can be detrimental to your investment performance. It is essential to resist the temptation to deviate from your method, even in the face of daily market fluctuations or news unless such developments genuinely impact the fundamentals and business prospects of the companies in your portfolio.

While strict adherence to your method is paramount, this does not preclude periodic review, analysis, and refinement. Regularly evaluating the effectiveness of your chosen method is a healthy practice. If, over time, it becomes evident that your method is not producing the desired results, you should consider adjustments or even adopting a new approach that has the potential for success. This is a proactive way to adapt to changing market conditions and refine your strategy to align better with your financial goals. In summary, a disciplined and unwavering commitment to your method, combined with a willingness to adapt and evolve, when necessary, is essential for achieving long-term success in the world of investing.

Have a Long-Term Horizon

Embracing a long-term horizon is a fundamental principle of successful investing. While trading can be a profitable strategy for some, it is important to distinguish between the objectives, techniques, and methods of traders and investors, as they are inherently different. Investors are focused on building wealth over the long term and should resist becoming overly concerned with the day-to-day fluctuations and market gyrations that traders may prioritize. Patience is a key attribute for investors, and it is crucial to remain committed to stocks with the potential to outperform the market. Having the discipline to hold onto or even add to your investments during both declining and rising market conditions is essential for capitalizing on long-term opportunities.

It is vital to adopt an attitude that acknowledges the inevitability of some investments underperforming or encountering setbacks. Over time, learning from these experiences and continually striving to improve your investment performance is the path to outpacing the average investor. This process of continuous learning and adaptation allows investors to refine their strategies, make more informed decisions, and enhance their overall investment outcomes. By embracing a long-term mindset, remaining patient, and learning from both successes and setbacks, investors can position themselves for greater success in building and preserving wealth over time.

STRATEGY AND APPROACH FOR STOCK MARKET INVESTING

This section delves into the nuanced art of crafting effective investment strategies, adopting proven approaches to navigate the dynamic stock market landscape with confidence.

Do Not Invest Without a Strategy

Having a well-defined investment strategy is an absolute imperative for anyone looking to enter the world of investing. The key is not necessarily the sophistication of the strategy, but the discipline in following one. A strategy provides you with a structured framework for your investments, helping you make informed decisions that align with your objectives and risk tolerance. A myriad of established investment strategies and techniques, developed based on the cumulative experience of successful investors over many years, are available to guide you. These strategies encompass various approaches and objectives, catering to different financial goals and market conditions. Some of the most prominent strategic approaches include growth, momentum, and value investing, each with its own unique principles and methods.

It is important to acknowledge that not all investment strategies work equally well in all investment environments, and some may falter due to changing market conditions. This underscores the significance of staying informed and adaptable in your approach. Markets are dynamic, and what was successful in the past may not yield the same results in the future. Thus, investors should periodically review and assess the effectiveness of their chosen strategy and be prepared to make adjustments when necessary to stay aligned with evolving financial landscapes. The overarching principle is that a well-considered strategy provides you with a roadmap for your investments, enabling you to navigate the complexities of the financial markets with greater confidence and purpose.

Select an Investment Strategy Before You Start Investing

Selecting your investment strategy is a pivotal step that should precede any actual investment. This decision should be grounded in a thorough understanding of your investment objectives, your expectations regarding returns, and the level of risk you find acceptable. Your chosen strategy serves as the compass that guides your investment journey and helps you make informed decisions that align with your financial goals. By identifying and selecting a strategy that matches your individual circumstances, you are laying the foundation for a more purposeful and potentially successful investment approach.

Once your strategy is in place, it is essential to implement it methodically and with unwavering discipline. Regardless of the specific strategy you choose, whether its growth, value, income, or a combination thereof, successful investors tend to be those who rigorously adhere to their chosen strategy's rules. By consistently following these rules, investors can mitigate impulsive decisions and emotional reactions to market fluctuations. Investors who fail to implement their strategy with discipline often find themselves on the losing side in the stock market, as they may succumb to erratic and inconsistent decision-making that is disconnected from their defined investment strategy.

Create Your Own Strategy for Better Alignment

Experienced investors often tailor and fine-tune established strategies to better align with their individual financial goals, risk tolerance, and personal experiences. These adjustments prove advantageous, especially when circumstances or objectives deviate from the standard framework of commonly recognized strategies. Some seasoned investors go a step further, venturing into the creation of entirely new investment approaches tailored to their unique needs and preferences. Such strategies may result from innovative thinking or a creative synthesis of existing principles. It is crucial to recognize that developing new strategies carries inherent risks, demanding only those with extensive experience and a high degree of sophistication in the field of investing to undertake significant experimentation.

Creating a novel investment strategy, particularly one based on untested or unconventional principles, requires a deep understanding of financial markets and a willingness to accept potentially high levels of risk. While such experimentation can yield valuable insights and substantial rewards, it also entails the potential for significant losses. For the majority of investors, adhering to established and proven strategies is generally a more prudent approach. Those with extensive knowledge and a strong risk appetite are best suited for engaging in the creation and testing of new investment approaches, while others may be better served by following established methodologies.

Do Not Use Unproven Strategies

Utilizing unproven or experimental investment strategies should be approached with caution, and it is generally advisable to avoid them unless you are a highly experienced investor who is comfortable with the associated risks. Unproven strategies lack a track record of success and may not have been thoroughly tested in real-world market conditions. For less experienced investors or those who have not fully analyzed the potential risks, it is often wiser to stick with well-established and time-tested strategies that have demonstrated their efficacy in various market cycles.

Combining multiple established strategies, such as growth, value, and momentum, can indeed be complex and may present challenges due to the potential for conflicting signals. Each of these strategies has its own set of principles and objectives, and they may not always align cohesively. When combining them, investors should be aware of the inherent trade-offs and complexities involved. Unless you have a profound understanding of how these strategies interact and have the expertise to navigate potential contradictions, it is generally safer to opt for a single, well-defined strategy that aligns more clearly with your investment goals and risk tolerance. In doing so, investors can maintain a more focused and disciplined approach, which is often conducive to more consistent and informed investment decisions.

Growth Investing Approach

The growth investing approach is one of the most widely practiced strategies in the world of investing. This approach is characterized by its primary objective, which is to invest in companies that are experiencing rapid growth in their business operations. The rationale behind growth investing is that companies with above-average growth rates and strong earnings prospects are likely to witness substantial price appreciation in their stock values over time. Investors who follow this approach have an underlying expectation that a growth stock's earnings will continue to expand at a superior rate, leading to the assumption that this growth will be reflected in a higher stock price.

The specific level of growth sought in a growth investment can vary significantly according to individual investor needs and requirements. The minimum requirement typically involves seeking a growth rate that surpasses the overall market's average. Beyond this baseline, the criteria for growth investing are determined by various factors, including the investor's risk profile (conservative, moderate, or high-risk) and the nature of the growth company in question. Established, large-cap companies might provide more stable growth opportunities, whereas smaller, more aggressive firms may offer greater growth potential but come with increased risk.

Value Investing Approach

Value investing is a widely practiced investment approach that focuses on identifying and investing in undervalued companies. The primary objective of value investors is to locate companies whose current market prices significantly undervalue their true intrinsic or liquidating value. These undervalued stocks are often viewed as opportunities to generate substantial profits with a comparatively lower level of risk because the downside potential for these beaten-down stocks is perceived to be limited. Value investors assess the genuine worth of these companies by examining factors such as their earnings and dividend potential, as well as their asset values. A crucial metric that value investors frequently look at is the P/E ratio, preferring companies with lower P/E ratios as they are seen as more attractively priced. However, it is important to recognize that an exceptionally low P/E ratio can signal the market's concerns about the company's performance and reduced earnings expectations. As a result, there is a risk that such undervalued stocks may stagnate, potentially tying up capital for an extended period. Before investing in an undervalued stock, it is imperative to understand the reasons behind its undervaluation and assess the potential for a turnaround.

Successful value investing requires a careful evaluation of the reasons for a stock's undervaluation and a comprehensive assessment of the prospects for the company to regain favor among investors. Value investors are often looking for companies that are temporarily out of favor or have been overlooked by the broader market, and they believe that these companies have the potential to recover in the long run. A thorough analysis of a company's financial health, competitive positioning, and management quality is essential to determine whether the undervaluation is justified and if there is a reasonable expectation for the stock to appreciate in value over time. Therefore, value investing is a strategy that involves in-depth research and a focus on acquiring assets that are perceived to be trading below their true worth, with the expectation that their value will ultimately be recognized by the market.

Momentum Investing Approach

Momentum investing is one of the three predominant approaches in the world of stock investing and is often characterized as "buying because others are buying." In this strategy, investment decisions revolve around chart patterns and the momentum of stock prices and earnings. Momentum stocks are typically defined by their rapidly growing earnings and/or strong price appreciation trends. However, it is crucial to understand that momentum investors have a strong proclivity to swiftly sell a stock at the first sign of a slowdown in either earnings growth or price appreciation momentum. This approach is associated with a high level of risk, as it can lead to substantial losses. The underlying reason for this risk is that, when any hint of trouble arises, momentum investors tend to exit en masse, which can amplify what might have been a minor decline under normal circumstances.

Momentum investing is characterized by its dynamic and responsive nature, with investors making quick and reactive decisions based on short-term trends and signals. The primary allure of this approach is the potential for rapid and substantial gains when stocks are in favor, but it also carries a heightened level of risk due to the speed at which investors can exit positions when momentum starts to wane. As a result, momentum investing is often viewed as a strategy best suited for experienced and disciplined investors who are adept at closely monitoring market conditions and reacting swiftly to changes in momentum. For those who employ this approach, it is essential to have a solid understanding of the potential risks and to exercise caution in order to mitigate potential losses.

How to Combine Investment Strategies

Combining investment strategies can be a prudent approach to diversify your portfolio and potentially mitigate risk while seeking opportunities for growth. One way to achieve this is by allocating a specific percentage of your portfolio funds to different strategies. For instance, you could allocate 75% of your portfolio to the growth strategy while simultaneously, the remaining 25% of your portfolio funds could be dedicated to the value or momentum strategy, depending on your objectives. This combination allows you to harness the strengths of different strategies, balancing the potential for capital appreciation and the opportunities presented by undervalued or momentum-driven stocks.

However, it is vital to establish clear guidelines and allocate percentages for each strategy at the outset. These guidelines should be informed by your investment objectives, risk tolerance, and the specific characteristics of the strategies you are employing. This structured approach ensures that your portfolio is well-diversified and aligns with your individual financial goals. By adhering to these predetermined allocations, you can benefit from the merits of each strategy while maintaining a disciplined and well-balanced investment approach. This flexibility can be particularly advantageous for investors who seek a multifaceted approach to portfolio management.

RESEARCH SOURCES AND TECHNIQUES

This section guides investors in their quest for sourcing reliable information and employing effective research techniques, empowering them to make informed decisions, and conduct thorough analyses for successful stock market investing.

Research Using Multiple Sources

Conducting thorough and extensive research is a fundamental step in making informed investment decisions. It is important to recognize that there is a multitude of sources available to assist you in your investment research. Initially, it may require some time and effort to identify reliable sources that align with your specific investment research objectives. It is a crucial point to understand that no single source can provide you with all the information you need to make well-informed investment choices. To that end, diversify your research by leveraging various sources, which can include the Internet, newspapers, newsletters, personal contacts, brokerage firms, and even direct communication with the companies you are considering for investment.

The Internet, in particular, has become a valuable and easily accessible resource for gathering information about companies, markets, and financial news. It provides a vast repository of data, research reports, and insights that can be instrumental in your research process. Newspapers and newsletters often offer in-depth analyses, expert opinions, and financial news that can provide a well-rounded perspective on the investment landscape. Additionally, personal contacts and communication with brokerage firms can provide valuable insights and recommendations based on their expertise and experience. Connecting directly with the companies you are interested in can also yield insights into their operations, strategies, and financial health. By diversifying your sources of information and conducting extensive research, you can enhance your ability to make well-informed investment decisions that align with your financial goals and risk tolerance.

Make the Internet Your Friend

Leveraging the Internet is an invaluable strategy for investors looking to gather comprehensive and up-to-date information. The digital realm offers a wealth of resources that can cater to virtually any investment research need. Numerous websites provide free access to a plethora of investment research materials. These resources encompass a wide range of information, such as concise business summaries and in-depth analyses, up-to-the-minute stock quotes and charts, company-specific research reports, the latest company news, updates on competitors, earnings reports, stock screening and analysis tools, summary recommendations, investment newsletters, market summaries, details on investment conferences, historical market data, and much more.

One of the key advantages of using the Internet for investment research is the accessibility to real-time data and a vast array of resources that can facilitate a more thorough understanding of the companies and markets you are interested in. Investors can conveniently track news, market trends, and company-specific information from the comfort of their own devices. This immediate access to a wide spectrum of financial information empowers investors to make more informed decisions, identify emerging opportunities, and stay attuned to market developments, all of which are critical for successful investment management.

Use the Investor's Business Daily

An invaluable resource for investment research is Investor's Business Daily (*IBD*), which is widely regarded as one of the top investment newspapers. *IBD*, available online at investors.com, offers a comprehensive suite of tools and information to aid in research on individual stocks and the broader market. Beyond delivering basic daily stock prices and performance data, *IBD* provides a wealth of additional features and insights, making it a valuable asset for investors. The newspaper offers daily market analysis and charts, facilitating an in-depth understanding of market trends and conditions. Furthermore, *IBD* offers extensive research on individual companies with the potential to become market leaders, providing investors with critical information for stock selection.

In addition to individual stock research, *IBD* offers a host of other essential resources, including industry, group, and sector charts that help identify trends and relative performance. Psychological indicators and options data are also available, aiding investors in making informed decisions and managing their portfolios. *IBD* goes beyond the numbers by providing pertinent business news and analysis that can impact investment decisions. It is a must-read for serious investors who value comprehensive, data-driven insights and wish to stay ahead in the fast-paced world of investing. With *IBD*'s comprehensive suite of tools and resources, investors can gain a more profound understanding of the market and individual companies, enabling them to make well-informed investment choices.

Do Not Use Unreliable Research Sources and Data

Caution is paramount when it comes to choosing research sources for investment decisions. While there is a wealth of information available, it is essential to recognize the limitations and potential pitfalls that can arise from unreliable or outdated data. One major concern is the accuracy of information and data from various sources. Inaccurate or flawed data can lead to misguided investment decisions, as it can create a false basis for analysis and conclusions. Therefore, it is crucial to scrutinize and validate the sources to ensure that the data you rely on is trustworthy and precise.

Another issue to watch out for is the timeliness of the information. Outdated data, especially regarding financial metrics like the P/E ratio or earnings reports, can seriously impact your investment analysis and decision-making. Using data that is several months old may not accurately represent a company's current financial health or the market's current conditions. Hence, it is essential to seek out sources that provide up-to-date and relevant data, which is critical for making informed investment choices. Furthermore, in the age of the Internet, some sources may have hidden agendas or biases, potentially disseminating information or news articles with ulterior motives. It is essential to approach sources with a discerning eye and be cautious about the credibility and intentions behind the information they present. To make well-informed investment decisions, select your research sources carefully, prioritize data accuracy and timeliness, and remain vigilant for potential biases or hidden agendas that could skew your understanding of the market and investment options.

Use Reliable Sources for Earnings Data

When it comes to earnings data, accuracy and timeliness are paramount, as this information forms the bedrock of many crucial investment decisions. Serious investors understand that using inaccurate or outdated earnings data can lead to misguided conclusions and investments. To ensure the reliability of your earnings data, it is imperative to turn to trusted and reputable sources. Several established sources excel in providing accurate and up-to-date earnings data, making them invaluable to investors. Some of the most esteemed sources for earnings data include Thomson Reuters, Zacks, Standard & Poor's, and Value Line.

These sources are renowned for their commitment to data accuracy and their ability to deliver earnings data in a timely manner. Investors can rely on them for insights into estimated and historical earnings, enabling them to make well-informed investment decisions based on a solid foundation of financial information. By utilizing these trusted sources, investors can enhance their ability to assess companies and industries with confidence, knowing they have access to reliable earnings data that is instrumental in their investment research and strategy development.

Study Research Reports

Studying company research and earnings estimate reports is an essential practice for any serious investor before making investment decisions. These reports offer a wealth of consolidated information, presenting a comprehensive view of the company's performance and prospects. A typical research report includes vital data on various aspects of the company, encompassing its business operations, financial health, earnings estimates, insider trading activities, as well as insights on competitors and the industry in which the company operates. These reports are invaluable for investors as they provide both current and historical data, allowing for a thorough analysis of a company's past performance and future potential.

The information contained within these reports serves as a critical resource for investors seeking to make informed investment choices. By delving into the details of a company's research report, investors can gain a deeper understanding of its strengths and weaknesses, competitive positioning, and potential growth prospects. These reports often come from trusted sources, such as brokerage firms and financial research institutions, and are compiled by experienced analysts who provide valuable insights and guidance. In essence, studying research reports enhances an investor's ability to make well-informed investment decisions grounded in a robust foundation of data and analysis.

Sources for Research Reports

Acquiring company research reports can be a straightforward process with a range of accessible sources. The initial point of contact for obtaining these reports is often the company itself. Companies maintain access to a variety of research reports from multiple sources and are typically willing to share them with interested investors. Contacting the company's investor relations department or visiting their official website is a common approach to requesting these reports.

Brokers are another convenient and reliable source for obtaining research reports. Many brokerage firms offer access to a wide array of research reports on companies, industries, and markets. They often provide these reports to their clients as part of their services, making it easy for investors to access valuable information to aid in their decision-making process. In addition to these traditional sources, numerous online platforms offer research reports from trusted providers. These online resources give investors the flexibility to access research reports at their convenience and offer a wide selection of reports that cater to various industries and companies. By tapping into these diverse sources, investors can equip themselves with the research reports needed to make informed and well-rounded investment decisions.

Study the 10K Report

When conducting investment research, it is crucial to approach company reports with a discerning eye, as annual reports published by companies tend to be marketing-oriented and often emphasize the positive aspects of their performance. Relying solely on these reports can lead to a skewed perspective, and serious investors understand the importance of considering additional sources of information that provide a more balanced view. One such source that plays a pivotal role in this regard is the 10K report, a comprehensive document that all companies are mandated to submit to the Securities and Exchange Commission (SEC). The 10K report offers a deeper and more accurate insight into the true financial health and operational standing of the issuing company. It goes beyond the glossy image portrayed in annual reports and delves into crucial details such as risks the company faces, business conditions, and other relevant information that is instrumental in evaluating whether the company's stock is a sound investment.

By studying the 10K report, investors can access an in-depth understanding of the company's operations, performance, and potential challenges. This document provides a more transparent and objective view, highlighting both the strengths and weaknesses of the company. It is an invaluable resource for investors who seek a comprehensive and balanced perspective, which is critical for making well-informed investment decisions. The 10K report can help investors navigate beyond the marketing rhetoric and gain a clearer picture of the risks and opportunities associated with a particular company.

Reach Out to the Company

Engaging directly with the company is a proactive and valuable approach for obtaining investment information. Companies typically maintain investor relations departments that are dedicated to assisting shareholders and potential investors. When inquiring about investment research data and relevant information pertaining to the company, do not hesitate to reach out to these departments. They can provide a range of materials beyond the annual report, including press releases, product information, the 10K report, and analysts' research reports on the company. These resources offer a more in-depth and up-to-date understanding of the company's operations, performance, and strategic initiatives.

Most companies are receptive to shareholders' and potential investors' concerns and requests, and they prioritize providing accurate and relevant information. Establishing contact with the Investor Relations department is often a straightforward process, and it can yield valuable insights that contribute to your investment research and decision-making. Whether you have specific questions or require additional data to inform your investment choices, companies are typically willing and able to assist, ensuring that you have the resources needed to make well-informed investment decisions. This direct line of communication with the company can be an invaluable asset for investors looking to gain a more comprehensive view of the company's financial health and prospects.

Listen in on Conference Calls

Listening in on company conference calls is an effective and insightful way for investors to gain valuable information about the company and its business prospects. These calls are typically scheduled following the release of a company's quarterly earnings results and provide a platform for executives to elaborate on the key points and implications of the reported performance. During these calls, company executives delve into the details of their recently announced results, offering a comprehensive perspective on the factors influencing their financial performance, strategic initiatives, and future outlook. Conference calls can offer an opportunity for investors to gain direct insights from the company's leadership, making them a vital resource for those looking to make informed investment decisions.

To participate in or listen to these conference calls, investors can access schedules through various Internet platforms. This accessibility enables investors to stay up to date with the latest developments and assessments presented by the company's management, further enriching their understanding of the company's operations and future prospects. By tuning into these calls, investors can access valuable firsthand information that complements their investment research, allowing for a more comprehensive assessment of the company and its potential as an investment.

What to Focus on During Conference Calls

Conference calls provide a treasure trove of essential information that investors can leverage for making well-informed decisions. During these calls, company officials typically outline the key highlights of the recently completed quarter, offering a detailed examination of their financial performance. This includes a breakdown of the results; including revenue, earnings, and other crucial financial metrics. Additionally, these calls often feature the presentation of strategic insights and discussions about the implications of financial statements.

Perhaps one of the most valuable aspects of conference calls is the forward-looking guidance provided by company executives. This guidance offers investors insight into the company's future prospects and strategies, helping them gauge the potential for growth or challenges in the coming quarters. Furthermore, these calls often feature questions from participants, including analysts, which can offer valuable insights that may not be readily available elsewhere. Listening to the conference calls, especially for the companies within your portfolio and particularly your largest holdings, is a prudent practice. It equips you with a deeper understanding of the company's performance and future outlook, allowing you to make investment decisions based on a comprehensive view of the company's operations and prospects.

Attend Shareholders' Meetings

Attending a company's shareholders' meeting is a valuable opportunity for investors to gain firsthand insights and information about the company's operations and prospects. These meetings often feature formal company presentations that provide a detailed overview of the company's performance, highlighting successes, challenges, current conditions, and future business prospects. This information, presented by company executives, offers investors a direct and comprehensive understanding of the company's strategies and outlook, serving as a critical resource for informed investment decisions.

One of the most beneficial aspects of shareholders' meetings is the interactive nature of these gatherings. The question-and-answer sessions that follow the presentations provide a platform for investors to seek clarification on specific issues, request additional information, or gain insights into aspects of the company's performance that may not be readily available elsewhere. Informal exchanges with the company's officers and other shareholders also provide opportunities for productive discussions and networking. These interactions can enhance an investor's understanding of the company and offer insights into its operations and strategies from multiple perspectives. By attending shareholders' meetings, investors can fortify their knowledge and develop a deeper appreciation of the company.

SCREENING

In this section, investors will discover the art of systematically filtering and evaluating stocks based on specific criteria, honing their skills to identify promising opportunities, and build a resilient portfolio.

Use a Proven Method for Picking Winners

In the dynamic and often unpredictable realm of the stock market, employing a proven method for picking winners is a prudent approach, particularly for investors who may not have the extensive experience of seasoned professionals. The stock market is not an arena for experimentation unless you are a highly experienced investor who has witnessed the market's multifaceted nature over many years and economic cycles. Until reaching that level of expertise, utilizing established methods such as the CANSLIM method, developed by the renowned investor William O'Neil, is a wise strategy. CANSLIM represents seven key characteristics that underpin the method, each serving as a fundamental pillar for stock selection. This approach is rooted in sound fundamentals and combines both fundamental and technical analysis to identify promising investment opportunities.

The CANSLIM method relies on a set of variables to pick winners, including crucial factors like current quarterly earnings per share, annual earnings per share growth, and price performance. By integrating these essential metrics, investors can assess a company's financial health, growth prospects, and stock price momentum, enabling them to make well-informed investment choices. Employing a proven method like CANSLIM offers a structured and systematic approach to identifying winning stocks in a market characterized by volatility and complexity. It provides a robust framework that enhances the investor's ability to make sound investment decisions in line with their financial goals and risk tolerance.

Search for Growth Companies

When seeking profitable stock investments, a primary focus should be on identifying fast-growing growth companies. These companies can be found across a spectrum of industries and sectors within the economy. However, it is important to note that a significant concentration of fast-growing companies lies within the technology sector. The tech industry is renowned for its innovation and disruptive potential, making it a fertile ground for discovering companies with rapid growth trajectories. Beyond technology, other sectors also offer notable opportunities, with financial services and the health-care sector, particularly biotechnology, standing out as potential growth hotspots. These sectors are poised for substantial expansion over the coming decades, primarily due to the anticipated high demand driven by the aging of the baby boomer generation.

By focusing your search on growth companies within these industries, you can position yourself to benefit from their potential for robust and sustained expansion. These companies are often characterized by innovation, strong revenue and earnings growth, and the capacity to tap into emerging trends and markets. Investing in such companies can offer the prospect of significant capital appreciation, making them a valuable component of a diversified investment portfolio.

Recognize and Pick Winning Indicators

When it comes to stock market analysis, selecting and using the right indicators is a crucial aspect of the screening and selection process. While there are countless indicators available for investors to consider, it is essential to exercise selectivity and focus on a few key indicators that are practical, powerful, and compatible with your chosen investment approach, whether its growth, momentum, or value. These indicators serve as tools for gauging a company's financial health, performance, and potential, and they play a significant role in your investment strategy.

While the indicators employed by the various investment approaches may differ, there are some common indicators that have relevance across the board. These universal indicators serve as valuable tools in assessing potential investment opportunities and can help investors make well-informed decisions regardless of their chosen investment strategy. By recognizing and picking these winning indicators, investors can equip themselves with a comprehensive set of tools to evaluate and select stocks that align with their investment objectives and risk tolerance.

Indicator Values to Use

It is crucial to recognize that the values assigned to indicators can vary significantly among different investment approaches, and these values are often tailored to match the specific strategy's objectives and risk tolerance. Take, for example, the earnings growth indicator. A momentum investor, who seeks stocks with rapid price appreciation, may set a high bar, requiring a minimum of 40% earnings growth as a screening criterion. This investor places a premium on companies exhibiting explosive growth potential. In contrast, a growth investor may opt for a slightly lower threshold, being content with a 25% earnings growth rate, as they still prioritize strong growth but may not require the same level of explosive earnings expansion.

Conversely, a very conservative value investor, who prioritizes safety and stability, may set a more modest benchmark of 10% for earnings growth. This approach emphasizes companies with consistent and reliable financial performance, even if the growth rate is more modest. These variations in indicator values underscore the significance of aligning the selection criteria with the chosen investment approach, ensuring that the chosen indicators reflect the specific goals and risk tolerance of the investor. By customizing indicator values in accordance with the investment approach, investors can effectively screen for stocks that match their unique investment objectives.

Use Indicators That Highlight Different Perspectives

Effective stock analysis requires a diversified set of indicators that provide insights from various angles, encompassing monetary, psychological, and valuation perspectives. This multifaceted approach adds depth and dimension to the assessment of potential investments, as different indicators shed light on distinct aspects of a company's performance and potential. By combining these varied perspectives, investors gain a more comprehensive understanding of the opportunities and risks associated with a particular stock. It is essential to recognize that the selection of indicators is an art rather than a science. Investors refine their indicator choices over time through experience, learning from both successes and mistakes. The process of identifying the ideal combination of indicators to align with one's investment objectives and goals is a dynamic and evolving one.

Incorporating a range of indicators can help investors capture the nuances and subtleties of the stock market. For instance, monetary indicators can provide insights into a company's financial health, while psychological indicators offer information on market sentiment and investor behavior. Valuation indicators, however, focus on the intrinsic worth of a company's stock. By thoughtfully integrating these different perspectives, investors can develop a well-rounded analysis that takes into account the multifaceted nature of the stock market, ultimately enhancing their ability to make sound investment decisions.

Earnings Indicators Favored for Screening and Selecting Stocks

Earnings indicators play a central role in stock screening and selection, and they are essential components of the assessment process for various investment approaches, including growth, momentum, and value strategies. Here are some of the key earnings indicators commonly used across these approaches:

- Earnings per Share (EPS)—Quarterly and Annual: EPS reflects a company's profitability on a per-share basis. Analyzing both quarterly and annual EPS allows investors to assess the consistency and growth of earnings over time, providing valuable insights into a company's financial performance.
- Projected Long-Term Earnings Growth Rate: This indicator gauges a company's expected future earnings growth over an extended horizon. It assists investors in identifying stocks with the potential for sustained growth, a critical consideration for growth-focused investors.
- Earnings Estimate Revisions: Examining changes in earnings estimates by analysts can provide valuable information about market sentiment and expectations regarding a company's future earnings. Positive revisions may signal bullish sentiment, while negative revisions can raise concerns about the company's prospects.
- Earnings per Share Rank: EPS ranking allows investors to compare a company's earnings performance against its industry peers. This indicator can help identify companies with strong earnings relative to their competitors, a valuable insight for both growth and value investors.
- Price-to-Earnings (P/E) Ratio and Relative P/E Ratio: The P/E ratio is a fundamental valuation metric that compares a company's stock

price to its earnings. Both the P/E ratio and the relative P/E ratio (comparing a stock's P/E to its sector or industry) offer insights into a company's valuation, which is essential for value investors assessing the attractiveness of a stock's price relative to its earnings.

- P/E-to-Growth (PEG) Ratio: The PEG ratio is a hybrid indicator that combines the P/E ratio with expected earnings growth. It helps investors evaluate whether a stock's price is justified by its growth prospects, making it particularly useful for growth-focused investors.

These earnings indicators are pivotal tools for investors, allowing them to evaluate companies from multiple angles and align their investment decisions with their chosen strategy. Whether it is assessing growth potential, market sentiment, or valuation, these indicators are valuable for making well-informed stock selections that support an investor's financial goals and risk tolerance.

Additional Indicators Used for Screening and Selecting Stocks

In addition to the core earnings indicators, investors often rely on a range of supplementary indicators to comprehensively assess stocks. The choice of these additional indicators depends on an investor's specific investment approach and objectives. Here are some additional indicators commonly used for screening and selecting stocks:

- Revenues (Sales) Growth: Monitoring a company's revenue growth is crucial for understanding its top-line performance. This indicator helps investors evaluate the company's ability to increase its sales over time, providing insights into its overall financial health and growth potential.
- Relative Strength (RS) Rank: RS rank measures a stock's relative performance compared to its peers or the broader market. It is a critical indicator for momentum investors, enabling them to identify stocks showing strong price momentum and potentially outperforming their competitors.
- Moving Averages: Moving averages are technical indicators that provide insights into a stock's price trends and momentum. They are commonly used for identifying potential entry and exit points, especially for technical and momentum-oriented investors.
- Accumulation and Distribution: This indicator assesses the flow of money into and out of a stock. It helps investors understand market sentiment, particularly when it comes to accumulation (buying pressure) and distribution (selling pressure).

- Daily Trading Volume: Trading volume reflects the number of shares traded in a stock on a daily basis. It offers insights into a stock's liquidity and can help investors gauge the level of market interest in a particular stock.
- Float: The float represents the number of a company's shares available for trading in the open market. It can impact a stock's price volatility and liquidity, making it a relevant consideration for investors focused on trading dynamics.
- Institutional Ownership: This indicator tracks the percentage of a company's shares held by institutional investors, such as mutual funds, pension funds, and hedge funds. High institutional ownership can signal confidence in a stock's potential, and some investors consider it a positive factor.
- Insider Buying: Monitoring insider buying activity can provide insights into the sentiments of a company's management and executives. It can be a valuable indicator for gauging the company's prospects and overall health.
- Stock Price: The stock price itself serves as a fundamental indicator. Investors may consider a stock's current price level in relation to its historical prices or its price relative to its peers or the broader market.
- Market Capitalization: Market capitalization, or market cap, measures a company's total value in the stock market. It is an important consideration for investors assessing a stock's size and scalability.
- Return on Equity (ROE): ROE assesses a company's profitability by measuring its ability to generate earnings relative to shareholder equity. It is a key financial indicator, particularly for value and fundamental investors.
- Debt/Equity Ratio: The debt/equity ratio evaluates a company's leverage and financial stability by comparing its debt to its equity. Investors concerned about a company's financial health consider this indicator when making investment decisions.
- Cash Flow Growth Rate: Evaluating a company's cash flow growth rate provides insights into its ability to generate cash and manage its finances effectively. It is a valuable indicator for assessing financial strength and sustainability.

These additional indicators offer investors a comprehensive toolkit for evaluating stocks based on their unique investment objectives and strategies. Whether it is assessing price momentum, liquidity, financial health, or market sentiment, the choice of these indicators enables investors to make informed decisions that align with their financial goals and risk tolerance.

Combining Indicators From Different Investment Approaches is Risky

Combining indicators from different investment approaches can indeed be a double-edged sword, offering the potential for comprehensive insights but also introducing the risk of conflicting signals. The diverse array of available indicators, when combined thoughtlessly, can yield discordant and confusing messages for investors. To mitigate this risk, it is advisable to adopt a simple yet focused approach that aligns with your chosen investment strategy. By selecting only a few key indicators that are compatible with your approach, you can maintain clarity in your decision-making process.

For instance, an investor adhering to a specific strategy, such as growth investing, should opt for indicators that are in harmony with the principles of growth. This includes using indicators that emphasize earnings growth, revenue expansion, and momentum. Conversely, it is generally unwise to combine indicators from distinct investment approaches, particularly if they have the potential to generate conflicting signals. For example, a value investor, who prioritizes undervalued stocks with strong fundamentals, should avoid incorporating indicators favored by momentum investors, like RS rank, which might emphasize price momentum over intrinsic value. This deliberate and strategy-aligned approach reduces the chances of receiving mixed signals and ensures that investors adhere to a consistent and clear investment path.

Never Use a Single Indicator

Relying on a single indicator for investment decisions is a precarious practice, as it neglects the multifaceted nature of stock analysis. Stocks and the broader market are influenced by a multitude of factors, and thus, a comprehensive evaluation requires the consideration of a well-balanced set of indicators. Depending solely on one indicator can lead to suboptimal decision-making, as it may fail to account for the intricate interplay of variables impacting a stock's performance. To make sound investment decisions, it is essential to employ a diverse mix of indicators that collectively provide a more holistic perspective. However, it is equally important to strike a balance in indicator selection.

Overloading on a large number of indicators can lead to information overload and confusion. Investors should aim for a manageable and focused set of indicators, prioritizing those they believe to be most significant in line with their investment objectives. By selecting a limited but well-chosen set of indicators, investors can better discern meaningful signals and maintain a clear and efficient decision-making process. Furthermore, the indicators should be harmonious with the chosen investment approach, avoiding combinations that might generate conflicting or incongruous signals.

Limit the Number of Indicators to Track

In the complex world of the stock market, a multitude of indicators, variables, and forces are constantly in play, making it a dynamic and often unpredictable environment. These indicators can exert varying degrees of influence, depending on the prevailing market conditions, economic climate, and specific investment goals. The significance of any given indicator is not fixed and can fluctuate with changing circumstances, such as economic downturns, bull markets, bear markets, or earnings seasons. Additionally, the relative importance of different indicators can differ significantly among investors, based on their individual investment philosophies, experiences, and objectives.

Given this intricate landscape, it is crucial for investors to recognize that they do not need to track an overwhelming number of indicators to make informed decisions. Instead, they should focus on identifying and monitoring a select few that align with their investment approach and objectives. By honing in on a manageable set of indicators that hold particular relevance to their chosen strategy, investors can reduce complexity, increase efficiency, and maintain a clear and purposeful investment process. This selective approach empowers investors to better navigate the multifaceted world of the stock market while emphasizing the indicators most relevant to their financial goals.

Use Online Screening Tools

Leveraging online screening tools is a smart and efficient way for investors to sift through vast stock databases and identify potential investment opportunities. These user-friendly tools, often accessible through popular financial websites, empower investors to customize their screening criteria by selecting specific indicators and their corresponding values. With easy-to-use menus and screens, investors can iteratively refine their searches, gradually narrowing down their criteria to pinpoint stocks that align with their investment objectives.

Prominent financial websites and apps offer comprehensive screening tools that cater to a range of investment strategies and goals. These platforms enable investors to efficiently filter through stocks, applying indicators and values tailored to their unique preferences. By harnessing the power of these screening tools, investors can streamline their stock selection process, saving time and effort while uncovering potential investment candidates that align with their criteria.

CHAPTER 2

BUYING

WHERE TO INVEST

This section guides investors in their quest to identify companies with the potential to become winners, so that their resources are invested effectively in the stock market.

Invest in What You Know the Best

Investing in areas you are most familiar with is a shrewd strategy that can provide you with a competitive advantage and increase your chances of making successful investments. The principle behind this approach is that your in-depth knowledge and firsthand experience in a particular company, industry, or sector can give you valuable insights and an edge in identifying investment opportunities before they gain widespread attention. Early identification of promising stories, often before they become mainstream news or attract media attention, can be a significant advantage in the world of investing.

In many instances, the best investment opportunities may be found right in your own backyard, within the companies or industries you have personal or professional connections with. This level of familiarity allows you to have a deeper understanding of the company's fundamentals and business prospects, offering you an informational advantage over Wall Street analysts who may not possess the same level of insight. By keeping a keen eye on these potential investments and leveraging your unique knowledge, you can seize opportunities at an early stage and potentially benefit from the growth and success of these ventures.

Buy Into a Theme

Focusing on themes rather than fleeting fads is a prudent approach to investment that can lead to more sustainable and profitable outcomes. While fads may attract temporary attention and speculative interest, they often lack the enduring qualities needed to provide long-term returns. Instead, investors should aim to identify and invest in themes or trends that have the potential to persist over an extended period. These themes capitalize on the transformative power of changing lifestyles, technological innovations, and evolving consumer preferences, aligning with the ongoing growth of the economy.

Recognizing and investing in a theme at its nascent stage is a challenging task, but it offers the potential for substantial rewards. Identifying and understanding these long-term trends can lead to the discovery of stock market leaders that stand to benefit from the sustained growth and evolution associated with the theme. While many investors may struggle to identify such themes early on, those who succeed in doing so can position themselves to capture significant gains as the theme unfolds and takes root in the market.

What Are The Current Themes

One prominent and clearly observable theme in contemporary investing is the growing influence of artificial Intelligence (AI) across various sectors of our economy and daily lives. As AI continues to advance, it is poised to play a pivotal role in shaping the future. Companies involved in AI development, software, machine learning, and data analytics are likely to thrive in this technological revolution. From autonomous vehicles to health-care diagnostics and financial risk assessments, AI is expected to permeate almost every aspect of our society. Investors can anticipate substantial growth and innovation within the AI sector, making it a promising area for long-term investment.

Another notable trend is the demographic shift, particularly with the aging baby-boomer generation. As this population segment ages, there will be a heightened demand for services in the health care and financial sectors. Health-care companies offering medical treatments, elderly care, and pharmaceuticals, as well as financial institutions providing retirement planning, wealth management, and insurance services, are expected to witness increasing demand for their offerings. Investors with a long-term horizon may consider these areas as opportunities for investment, given the foreseeable growth potential over the next couple of decades.

Invest in Growth Companies

One prominent and clearly observable theme in contemporary investing is the growing influence of artificial intelligence across various sectors of our economy and daily lives. As AI continues to advance, it is poised to play a pivotal role in shaping the future. Companies involved in AI development, software, machine learning, and data analytics are likely to thrive in this technological revolution. From autonomous vehicles to health-care diagnostics and financial risk assessments, AI is expected to permeate almost every aspect of our society. Investors can anticipate substantial growth and innovation within the AI sector, making it a promising area for long-term investment.

Another notable trend is the demographic shift, particularly with the aging baby-boomer generation. As this population segment ages, there will be a heightened demand for services in the health-care and financial sectors. Health-care companies offering medical treatments, elderly care, and pharmaceuticals, as well as financial institutions providing retirement planning, wealth management, and insurance services, are expected to witness increasing demand for their offerings. Investors with a long-term horizon may consider these areas as opportunities for investment, given the foreseeable growth potential over the next couple of decades.

Buy Leading Companies in an Industry or Niche

Investing in leading companies within a particular industry or niche area is a sound strategy that can enhance the quality of your investment portfolio. Instead of purchasing stocks from mediocre or average companies solely based on their lower stock prices compared to industry leaders, it is advisable to prioritize quality and performance. High-quality, premier companies that consistently outperform their peers should be the primary focus for investors. Selecting the top two or three companies in an industry ensures that you are investing in companies with proven track records of success and market dominance.

While the top companies in an industry are often the preferred choices, there can be opportunities for investment in smaller companies that control a niche market or offer unique and innovative products or services. However, investing in such smaller companies should be approached cautiously. Thorough risk assessment and evaluation of the potential rewards are essential before considering an investment in these niche players. The key is to strike a balance between industry leaders and smaller, specialized companies to build a well-diversified and risk-managed investment portfolio.

Invest in a Company—Not the Market

Investing in a specific company rather than the stock market as a whole is a fundamental principle of sound investment strategy. Although the overall performance of the stock market can influence the short-term price movements of your stocks, the long-term success or failure of your investments hinges primarily on the performance and profitability of the individual companies in which you invest. A company's business success is not intrinsically tied to the overall performance of the stock market, emphasizing the importance of conducting in-depth research and analysis on the specific company you are considering for investment.

Understanding the business, financials, and fundamentals of a company is critical when evaluating it as a potential investment. Even in a thriving stock market, a weak company is likely to face challenges and may not experience significant success. Therefore, your investment decisions should be driven by the company's intrinsic qualities, growth prospects, and profitability rather than being solely influenced by broader market trends. This approach helps you make informed investment choices that are more closely aligned with the company's individual merits and future potential.

Invest in Small Companies

Investing in small companies can be an attractive strategy due to the potential for larger price movements compared to their larger counterparts. Smaller companies often experience more significant price fluctuations, which can result in substantial gains for investors. This heightened volatility can be attributed to the fact that small companies typically have smaller market capitalizations and, as a result, can undergo more dramatic shifts in response to various market events.

Furthermore, small companies have greater growth potential as they operate from a smaller base compared to larger, more established corporations. Smaller companies are often in a position to expand their sales and market presence more rapidly, allowing investors to benefit from their growth. They can explore new markets and opportunities with greater ease, whereas larger companies often face the challenge of operating in saturated markets where expansion may be more limited. Investing in small companies can provide investors with the opportunity to tap into emerging growth stories and witness significant price appreciation. However, it is essential to be aware that this approach can also involve higher levels of risk and volatility, so thorough research and risk management are crucial when considering such investments.

Favor Small-Cap Companies

Investors who favor small-cap companies often do so with the expectation of experiencing more significant price movements compared to their large-cap counterparts. Smaller companies, or small caps, tend to be more nimble and agile in responding to market conditions and opportunities. Due to their smaller market capitalization, small-cap stocks can make substantial price moves, driven by rapid growth, innovative products or services, or breakthroughs in their industries. These stocks often have fewer outstanding shares available for trading, contributing to greater price volatility as each trade has a more significant impact on the stock's price.

Additionally, small-cap stocks are often overlooked by institutional investors and analysts, making them less well-researched and less widely followed. This relative obscurity can present an opportunity for investors, as when these companies begin to attract attention from institutional investors and analysts, demand for their shares can increase rapidly, potentially leading to substantial price appreciation. Favoring small-cap companies can provide investors with the potential for significant returns, but it is important to note that these investments come with higher risk and may exhibit greater volatility compared to their larger counterparts. Therefore, thorough research, due diligence, and risk management are essential when considering investments in small-cap stocks.

Favor Stocks With Market Cap Below $1 Billion

Favoring stocks with a market capitalization below $1 billion is a strategy often associated with investing in small-cap companies. Smaller market capitalizations indicate that a company is considered a small-cap stock, which typically implies it is relatively less well-established or less known in the financial markets. Smaller companies may still be in a phase of rapid growth and have significant potential for future expansion, making them attractive investment opportunities. These companies may be focused on niche markets, innovative products, or emerging trends, and investors often seek them out for the potential to realize substantial price appreciation.

Investors who favor stocks with market caps below $1 billion are often looking for opportunities to capitalize on underrecognized or underappreciated companies that have room for significant growth. It is important to note that while small-cap stocks offer potential for higher returns, they also come with higher risk and greater price volatility. As a result, due diligence, diversification, and risk management are essential when considering investments in small-cap stocks, and investors should be prepared for the potential for more significant price fluctuations in exchange for the possibility of substantial gains.

Do Not Be Misled By Large Price Moves

When evaluating stocks, it is crucial not to be misled by large dollar price movements. The absolute dollar value of price moves can be deceptive, as it doesn't necessarily reflect the significance of the change in percentage terms. High-priced and larger companies may experience more substantial dollar price fluctuations compared to smaller, lower-priced stocks, but these moves may represent a relatively lower percentage change in the stock's value. Understanding the percentage change is essential because it provides a clearer indication of the stock's performance and the impact on your investment.

For example, if a $100 stock increases by $10, it represents a 10% price movement. In contrast, a $20 stock that increases by the same $10 represents a 50% price movement. Therefore, investors should not solely focus on the dollar amount of a stock's price movement but instead consider the percentage change to gauge its significance. This perspective is critical for making informed investment decisions, especially when comparing stocks with varying prices and market capitalizations.

Laggards Can Occasionally Become Winners

Occasionally, overlooked and underestimated companies have the potential to emerge as winning investments. These companies might be overlooked by Wall Street, leading to a lack of attention from investors, and this neglect can create opportunities for astute investors. However, it is important to be patient, as it may take some time for these hidden gems to gain recognition and for their stories to become known to a wider audience. Typically, these are not companies facing financial difficulties; instead, they often boast a robust track record of profitability spanning several years.

One common characteristic of these companies is their consistent and strong earnings growth, yet their stock prices may not reflect their financial performance, resulting in low P/E ratios. When the market finally recognizes the growth potential of such profitable companies, especially among growth stocks, there is potential for substantial profit as the P/E ratios expand. This growth in P/E ratios indicates growing investor confidence and interest in these companies, which can lead to significant gains for those who identified the opportunity early on.

WHEN TO BUY

In this section, investors will learn the intricacies of identifying buying opportunities, which will enable them to avoid investing in stocks that will turn out to be poor investments.

Buy Low, Sell High

"Buy low, sell high" is a fundamental principle in investing, and it encapsulates the core concept of seeking to purchase assets at undervalued or discounted prices and then selling them at a profit when their value appreciates. The challenge for investors is determining what constitutes a "low" or undervalued price and what is a "high" or overvalued price for a particular stock. To apply this principle effectively, investors must develop an understanding of valuation methods, which can help them assess both the buying and selling points for a stock.

Valuation involves analyzing various financial metrics and indicators, such as P/E ratios, earnings growth rates, and other fundamental factors to estimate a stock's intrinsic value. By comparing a stock's market price to its intrinsic value, investors can make informed decisions about whether a stock is currently trading at a low or high price relative to its potential worth. This helps investors identify buying opportunities when a stock appears undervalued and selling opportunities when it becomes overvalued, aligning with the timeless wisdom of "buy low, sell high." While there is no one-size-fits-all approach to valuation, understanding these principles can provide a solid foundation for investors seeking to make well-informed and profitable decisions in the stock market.

Remain Invested at All Times

Remaining invested in the stock market at all times is a prudent strategy for most investors because attempting to time the market consistently can be challenging. Market timing involves predicting when to enter and exit the market to maximize gains or minimize losses, and it often leads to suboptimal outcomes due to its inherent uncertainty. Investors who try to time the market may miss out on significant market rallies or lock in losses during downturns. Instead, a more effective approach is to ride the market's natural fluctuations and maintain a diversified portfolio that can withstand various market conditions.

During market declines or bear markets, it is crucial not to panic and sell all your holdings. Lightening up on your stock positions or rebalancing your portfolio by selling some overvalued assets can be a more reasonable response. Continuously investing a fixed amount of money, regardless of market conditions, can help you take advantage of opportunities when the market is down, as you will be buying stocks at lower prices. Conversely, in bullish markets when signs indicate strong performance, you may choose to be fully invested. Timing the market based on a rational assessment of market conditions, rather than emotions or speculation, is a more strategic way to navigate the ever-changing landscape of the stock market.

Buy on Weakness—Sell on Strength

The principle of buying on weakness and selling on strength is a strategy that acknowledges the importance of timing in the stock market. When a stock experiences weakness, it may present an opportunity for value-oriented investors to buy at a lower price, provided that the company's fundamentals remain strong. This strategy aligns with the idea of purchasing stocks with a margin of safety, where investors aim to acquire shares at a discount to their intrinsic value. The key to success here is thorough research to confirm the company's financial health and prospects before capitalizing on the weakness.

Selling on strength, however, is more applicable to traders or those with a specific exit strategy in place. While long-term investors often follow the approach of letting their profits run, traders may opt to sell when a stock exhibits strong momentum or reaches a predefined target price. This can help traders lock in gains and manage risk more effectively. For long-term investors, it is generally advisable to remain invested in fundamentally sound companies and only consider selling if there is a significant change in the company's fundamentals or if you have specific financial goals that require liquidating some of your positions.

Buy High, Sell Higher

The strategy of "buy high, sell higher" is a characteristic approach of momentum investing. Momentum investors focus on a stock's recent price and earnings momentum, rather than traditional fundamental analysis or valuations. They are driven by the belief that stocks with strong recent performance will continue to exhibit that momentum and climb even higher. This strategy can be seen as a way to capitalize on market trends and is characterized by a focus on short- to medium-term price movements.

However, it is important to note that momentum investing comes with inherent risks, and it may not be suitable for all investors. It requires a keen understanding of technical analysis, as momentum investors rely heavily on charts and patterns to identify entry and exit points. For those not well-versed in these techniques, the strategy can be particularly risky, as it may be challenging to identify when a stock has lost its momentum, leading to potential losses. It is crucial for investors to be aware of their own risk tolerance and investment goals before considering a momentum-based approach to stock investing.

Buy Stocks Six Months After a Recession Starts

Investing in stocks approximately six months after a recession has begun is a strategic move to maximize potential profits. It is based on the idea that stock markets are forward-looking, and they often begin to anticipate the economic recovery before it becomes evident to the broader public. During the early stages of the economic rebound, the stock market typically experiences its most significant gains as investors regain confidence and optimism starts to outweigh pessimism.

By entering the market during this period, you position yourself to capture the substantial upswing in stock prices that often occurs as the recession comes to an end. However, it is important to remember that economic cycles and market dynamics can vary, so it is not a foolproof strategy. Economic conditions, monetary policy, and other factors can influence the timing and trajectory of market recoveries. As such, it is essential for investors to conduct thorough research, understand their risk tolerance, and consider their individual financial goals when applying this strategy or any investment approach.

Dollar Cost Average to Avoid Mistiming

Dollar cost averaging is a prudent investment strategy for ordinary investors who seek to avoid the pitfalls of market timing. It helps mitigate the risk of buying at the peak of market exuberance or selling in a panic when prices are depressed. By investing a fixed amount of money at regular intervals, regardless of market conditions, investors acquire more shares when prices are low and fewer shares when prices are high. This approach, over time, can result in a lower average cost per share, enhancing the potential for long-term gains.

Dollar cost averaging aligns with the concept of disciplined investing, as it encourages investors to focus on their long-term financial goals rather than reacting to short-term market fluctuations. It is especially beneficial for those who lack the expertise, resources, or time to engage in intricate market timing strategies. By consistently investing over time, investors can accumulate shares in a diversified portfolio, potentially benefiting from the natural upward trajectory of the stock market in the long run.

Average Up—Not Down

Averaging up, as opposed to averaging down, is a strategy that focuses on building on success rather than trying to rescue a declining investment. It involves adding more shares to a winning position as the stock's price appreciates. This approach can be psychologically challenging for some investors because it requires them to buy a stock at a higher price than their initial entry point. However, it is essential to remember that stocks that are already performing well often continue to do so, provided that the underlying fundamentals and growth prospects remain strong.

Before averaging up, investors should conduct a thorough analysis to ensure that the stock is not overvalued and that the reasons for their initial investment thesis remain valid. By adhering to a disciplined approach, investors can capitalize on their successful picks and potentially increase their profits as their stocks continue their upward trajectory.

SEASONAL CONSIDERATIONS

In this section, investors will learn about the role of seasonal factors in the stock market, which will enable them to take advantage of the positive factors, while avoiding their adverse impact.

Take Advantage of Seasonal Factors

Seasonal factors can play a significant role in stock market performance, and investors who pay attention to these patterns can enhance their investment strategies. These factors can impact various industries and sectors differently, and understanding them can provide a tactical advantage. For example, the retail sector often experiences strong performance during the holiday season, while the energy sector may benefit from increased demand for heating during the winter months.

Incorporating seasonal factors into your investment strategy can involve timing your stock purchases to coincide with the start of favorable seasonal periods for specific industries or sectors. You can also adjust

your portfolio allocation based on these factors to capitalize on anticipated market movements. By paying attention to these seasonal patterns,
investors can make more informed decisions and potentially achieve better results in their stock market investments.

Take Advantage of the January Effect

The January effect is a well-documented market phenomenon characterized by a historical tendency for stocks, especially smaller ones, to perform well in the first month of the year. One of the key drivers of the
January effect is the influx of new funds into the stock market during this
time, including contributions to retirement accounts, year-end bonuses,
and investment reallocations. This increased demand for stocks can create
a positive bias in the market, particularly benefiting smaller-cap stocks
that tend to outperform their larger counterparts during January.

Investors can take advantage of the January effect by carefully analyzing the market's overall trend and bias before making investment decisions. While January typically exhibits an upward bias, it is crucial to assess
the broader economic and market conditions to avoid getting caught in a
market that may be on the verge of a downturn. By being aware of this
historical pattern and conducting thorough research, investors can potentially leverage the January effect to enhance their investment strategies
and potentially achieve more favorable outcomes.

Beware of September

September has gained a reputation as a historically challenging month for
stock performance, primarily attributed to factors like the pre-announce-
ments of disappointing earnings results and concerns about companies
falling short of their yearly targets. As the month progresses, investor
sentiment can become more pessimistic, and this negativity can cast a
shadow over the broader market. Even well-performing companies that
meet their expectations may experience downward pressure on their
stock prices due to the prevailing negative sentiment.

In light of these historical patterns, many investors opt to reduce
their overall exposure to stocks before the arrival of September. By taking
a more cautious approach during this month, investors aim to mitigate the
potential adverse impacts of unfavorable market conditions. While past
performance does not guarantee future results, the awareness of historical trends can inform investment strategies and help investors make more
informed decisions.

Take Advantage of Window Dressing

"Window dressing" is a practice often employed by mutual fund managers at the end of each quarter. During this time, fund managers sell off the underperforming stocks in their portfolio. The primary motivation behind this practice is to present a more favorable picture of the fund's holdings in their quarterly reports to investors. By eliminating the poor-performing stocks from the list, the fund can avoid showcasing these underperformers. When multiple mutual funds engage in this practice and simultaneously divest from particular stocks, it increases selling pressure on those stocks, contributing to the phenomenon known as "window dressing."

Investors can potentially take advantage of this situation when they recognize that a stock's underperformance is primarily due to window dressing rather than deteriorating fundamentals. If a stock has faced challenging times but is now on an upward trajectory in terms of its underlying financial health, and it experiences a decline due to window dressing, investors may have an opportunity to purchase the stock at a more attractive, discounted price. By understanding the dynamics of window dressing, investors can navigate the market more effectively and identify potential opportunities for profitable investments.

WHAT TO DO BEFORE YOU BUY

This section identifies the pre-purchase steps that should be taken before investing, ensuring a comprehensive approach that empowers informed decision-making and strategic planning.

Select the Broker

The choice of a broker depends on your investment approach and level of expertise. If you are a self-reliant investor who prefers to make your own investment decisions, a discount broker is suitable for your needs. These brokers offer the essential service of executing your trades at a lower cost compared to full-service brokers, but they do not provide personalized advice or guidance on investment decisions. Discount brokers are ideal for experienced investors who have a clear investment strategy and do not require additional support.

If you are seeking guidance and advice in your investment decisions, a full-service broker is a better choice. Full-service brokers provide a range of services, including investment advice, research, and personalized recommendations. They can help you navigate the complexities of the stock market and make informed investment choices. For traders, having access to a full-service broker with an efficient online trading platform is essential, as it can offer tools and resources to facilitate your trading activities, minimize risks, and optimize your investment strategies. Therefore, the decision regarding which broker to use should align with your investment goals and preferred level of involvement in the decision-making process.

Who Are the Leading Brokers

Brokers play a crucial role in facilitating stock trading and investment. They act as intermediaries between investors and the stock market, executing buy and sell orders on behalf of clients. The brokerage industry encompasses a wide range of firms, providing investors with a variety of choices to suit their specific needs. Full-service brokers like Merrill Lynch, Morgan Stanley, UBS Wealth Management, J.P. Morgan Securities, and Goldman Sachs offer comprehensive services that include personalized investment advice, research, and financial planning. They are often a preferred choice for investors seeking guidance and a higher level of service.

Alternatively, discount brokers, such as Charles Schwab, e-Trade, Fidelity Investments, and Interactive Brokers cater to investors who prefer a do-it-yourself approach. These brokers typically offer lower fees and commissions for executing trades but do not provide personalized investment advice. Investors can choose the type of broker that aligns with their investment goals, expertise, and level of involvement in their investment decisions. The brokerage industry's diversity allows investors to select the most suitable option based on their preferences and financial objectives.

Get Information Before, Not After, Buying a Stock

Obtaining information before making an investment decision is a fundamental principle in the world of stock market investing. Rushing into buying a stock without conducting proper research can expose investors to unnecessary risks. This diligence involves studying the company's financial health, its competitive landscape, and the broader economic environment in which it operates. By delving into these aspects, investors can better understand the company's potential and the risks associated with its stock.

One common pitfall is being lured by a stock that appears attractive due to a sudden price drop. Such a scenario can indeed present opportunities, but it also necessitates a comprehensive investigation before making a move. Rushed decisions based solely on short-term market fluctuations can lead to suboptimal investment outcomes, so prudent investors should ensure they have the necessary information and insight to make well-informed choices.

Analyze Fundamentals Before Investing

Analyzing a stock's fundamentals before making an investment decision is a key practice in successful stock market investing. Whether a stock has declined significantly over an extended period or experienced a sudden drop in price, it is crucial to resist the impulse to buy immediately. Instead, take the time to investigate the reasons behind the decline. It is important to discern whether the worst is already reflected in the stock's price or if there may be further declines on the horizon. Conducting a thorough analysis of the company's fundamentals using fundamental analysis techniques is essential before arriving at any investment decision.

The same principle applies when a stock is on a fast upward trajectory. Investors should exercise caution and not jump on the bandwagon without conducting a comprehensive fundamental analysis of the company. The goal is to understand the underlying reasons for the stock's rapid ascent and assess whether it is justified by the company's financial health and outlook. When evaluating a stock that has remained relatively stagnant for some time, it is essential to determine the reasons for its lack of movement. This assessment can help investors determine whether there are underlying issues or potential catalysts that may impact the stock's future performance.

Determine Risk Associated With a Stock

When considering an investment in stocks, it is crucial to understand the risk associated with the specific type of stock you are interested in. Different stocks exhibit varying levels of risk and reward. For instance, stocks in the food industry are known for their relative stability and tend to experience minimal intraday fluctuations and moderate price changes over time. Contrastingly, technology stocks are renowned for their high volatility and significant price swings. These stocks carry inherent risk as their success is closely tied to rapidly evolving technology that can quickly become outdated once a superior alternative emerges. Therefore, it is essential to evaluate the potential risk and reward of a stock before making an investment decision.

Assessing the risk associated with a stock involves examining various factors, including the industry it belongs to, the competitive landscape, the company's financial health, and its exposure to market and economic conditions. By gaining a comprehensive understanding of these elements, investors can make informed decisions about the level of risk they are willing to take on and the potential rewards they can expect from a particular stock.

Analyze Business Conditions and Prospects

Before making any investment in a stock, it is imperative to conduct a thorough analysis of the company's business conditions and prospects. This analysis should encompass a broad spectrum of factors that can influence the company's performance. You should begin by assessing the immediate business environment in which the company operates, considering elements such as market dynamics, regulatory changes, and economic conditions. Evaluating the current and future business conditions is essential, as it provides insights into the company's ability to thrive in its industry. Additionally, examining the expected market growth rate and potential for saturation is critical, as it can determine the company's future growth prospects and overall health.

A comprehensive analysis should also delve into the competitive landscape, as understanding the company's position relative to its competitors is vital. Product offerings, pricing strategies, and market share should be considered. By evaluating these factors, investors can gauge the company's competitive advantage or potential weaknesses. Furthermore, it is crucial to consider the outlook for the company's products and services, as this can impact its long-term sustainability and growth potential. To make well-informed investment decisions, it is equally important to extend the analysis to the broader industry and sector in which the stock operates, as these external factors can significantly influence its performance. By thoroughly assessing business conditions and prospects, investors can better position themselves for success.

Check the Market Health

Once you have identified a promising investment opportunity, it is essential to assess the overall health of the stock market since it can significantly impact the performance of individual stocks. While attempting to perfectly time the market is not advisable, it is prudent to consider the broader market conditions before making an investment. If you perceive that the market is approaching a top, is in a declining phase, or has entered a bear market, it may be wise to delay your purchase. During such periods, market instability and uncertainty can negatively affect stock prices.

Waiting for the market to stabilize and potentially identifying a bottom could help you make a more informed investment decision and reduce your risk exposure.

The state of the market also affects the risk level associated with your investment. In a bull market, where stock prices are generally rising, investments may carry less risk. However, in a bear market or during a market decline, stocks become riskier investments. By assessing the market's health and conditions, you can better align your investment strategy with the overall market trend, potentially making more informed and risk-adjusted investment decisions.

Analyze Economic Conditions and Cycle

Analyzing economic conditions and the broader economic cycle is crucial in making informed investment decisions. Economic conditions have a significant influence on the performance and earnings potential of companies. Different stocks respond differently to changes in the economic cycle. Defensive stocks tend to perform well in a slowing economy or during a recession as they are relatively immune to economic downturns. These stocks often belong to sectors such as utilities, health care, or consumer staples, where demand for products or services remains consistent even in challenging economic times. Conversely, cyclical stocks are highly sensitive to the economic cycle. They are often associated with industries like manufacturing or construction and are likely to experience significant impacts during economic downturns.

Understanding the economic cycle allows investors to adjust their investment strategies accordingly. For example, during a recession, growth stocks may be favored because they can sustain their earnings growth even as the broader economy slows down. However, as the economy starts to recover, cyclical stocks become more attractive. By analyzing economic conditions and their impact on different sectors, investors can make well-informed decisions that align with the current economic environment and the expected trajectory of the economic cycle.

CHAPTER 3

PICKING WINNING CHARACTERISTICS

FAST AND CONSISTENT GROWTH

This section delves into the art of identifying stocks with dynamic and steady growth patterns, providing investors with valuable insights for bolstering their portfolios with resilient and high-performing assets.

What Are Growth Stock Characteristics?

A growth stock is a company that exhibits a growth rate significantly higher than the market average. What makes a growth stock attractive to investors is its potential for rapid expansion and profitability. Growth stocks tend to outperform during periods of economic slowdown or recession because they are less dependent on the overall economic cycle. When the broader economy is sluggish, growth companies can maintain or even increase their earnings, making them appealing investments.

Investors looking for growth stocks should focus on small companies that have the potential for substantial growth, especially in sectors or industries experiencing rapid expansion. The key is to identify companies with growth rates that surpass not only the market average but also their own industry, sector, and benchmarks like the S&P 500, which tracks the 500 largest companies in the United States. This emphasis on outperforming peers and benchmarks is what distinguishes growth stocks and makes them an attractive choice for those seeking above-average returns.

High Growth Rate Should Be Sustainable

A strong growth stock should have a solid track record of high growth in both revenues and earnings. This growth should consistently outpace the market average, ideally exceeding 20%. However, it is not merely the current growth rate that matters; a promising growth stock should demonstrate the potential to accelerate from, for example, 10%–15% growth to 25%–30% or more. What sets a growth stock apart is the ability to sustain this high growth rate for more than just a few quarters. This sustainability is a key factor in evaluating a growth company.

Furthermore, a sustainable growth stock is often found in an industry that is experiencing growth itself. Being part of an expanding sector allows the company to maintain or even increase its growth rate in the years to come. Investing in companies poised to capitalize on the growth of their industry can provide investors with an opportunity to benefit from not just current growth but future prospects as well.

Stock Should Have Small Capitalization

The market capitalization of a stock, which is calculated by multiplying the stock price by the number of outstanding shares, is a key determinant of how stocks are classified. One common classification designates a stock with a market capitalization of less than $1 billion as a small-cap stock. However, to identify the most promising investment opportunities in the growth stock arena, you should focus on small-cap stocks that have strong growth potential. These stocks are often found in the market cap range of $500 million to $1 billion, where the company's size and the growth prospects can be well balanced.

When searching for growth stocks, you can also consider those with a market capitalization in the $1–$2 billion range, as they may still offer substantial growth opportunities while having a bit more financial stability than smaller, riskier small-cap stocks. Stocks with a market capitalization below $500 million are typically considered more speculative and should be approached with caution, as their shorter track record makes it challenging to effectively evaluate their growth potential and stability.

Growth Must Be Accompanied By Profits

Growth is indeed essential, but it must be sustainable and accompanied by profits to create long-term value for investors. Many companies have experienced rapid revenue growth without generating corresponding profits, which often leads to disappointment for investors. The dot-com bubble is a prime example of companies that exhibited explosive revenue growth but failed to translate that into profits, ultimately leading to investor losses. A company should not just focus on growth for growth's sake; it should aim to achieve a balance between growth and profitability.

A sustainable and robust growth strategy is one in which a company can expand its top line (revenues) while also demonstrating a healthy bottom line (profits). Sustainable profits indicate that a company can reinvest in its operations, research, and development, which are essential for future growth. When analyzing a company's profitability, it is important to ensure that these profits are not achieved through temporary means like cost-cutting, restructuring, or asset sales, as such methods are not sustainable and may not bode well for the company's long-term prospects. Instead, true profitability growth should stem from the company's core operations and business model.

Revenue Should Be Increasing at a Healthy Pace

Healthy revenue growth is a fundamental indicator of a company's strength and potential. When a company's revenues increase, it means it can sell more of its products or services, which is a sign of strong demand and effective business operations. Revenue growth is crucial for long-term earnings growth because, without it, the potential for increasing profits is limited. Consistent and sustained revenue growth is a key factor in driving earnings growth over time.

Investors should keep a close eye on a company's revenue growth and view it as a warning sign if this growth begins to stagnate or decline. Declining sales can signal issues such as market saturation, competition, or a decrease in demand for the company's products or services. In such cases, the company may struggle to maintain or improve its profitability, making it less attractive to investors. Consequently, when evaluating a potential investment, assessing the trend and sustainability of a company's revenue growth is a critical analysis component.

Learn How to Analyze Revenue

Analyzing a company's revenue can be approached in various ways to gain a more comprehensive understanding of its performance and prospects. One crucial metric to track, in addition to annual sales, is the "quarterly sales percent change," which measures the percentage change in a company's quarterly sales compared to the same quarter of the previous year. This metric provides insights into the company's recent performance and its ability to maintain growth over time. Additionally, examining seasonal patterns and any variations in sales categories can help identify strong and weak areas within the company's revenue streams. This can be especially valuable in understanding the dynamics of the business and potential growth drivers.

When analyzing revenue, it is essential to be cautious when a company exhibits extremely high growth rates, such as 50%–100%, as such rates may be unsustainable and could indicate that the company is in a speculative or risky phase. Furthermore, closely monitoring the sales growth of a company's flagship product(s) is crucial. If these products start to experience declining sales, it can serve as an early warning sign of potential problems within the company. A decline in sales for key products may indicate increased competition, shifting customer preferences, or potential difficulties in maintaining market share. This makes it an important indicator to assess when evaluating the overall health and potential future success of the company.

Growth Rate Should Be Greater Than the P/E Ratio

When considering an investment in a growth stock, it is essential to verify that the stock's P/E ratio is lower than its earnings growth rate. This comparison helps investors assess whether the stock is trading at a reasonable valuation relative to its growth prospects. For example, if a growth stock has an annual earnings growth rate of 30%, its P/E ratio should ideally be less than 30. Some investors are more lenient and allow for a P/E ratio up to 125% of the growth rate, but when the P/E ratio exceeds the growth rate, it typically indicates that the stock may be overvalued. This is an important consideration for value-oriented and growth investors, as it helps in determining whether the stock's current price is justified based on its expected earnings growth.

It is worth noting that small companies in a high-growth phase can sometimes have significantly higher P/E ratios than the general guideline suggests. This is because investors may be willing to pay a premium for the potential rapid expansion and growth opportunities associated with smaller firms. In such cases, the assessment should also consider the company's overall growth prospects and the specific industry or sector dynamics influencing its valuation. While this guideline provides a helpful reference, investors should conduct a comprehensive analysis of a growth stock, taking into account various factors, to make informed investment decisions.

PROFITABILITY

This section helps uncover the vital metrics and financial indicators essential for identifying stocks with sustainable profitability, empowering investors to make informed decisions.

The Company Must Be Profitable

Earnings are a fundamental driver of stock prices over the long term. For this reason, it is crucial to invest in companies with a track record of profitability and those that are currently generating profits. Companies in their early development stages, particularly those accumulating losses, should be approached with caution. When evaluating small companies, it is advisable to focus on those with a consistent positive earnings trend over a period of three to five years, unless there is a justifiable reason for an occasional off year. A single year of underperformance can be over-looked if the company demonstrates a rapid recovery and strong growth prospects.

Profitability is a vital indicator of a company's financial health and ability to deliver long-term value to investors. Sustained profitability reflects the effectiveness of the company's operations and its capacity to generate returns for shareholders. Investing in profitable companies with a solid earnings track record provides investors with greater confidence in the stock's stability and growth potential. However, it is also important to conduct a thorough analysis of the reasons behind any isolated earnings declines to ensure that they are not indicative of broader issues within the company.

Earnings Growth Rate Should Be High

When seeking investment opportunities, it is crucial to identify stocks with a strong potential for future profitability. To accomplish this, concentrate on the projected earnings growth for the next three to five years. An exceptional growth company will have a long-term, 3–5 year projected earnings growth rate exceeding 25%. A higher growth rate is generally considered more favorable for investment, as long as it is expected to be sustainable. These long-term projected earnings growth rates can be obtained from sources like Zacks, Thomson Reuters, Standard & Poor's, and other reliable online platforms.

A high earnings growth rate is a key indicator of a company's ability to expand its profitability over time. It reflects the company's capacity to generate higher earnings and deliver value to its shareholders, making it an attractive investment option. However, it is important to ensure that this growth rate is sustainable and supported by sound fundamentals, business prospects, and market conditions to avoid investing in companies with overly optimistic projections that may not materialize. Thorough research and analysis are essential to verify the accuracy and feasibility of these growth expectations.

Annual and Quarterly Earnings Should Be Increasing

When evaluating potential investments, it is essential to scrutinize a company's earnings, which are reported both on an annual and quarterly basis. A crucial aspect to consider is the consistent growth of these earnings. Wall Street generally favors companies that consistently outperform earnings expectations and deliver consistent growth. Conversely, companies that fail to demonstrate consistent earnings growth or report disappointing earnings often face severe consequences in the financial markets. As an investor, it is prudent to prioritize companies that exhibit rapid increases in both their annual and quarterly earnings, with growth rates ideally exceeding 20%. To make informed investment decisions, it is vital to develop the ability to analyze earnings data, such as year-over-year increases, and understand their implications for the stock's performance.

By closely monitoring earnings trends, you can gain valuable insights into a company's financial health and prospects. Consistently increasing annual and quarterly earnings are indicative of a well-managed and financially sound organization. Such companies are better equipped to create shareholder value, attract investor confidence, and potentially yield favorable returns for their shareholders. When considering stocks with consistent earnings growth, focus on their ability to maintain and potentially exceed these growth rates over time, thereby indicating a long-term commitment to profitability and financial stability.

Earnings Should Be Accelerating

Earnings acceleration is a key indicator of a stock's potential to succeed. Companies that consistently demonstrate increasing acceleration in both quarterly and annual earnings, such as transitioning from a growth rate of 20% to 25% and then 30%, tend to exhibit characteristics associated with winning stocks. These companies often outperform earnings estimates, which are released by a multitude of Wall Street analysts. Such outperformance typically results in positive assessments and upgrades from these analysts, frequently contributing to an upward movement in the stock's price.

For investors, focusing on stocks with accelerating earnings is a strategic approach that can yield substantial rewards. Companies that consistently show this pattern may signal a robust business model and strategic planning, leading to increased market valuation and the potential for higher returns for investors who seize the opportunity. Consequently, recognizing and investing in stocks with accelerating earnings can be a fundamental component of building a successful and profitable investment portfolio.

Earnings Estimates Are Being Raised

Earnings estimates play a significant role in evaluating a company's potential stock performance. While it is crucial for a company to meet its earnings estimates, it is equally vital to pay attention to the direction in which these estimates are moving. When analysts consistently raise their estimated earnings for a particular company, it is considered a positive signal. This upward revision indicates growing confidence in the company's prospects, which can have a positive impact on its stock performance. Conversely, if earnings estimates are being consistently lowered, it is viewed as a negative sign, often reflecting concerns about the company's ability to meet its financial targets.

Investors are generally advised to focus on stocks for which earnings estimates are trending upward. These are the stocks most likely to experience strong appreciation because the positive sentiment and increasing expectations from analysts suggest a bright future for the company. Conversely, it is recommended to be cautious with stocks that are experiencing downward revisions in earnings estimates, as they may indicate underlying issues or uncertainties about the company's financial health and growth prospects. By paying attention to the direction of earnings estimates, investors can make informed decisions and position themselves for potentially more favorable returns.

EPS Rank Is High

The earnings per share rank is a valuable tool for investors to gauge a company's earnings performance and growth trajectory. It provides a score, ranging from 1 to 99, based on a company's EPS growth over the past five years and the consistency of that growth. A higher EPS rank is indicative of better performance. Essentially, this metric measures how a stock's earnings momentum compares to that of all other stocks in the market. Therefore, companies with higher EPS ranks are considered leaders within their industry. For example, a company with an EPS rank of 90 indicates that its earnings have outperformed 90% of other companies, making it a leader in terms of earnings growth.

Investors are encouraged to favor companies with a high EPS rank, particularly those with an EPS rank of 80 or higher. Such companies typically demonstrate strong earnings momentum and have a track record of delivering consistent growth. High EPS ranks are often associated with fewer earnings disappointments, making these stocks attractive options for investors seeking reliable and potentially more lucrative opportunities in the market. Analyzing a company's EPS rank can be a valuable component of stock selection, helping investors identify businesses with robust earnings growth and a higher likelihood of positive stock performance.

EPS Rank Is Rising

While it is crucial to consider a stock's current EPS rank when making investment decisions, it is equally important to look for stocks whose EPS rank is on an upward trajectory. Stocks with rising EPS rank are often preferred by momentum investors who follow trends. Investing in a stock with a relatively modest EPS rank, say around 60 or 70, that eventually climbs to an EPS rank of 90 or higher can lead to significant gains. However, this strategy requires a solid foundation of fundamental analysis to ensure that there are valid reasons for anticipating an increase in the company's earnings in the future. It is essential that earnings are on an upward trajectory since this is the key driver behind an increasing EPS rank.

For investors who seek stocks with strong growth potential and the prospect of a rising EPS rank, it is imperative to monitor a company's financial health, business conditions, and other factors that can influence earnings growth. The ability to predict and anticipate a rise in earnings is critical in capitalizing on stocks with improving EPS rank, making fundamental analysis an indispensable component of your investment strategy.

Margins Are High and Rising

High and rising profit margins are significant indicators of a successful growth company. These companies often excel by introducing new products with increasingly shorter product cycles, resulting in higher profit margins. For these companies, the ability to charge a premium for their innovative products is a key factor contributing to rapid earnings growth. Leading-edge businesses tend to maintain high profit margins, which sets them apart from commodity businesses that typically operate with lower margins. When evaluating stocks through fundamental analysis, it is essential to favor companies that are experiencing rising profit margins, as this trend signifies an upswing in profitability that is likely to be reflected in the company's stock performance.

Rising profit margins not only signal growing profitability, but also indicate that the company may have a competitive advantage in its industry. This advantage can result from cost efficiency, superior product differentiation, or pricing power that enables the company to maintain those high margins. As such, it is crucial to track and consider the margin trends of companies in your investment analysis to make informed decisions and identify stocks with strong growth potential.

MOMENTUM

This section explores the dynamic world of momentum investing, providing investors with insights into identifying stocks with strong upward trends, and strategic entry points for maximizing returns.

RS Rank Is High

The relative strength rank is a valuable measure that assesses a stock's price performance over the past year, with more emphasis on the last quarter's performance and compares it to all other stocks in the market. It serves as a crucial tool for identifying strong-performing stocks, especially among market leaders. Therefore, in your stock selection process, it is wise to favor stocks with an RS rank of 80 or higher, as this indicates strong price momentum. These stocks are often sought after by momentum investors who prefer to invest in companies with a proven track record of outperforming their peers.

Conversely, if a stock's RS rank starts to decline, it should raise a flag of concern, and investors should consider taking appropriate action. A decreasing RS rank suggests a loss of relative price strength and could be indicative of the stock's weakening performance compared to the broader market or its industry peers. Monitoring the RS rank of stocks within your portfolio is a key practice, allowing you to identify potential changes in their price momentum and make informed investment decisions accordingly.

Stock Is Hitting New Price Highs

Hitting a new 52-week price high is an important indicator for investors, especially momentum and growth investors. When a stock achieves this milestone, it signifies that the stock is in an uptrend, and there is typically less resistance from sellers. Resistance often arises when current shareholders, who purchased the stock at a higher price, reach their breakeven point and decide to sell. For momentum investors, in particular, stocks hitting new price highs are highly attractive. These stocks tend to be favored because they often exhibit strong price momentum, which can lead to further gains.

Growth stock investors also appreciate stocks reaching new price highs, but they do so with a focus on the underlying fundamentals and valuations. It is important to ensure that the stock's current price is supported by its financial performance and future growth prospects. In cases where the fundamentals align with the new price highs, it presents a compelling investment opportunity, as such stocks have the potential for continued growth and positive returns.

Accumulation Is Taking Place

The accumulation/distribution rating is a valuable indicator when considering a stock for investment. It reflects the level of institutional interest in the stock and is typically reported on a scale from A to E. A rating of A or B indicates that institutions, such as mutual funds and other large investors, are actively accumulating the stock. This is a positive sign for investors as it suggests that well-informed market participants with significant resources are showing confidence in the stock's potential.

Institutional buying is a critical driver in pushing stock prices higher. When institutions are accumulating stock, it often leads to increased demand, which can result in price appreciation. Conversely, ratings of D or E signal that institutions are selling the stock, which can put downward pressure on its price. Therefore, when evaluating a stock for investment, the accumulation/distribution rating should be taken into account as it provides valuable insights into institutional sentiment and can be a contributing factor in your investment decision-making process. This rating is frequently reported in financial publications like the Investor's Business Daily.

Stock Is in an Uptrend

For investors who follow technical analysis and employ momentum-based strategies, the 200-day moving average is a valuable tool for identifying stocks in an uptrend. When a stock's price consistently trades above its 200-day moving average, it is seen as an indication that the stock is on an upward trajectory. This moving average helps chartists and momentum investors identify the prevailing direction of the stock's price movement. An uptrend can signal that the stock is experiencing positive momentum and is likely to continue rising in the near term.

However, for investors who primarily rely on fundamental analysis to make investment decisions, the 200-day moving average might not hold the same level of significance. They typically use it as an additional tool for timing their entry into a stock. After conducting thorough fundamental analysis and identifying a stock as a good investment candidate, the 200-day moving average can then be used as a technical indicator to help pinpoint an optimal entry point. This combination of fundamental and technical analysis can provide investors with a more comprehensive approach to stock selection and timing their investments.

LEADERSHIP

This section delves into the crucial aspect of evaluating corporate leadership, uncovering the traits and indicators that distinguish companies with effective and visionary leaders, guiding strategic investment decisions for long-term success in the stock market.

Stock Is a Leader

Investing in leading companies, also known as market leaders or sector leaders, can be a strategic approach for investors. These companies often have a competitive edge in their respective industries, with strong market positions and robust financial performance. Being leaders, they are more likely to benefit from economic growth and market upturns. When times are good, these companies often outperform their peers and tend to be the first to experience gains. This is why, in times of economic expansion and the start of a new bull market, investors should focus on identifying and investing in leading companies within the sectors they are interested in.

However, it is important to recognize that leadership in the stock market can shift over time. A company that was a star performer in the previous bull market may not necessarily continue as a leader in the next one. Therefore, investors should stay vigilant and continuously monitor the market dynamics to identify emerging leaders and not just cling to the past high flyers. This is crucial because a former high-flying stock, even after a significant price decline, might still be overvalued, and its best days of growth may already be behind it. By being selective and staying attuned to changes in market leadership, investors can adapt their strategies to stay ahead in the dynamic world of stock investing.

Stock Is a Leader Emerging From a Correction

Picking emerging leaders as they recover from a correction can be a rewarding strategy for investors. Corrections in the stock market can be challenging, and they often hit growth stocks particularly hard. During a typical bull market correction, growth stocks might decline by 1 1/2 to 2 times the market average. However, some stocks show resilience by either not correcting as much or even rising during this period. These are the stocks that often emerge as new leaders when the market rebounds.

To identify these emerging leaders, investors should look for several key indicators. New price highs, a high RS rank, and improving fundamentals are signs that a stock is on the path to becoming a potential leader. Stocks that maintain a high RS rank during a market correction stand out because the RS of leading stocks usually undergoes a sharp drop during these periods. When the market rebounds, these stocks have a higher likelihood of experiencing significant price appreciation, making them attractive candidates for investment. By focusing on emerging leaders coming out of a correction, investors can position themselves to capture strong growth potential and participate in the next phase of the market's upturn.

Company Has Superior Leadership

The leadership of a company plays a pivotal role in its growth and success. A capable and effective management team is a key factor in identifying a successful growth company. These leaders are responsible for shaping the company's strategy, execution, and adaptability to challenges and opportunities. Management teams with a strong track record are more likely to make informed decisions, set the right course for the company, and successfully execute their plans.

In contrast, companies with weak or incompetent leadership, even if they possess great products or services, are at a significant disadvantage. In such cases, a lack of strategic vision and ineffective execution can hinder the company's ability to adapt to changes in the market or effectively address unexpected challenges. Therefore, when evaluating potential growth stocks, it is essential to consider the quality and track record of the management team as a critical factor in the company's growth prospects.

Stock Market Leader Need Not Be a Household Name

It is important to recognize that stock market leaders often emerge from relatively young and fast-growing companies that may not be well-known household names. In many cases, these young and dynamic growth stocks are not the subjects of widespread public recognition. In fact, the best growth opportunities often come from companies that have yet to gain significant attention from the mainstream market or media. When a company starts to receive extensive media coverage and becomes widely known, it may already be approaching its peak potential in terms of price appreciation. This is because once a company becomes too popular, there are fewer new buyers entering the market to drive its stock price even higher.

Furthermore, smaller companies, particularly those in the early stages of their growth, are often not on the radar of institutional investors or Wall Street analysts. These under-the-radar companies are less likely to be influenced by institutional trading, and when they eventually attract the attention of these larger players, it can lead to substantial price appreciation in a relatively short timeframe. Therefore, identifying and investing in lesser-known small growth stocks can offer significant potential for capital appreciation.

Use Industry Groups to Identify Leadership

Industry groups can provide valuable insights for identifying potential stock leaders and winners. When evaluating stocks, pay attention to the industry groups that are in an uptrend and showing strength. In a well-performing industry group, you will often find many stocks achieving new price highs, which is a clear indicator of current leadership within that sector. This trend suggests that these groups are poised to maintain their positions in the market for the near future.

To maximize industry group performance rankings, concentrate on sectors where an increasing number of stocks are making new highs. This indicates sustained growth and leadership within the sector. Additionally, within these top-performing industry groups, consider stocks that have a high EPS rank, preferably above 90. Such stocks are more likely to be potential leaders, exhibiting strong growth and earning capabilities. By focusing on these industry groups and stocks with robust EPS ranks, you can enhance your chances of identifying and investing in market leaders well-positioned for future success.

Sources to Scan for Industry Group Leadership

To identify industry group leadership and potential market winners, investors can rely on various sources that provide data on sectors, groups, and industries. One of the most comprehensive resources for this information is the Investor's Business Daily, which tracks 197 industry groups. *IBD's* data allows investors to pinpoint the top-performing industry groups and identify those with the highest percentage of stocks achieving new highs. It is also a valuable tool for checking the performance of different market sector indexes, offering valuable insights for investment decisions. Other organizations that track industry groups include Standard & Poor's, Bloomberg, FactSet, and Zack's Investment Research.

These sources offer investors the essential data they need to make informed investment decisions based on industry group performance. By regularly monitoring industry rankings and analyzing the data provided by these sources, investors can stay up to date with current industry leaders and position themselves for potential market success.

OTHER CHARACTERISTICS

This section explores a diverse range of essential traits beyond the conventional metrics, providing a nuanced understanding of unique factors that contribute to identifying winning stocks, and fostering a well-rounded investment strategy.

High Demand for Products

A successful growth company's rise to prominence is often driven by several key factors. First and foremost, such a company will establish itself as a market leader with innovative products that align with broader market trends and themes. Its offerings will meet a significant demand, setting it apart from competitors and positioning it as a frontrunner in the industry. The company's products or services will typically have a competitive edge with unique advantages, allowing it to control a niche area within the market. This competitive advantage is further reinforced by high barriers to entry, making it difficult for new players to compete effectively.

Furthermore, a successful growth company will maintain a strong product cycle, consistently introducing new and improved offerings to meet evolving customer demands. A significant portion of its revenues will be reinvested in research and development (R&D), ensuring its ability to innovate and remain competitive. The company may also introduce groundbreaking products or services that disrupt the industry and generate significant customer interest. These characteristics contribute to its leadership in the market and its potential to become a winning stock.

Strategic Market Position

A successful growth company secures a strategic market position that enables it to maintain high prices for its products or services. This is typically achieved through a combination of factors. The company will have established a strong market presence, often based on a combination of proprietary technologies, intellectual property, or other competitive advantages. Also, its offerings are positioned as premium or unique within the industry, allowing it to command higher prices.

A growth company's marketing strength, achieved through effective advertising, branding, and strategic alliances, facilitates outreach to a diverse customer base. Diversification mitigates risks associated with relying on a single customer, enhancing stability. Barriers to entry, like complex technologies and regulatory requirements, protect market position and contribute to growth potential. These factors collectively fortify the company's strategic position, enhancing its attractiveness as an investment.

Institutional Ownership Is High

Institutional ownership is a factor to consider when evaluating a potential investment in a stock. Institutions such as mutual funds, pension funds, and hedge funds are considered influential market participants due to their substantial financial resources and professional expertise. High institutional ownership is a positive indicator because it reflects the confidence these professional investors have in the company's growth prospects. Institutional investors typically conduct thorough research and analysis before making substantial investments, and this can provide additional validation for your own investment thesis.

When selecting stocks, balancing institutional ownership is crucial. Stocks with excessive institutional ownership, often above 50%, may lack significant growth potential as available capital from institutions is saturated. It is advisable to target stocks with moderate ownership (25%–50%) showing increasing institutional interest. This balance allows for potential additional institutional capital, driving value higher, while preserving opportunities for individual investors. Avoiding stocks with excessive institutional presence is prudent, as they may have already reached their peak potential for institutional-driven price appreciation.

Insiders Should Have a High Stake

High insider ownership is a favorable indicator when evaluating a stock for potential investment. When company executives, directors, and other insiders hold a significant stake in the company through stock ownership, it aligns their interests with those of shareholders. This alignment can be beneficial for individual investors because it means that the company's leadership has a personal financial stake in the stock's performance. If the stock price rises, insiders will benefit directly from the financial gains, creating an incentive for them to make decisions that promote shareholder value. Conversely, if the stock price falls, insiders will also experience a decline in their own net worth, motivating them to take actions that help support the stock's value.

Furthermore, high insider ownership can result in a reduction in the number of shares available for trading in the open market, which can lead to increased scarcity and, potentially, increased demand. The concept of "skin in the game" is highly regarded because it suggests that insiders are more likely to act in the best interests of the company and its shareholders when their own wealth is directly tied to the company's stock price. As such, individual investors often view companies with a higher percentage of outstanding stock held by insiders as more trustworthy and reliable, particularly when it comes to making strategic decisions that impact the company's financial health and long-term growth prospects.

Insider Buying Is Taking Place

Insider buying, which occurs when company executives, directors, and other insiders purchase shares of their own company's stock on the open market, is a strong indicator of their confidence in the company's future prospects. It suggests that those who are most familiar with the inner workings of the business have a positive outlook and believe that the company's performance is likely to improve or remain strong. When insiders buy shares, it can be a signal to individual investors that the company's financial health and growth prospects are sound.

The reason insider buying is considered a valuable indicator is that it reflects a personal financial commitment on the part of the company's leadership. When insiders invest their own money in the company's stock, they have a vested interest in its performance. If the stock price rises, they stand to benefit directly from the financial gains. Conversely, if the stock price falls, they will also experience a decrease in their own net worth, providing them with a strong incentive to take actions that promote the stock's value. For individual investors, this can be seen as a positive sign that the company's management believes in its ability to deliver value to shareholders and that its business prospects are on an upward trajectory.

Stock With a Small Float Should Be Avoided

The size of a stock's float, which represents the number of shares available for trading on the open market, can have a significant impact on its price dynamics. For investors, it is important to consider the float when evaluating a stock because it can influence the supply and demand balance, and ultimately, how easily the stock's price can be moved in either direction. A stock with a reasonable float typically strikes a balance that allows for relatively stable price movements, reflecting the law of supply and demand.

If a stock has a relatively high number of outstanding shares, it means there is a greater supply available in the market. Consequently, it can be more challenging for buyers to drive the stock price significantly higher, as it requires a substantial increase in demand to overcome the available supply. On the other hand, a stock with a very small float can be more susceptible to sharp price swings, as relatively small trading volumes can have a more pronounced impact on the stock's price. When evaluating a stock, it is essential to consider the float size in the context of your investment goals and risk tolerance. Stocks with larger floats tend to be less volatile, making them suitable for conservative investors, while stocks with smaller floats can offer more substantial price movements but come with increased risk and potential for significant volatility.

CHAPTER 4

COMPANY, INDUSTRY, AND SECTOR ANALYSIS

THOROUGHLY EVALUATE THE COMPANY

In this section, investors will learn how to evaluate a company from different perspectives, such as its business, product cycle, and management before investing in it.

Perform Fundamental Analysis

Fundamental analysis is a critical step in the stock selection process, and it forms the foundation of informed investment decisions. This thorough examination of a company and its operating environment involves the assessment of various factors and indicators that collectively determine the company's health, growth potential, and suitability for investment. These factors can include the company's financial statements, earnings, revenue growth, market position, competitive advantages, and overall performance.

In a comprehensive fundamental analysis, you delve into the company's financial health, looking at income statements, balance sheets, and cash flow statements to assess its ability to generate profits and cash flows. Evaluating a company's competitive advantages, industry dynamics, and long-term prospects is also crucial, as these factors can significantly impact its growth potential. Additionally, you may explore technical and sentiment indicators to gain insight into market trends and investor sentiment. A sound understanding of these elements allows you to make informed investment choices, aligning your portfolio with your financial goals and risk tolerance. Whether you are a value investor focused on undervalued stocks or a growth investor seeking companies with strong growth prospects, fundamental analysis provides the necessary insights to make informed investment decisions.

Study the Company's Business

Studying a company's business is a fundamental step in the process of evaluating its investment potential. This in-depth examination requires assessing the core aspects of the company's operations, including its products and services. The sustainability and quality of these offerings are crucial considerations, ensuring they aren't just fleeting fads but have long-term value. Analyzing the product cycle and upgrades can provide insight into the company's ability to adapt to changing market demands and stay competitive. A company's market share, leadership position, and control of a niche are also important factors to gauge its industry dominance and growth potential.

Moreover, it is essential to scrutinize the competitive landscape and identify any unique advantages or differentiators that set the company apart from its rivals. By thoroughly evaluating the company's business, you can gain a deeper understanding of its financial prospects, its position within the industry, and its potential for future growth. This knowledge is pivotal in determining whether the stock price is likely to appreciate in sync with the company's business expansion, making it a valuable component of the stock selection process.

Evaluate the Company's Products

Evaluating a company's products is a pivotal aspect of fundamental analysis when considering potential investments. Innovation plays a significant role in a company's profitability, as businesses that continually introduce innovative and cutting-edge products tend to enjoy a competitive edge. Investors should favor such companies because innovation often translates to higher profit margins and growth opportunities. Innovative companies are more likely to be rewarded with superior stock price appreciation, making them attractive investment candidates.

Furthermore, diversification within a company's product line can reduce risk. A company with a broad range of products is better positioned to weather industry fluctuations and market challenges. In contrast, companies with a single product or a product line lacking diversity are exposed to more significant risk. If their primary product faces issues or fails, these companies can become highly vulnerable. It is advisable to limit exposure to such companies in your investment portfolio to mitigate the potential impact of such vulnerabilities on your overall returns.

Study the Product Cycle

Analyzing a company's product cycle is integral to fundamental analysis, offering insights into potential revenue growth and profitability. A robust product cycle, marked by timely releases meeting market demand, signals optimism for investors, and often results in increasing revenues and profits, positively impacting the stock price. Thoroughly investigating the company's product release schedule is vital to understanding fluctuations in the revenue stream, aiding investors in informed decisions on buying or selling. Additionally, monitoring this schedule helps identify potential delays, advising caution and potential avoidance of the stock to mitigate risks.

Understanding a company's product cycle is a dynamic aspect of fundamental analysis, involving tracking the timing and impact of product releases. Staying informed about the company's product development and launch schedule enables investors to align their investment strategies with expected growth and financial performance, facilitating informed decisions on entering or exiting positions in the stock.

Evaluate Management Strengths and Weaknesses

Evaluating the strengths and weaknesses of a company's management team is a crucial aspect of fundamental analysis. Effective management is often a deciding factor in a company's long-term success or failure. The competence, experience, and strategic vision of a company's leadership team can significantly impact its ability to not only survive but also thrive in a competitive business environment. The importance of sound management should not be underestimated, as it plays a pivotal role in guiding a company to success.

As part of the analysis process, it is important to scrutinize the past track records and achievements of key executives and management personnel within the company. Their prior experiences and successes in other organizations can provide valuable insights into their leadership abilities and effectiveness. For instance, if the CEO or other key executives have demonstrated exceptional performance in their previous roles, it can instill confidence in investors that the company is in capable hands. These past achievements can serve as an indicator of the potential for strong leadership, which is a fundamental driver of a company's future performance and, consequently, its stock price.

Evaluate Management Characteristics

The evaluation of management characteristics is essential for determining the potential success of a company. Management's integrity and ethical standards are foundational aspects, as it is vital for leadership to operate with transparency, honesty, and ethical behavior. A management team that adheres to high standards of integrity will build trust within the company and among shareholders, fostering a more positive relationship between the company and its investors. This trust, in turn, is critical for maintaining investor confidence and encouraging long-term commitment to the stock.

A company's management should also exhibit strategic vision and the ability to develop and execute effective business plans. Strategic thinking is necessary to navigate competitive markets and identify growth opportunities. The capability to execute plans and willingness to invest in the company's future are important indicators of management's dedication to long-term success. Furthermore, management should be responsive and adaptable to changes in the market and economic conditions. Strong communication and marketing skills are also crucial for conveying the company's vision to both the investment community and customers. By assessing these characteristics, investors can gain insight into how management is perceived by the investment community and how well they are equipped to lead the company to success.

STUDY ENVIRONMENT, COMPETITION, AND OWNERSHIP

In this section, investors will gain insights into the multifaceted factors shaping a company's performance, including the environment in which it operates, competitive landscape, and ownership.

Determine Market Growth Expectations and Expansion Plans

It is crucial to assess the market growth expectations and expansion plans of the company in which you have invested. First, examine the markets where the company operates, including both domestic and international markets. Understanding the geographical reach of the company provides insights into its exposure to different economic conditions, regulatory environments, and customer bases. Companies that have a diversified

geographic presence may be better equipped to weather economic fluctuations and capture opportunities in high-growth areas.

Expansion plans are crucial in assessing a company's potential for
future growth. Investigate whether the company has a clear strategy and
plans to enter new markets or extend its presence in existing ones. The
company's ability to execute these expansion plans and its understanding
of the competitive landscape in target markets are vital factors in assessing
future growth prospects. Evaluating market saturation and competition
will help you gauge the pace at which the company's sales and profits might
expand, providing insights into the potential direction of the stock price.

Determine the Company's Market Control Status

It is essential to evaluate the company's market control status relative to its
competition. This assessment involves understanding whether the company
operates in a niche market, holds a monopoly, or maintains a significant
market share within its industry. Each of these scenarios has unique implications for the company's profitability and, by extension, its stock price.

In the case of a niche market, you should examine the company's
ability to maintain control of that niche and the strength of the barriers to entry. Niche areas can be highly profitable, as they often face less
direct competition. Companies that effectively protect their niche positions can enjoy sustained profitability, which can positively impact their
stock prices. If the company operates as a monopoly, it may also thrive,
but it must navigate potential challenges, such as regulatory burdens and
constraints on growth. These regulatory factors could affect the company's future prospects and stock performance. Evaluating the company's
market control status is an important aspect of fundamental analysis that
can guide your investment decisions.

Analyze Existing Competitors as Well as Potential Competition

When evaluating a company for investment, it is essential to assess both
its existing competitors and potential competition in the market. A comprehensive understanding of the competitive landscape can provide
valuable insights that influence your investment decision. For instance,
your analysis may uncover a strong competitor that is on the verge of
introducing a groundbreaking product, making it an attractive investment
option. In this scenario, the company you are evaluating could face significant challenges and increased competition, potentially affecting its
future performance. Consequently, you might opt to avoid investing in

this company and, instead, consider the competitor that appears to have superior growth prospects and investment potential.

This thorough examination of competitors helps you make more informed investment decisions, ensuring that you select companies with a competitive advantage and the ability to thrive in their respective markets. It is an important aspect of fundamental analysis that allows you to identify companies with strong growth prospects and avoid potential pitfalls associated with intense competition.

Check If Insiders Have Been Buying

When evaluating a potential investment, it is crucial to examine insider trading activity, particularly instances of insider buying. This information can be obtained from an SEC filing, company website, as well as financial news websites. While insider selling can occur for various reasons and may not always be indicative of the company's future prospects, insider buying is often viewed as a highly positive signal. Insider buying typically reflects the belief of company insiders (who possess intimate knowledge of the company's operations) that the stock's price is poised to increase. The greater the number of insider buyers and the more significant their purchases, the stronger the signal of confidence in the company's prospects.

Insider buying is a notable aspect of fundamental analysis because it suggests that those closely connected to the company have a positive outlook on its future performance. This can serve as a valuable indicator for investors, indicating potential upward momentum in the stock's price and contributing to the investment decision-making process.

Check If Institutions Have Invested in the Stock

When analyzing a stock, it is essential to assess the level of institutional ownership, as it can provide valuable insights into the stock's potential for price appreciation. Institutional ownership refers to the percentage of a company's outstanding shares held by institutions such as mutual funds, pension funds, and other large investment entities. This metric is significant because institutions possess substantial buying power and can significantly influence the demand for a stock.

If the level of institutional ownership falls within the range of 10% to 20%, it suggests that institutions have started to accumulate the stock. While this indicates some institutional interest, it also implies that there is ample room for further institutional buying. Ideally, investors often prefer to see a higher level of institutional ownership, typically falling within the

25%–50% range. This level implies a more significant presence of institutional investors in the stock, indicating that the stock may have caught the attention of the investment community. However, if the institutional ownership exceeds this range, it may signify that the stock has already been widely "discovered," and there might be limited potential for additional institutional buying to drive the stock's price significantly higher.

CONFIRM COMPANY'S FINANCIAL HEALTH

In this section, investors will learn how to analyze a company's health from different perspectives, using key metrics and indicators, which are crucial for assessing the robustness and sustainability of its financial standing.

Company Must Have Financial Strength

Investing in a company with robust financial strength and a solid balance sheet is essential for minimizing risks and ensuring the company's ability to withstand economic challenges and market volatility. A financially sound company has the necessary resources to overcome setbacks and adapt to changing business environments. Moreover, it can seize opportunities for expansion without overreliance on debt financing, which can lead to increased financial risk.

When evaluating a company's financial strength, it is crucial to consider various financial ratios and metrics. Favor companies with low levels of debt and a debt-to-equity ratio that is below the industry average. Low debt levels provide a cushion against financial instability and reduce the risk of insolvency during economic downturns. Additionally, having sufficient cash reserves and access to lines of credit gives the company the flexibility to execute its growth strategies and navigate unforeseen challenges. High return on equity, typically exceeding 15%, is a strong indicator of a company's efficiency and ability to generate profits from shareholders' equity. Healthy profit margins and a cash flow growth rate exceeding the earnings growth rate further demonstrate the company's financial resilience and potential for sustainable growth.

Analyze Financial Statements

When conducting fundamental analysis, it is crucial to analyze the three primary financial statements: the balance sheet, income statement, and statement of cash flows. Each of these statements offers a distinct perspective on the company's financial health and performance, contributing essential insights to your evaluation. The balance sheet provides a snapshot of the company's financial position at a specific point in time. It reveals the company's assets, liabilities, and shareholders' equity. Analyzing the balance sheet helps assess the company's liquidity, solvency, and overall financial stability. It can reveal the company's ability to meet short-term and long-term obligations and its asset base; including cash, accounts receivable, and fixed assets.

The income statement, however, details the company's revenues, expenses, and profitability over a specific period, such as a quarter or year. It provides a comprehensive view of the company's performance, showcasing its ability to generate profits and manage costs. Lastly, the statement of cash flows traces the inflows and outflows of cash within the company, separating them into operating, investing, and financing activities. This statement is valuable for understanding the company's cash generation, capital investments, and sources of funding. By analyzing these financial statements, investors can assess a company's financial health and make informed investment decisions.

Determine Financial Performance Trends

When evaluating a company's financial performance, it is essential to assess both its present situation and the trajectory it follows. A company's current financial numbers can appear promising, but their significance becomes clearer when considered alongside historical trends. By analyzing the financial data over several years, you can identify whether the company's performance is improving, stable, or deteriorating. It is important to not only recognize the trend but also understand the underlying factors driving that trend. For instance, if a company's profits are consistently increasing, you will want to determine whether this growth results from effective strategies or temporary circumstances.

To gain a comprehensive understanding of the company's financial health, it is essential to compare its performance with both competitors and industry standards. This comparative analysis provides context for assessing the company's relative strengths and weaknesses. By benchmarking against peers and industry norms, you can identify where the company excels and where it may need improvement, contributing to a more comprehensive evaluation of its financial performance.

Important Items to Review in Financial Statements

In any thorough financial analysis, several key items within the financial statements demand close scrutiny. Starting with the balance sheet, it is crucial to assess the company's financial strength and stability, with a focus on its assets, liabilities, and equity. A strong balance sheet typically exhibits ample assets compared to liabilities, indicating a healthy financial position. Additionally, a rising trend in revenues reflects the company's ability to generate income consistently, which is essential for sustaining profitability. The net income and EPS figures are vital indicators of a company's profitability and can signal its ability to provide returns to investors.

Cash flow is another critical factor to evaluate, as it reflects the company's ability to generate cash from its core operations. A positive cash flow demonstrates that the company can effectively manage its finances and potentially invest in future growth. Examining profit margins, such as gross and operating margins, is essential as well, as they reveal the company's efficiency in generating profits. An uptrend in these margins indicates an ability to control costs and maximize profitability. Lastly, R&D expenditure can offer insights into a company's innovation and long-term growth potential. A company that consistently invests in R&D may be better positioned to adapt to changing market conditions and maintain its competitive edge. Conversely, reviewing items like outstanding shares, receivables, and inventory levels can help identify any concerning trends, while monitoring debt levels for stability or reduction is important to ensure manageable financial obligations.

Cash Flow Should Be Healthy

Healthy cash flow is essential for a growth company to sustain and expand its operations. It provides the financial flexibility required for investing in growth initiatives and navigating through economic downturns. The more cash a company generates from its core operations, the better it can manage its finances and respond to opportunities and challenges effectively. In contrast, poor cash flow can have adverse consequences, potentially forcing the company to resort to borrowing or issuing more stock. Both of these actions can negatively impact earnings and the earnings per share, which, in turn, can affect the stock price.

Analyzing cash flow per share, which is calculated as the cash provided by operations divided by the total number of outstanding common shares, offers valuable insights into the company's cash flow performance on a per-share basis. It is a useful metric for assessing the efficiency of a company in generating cash relative to the number of shares available to investors. Moreover, if the company's cash flow growth rate significantly surpasses its earnings growth rate, it is generally regarded as a positive sign. It indicates that the company is converting a larger portion of its earnings into cash, which can be used for reinvestment, debt reduction, or returning value to shareholders, potentially strengthening its overall financial health and outlook.

Debt-to-Equity Ratio Should Be Low

A low debt-to-equity ratio is a favorable sign for a company and its investors as it signifies that the company relies less on debt financing and has a more conservative financial structure. The lower the debt/equity ratio, the lower the financial risk associated with the company, making it a safer investment. High levels of debt can pose risks, especially during economic downturns or periods of financial stress, which could hinder a company's ability to meet its financial obligations and can lead to distress or bankruptcy. Therefore, investors often prefer companies with a low debt/equity ratio.

When evaluating a company's debt/equity ratio, it is not only important to look at the current ratio but also to examine its trend over time. A decreasing debt/equity ratio over the past two to three years or in recent quarters is generally seen as a positive sign. It suggests that the company is actively managing its debt and working toward a more favorable financial structure. Furthermore, comparing the company's debt/equity ratio to others in its industry is a valuable benchmark. It should ideally be in line with, or even lower than, the industry average, as this reflects prudent financial management and reduces financial risk, making the company a more attractive investment.

ROE Should Be High

Return on equity is a key financial metric that measures a company's ability to generate profits from its shareholders' equity. A high ROE indicates that the company is effectively utilizing the capital invested by shareholders to generate earnings. For investors, a high ROE is a favorable sign as it signifies the company's efficiency and its potential to provide strong returns. When analyzing stock market winners, you will often find a positive correlation between high ROE and stock market success. Companies that consistently deliver a high ROE tend to attract investors and see their stock price rise.

A high ROE is a reflection of a company's ability to manage its assets and liabilities effectively, generate profits, and grow its shareholders' equity. It suggests that the company is efficient in producing returns on its investments, which is attractive to shareholders. Investors often look for companies with a high ROE as it demonstrates financial health and management's ability to deliver strong returns to its owners. However, it is important to consider the industry and sector norms while evaluating ROE, as certain industries may naturally have higher or lower ROE based on their characteristics.

Return on Sales and Margins Should Be High

Return on sales and profit margins are essential indicators of a company's efficiency and profitability. Return on sales, often referred to as operating margin or profit margin, measures the percentage of sales revenue that a company converts into profits. A higher return on sales implies that a company is managing its operations efficiently, turning a greater portion of its revenue into profits. High return on sales is a positive sign for investors as it indicates strong financial performance.

Profit margins, which include gross margin, operating margin, and net profit margin, provide insight into a company's ability to manage costs and generate profits at different stages of its operations. A high profit margin suggests that the company can maintain healthy profitability levels, even in the face of competitive pressures or economic challenges. When analyzing potential investments, comparing profit margins across companies within the same industry can be a useful way to gauge a company's competitive position and profitability relative to its peers. Investors often favor companies with high return on sales and profit margins, as these metrics reflect a strong ability to convert sales into profits, fueling business growth and potential stock price appreciation.

ANALYZE THE INDUSTRY GROUP AND SECTOR

This section discusses how industry groups and sectors should be analyzed and monitored, as they can significantly impact the performance of their constituent companies.

Determine Stock's Industry Group/Sector

To make informed investment decisions, it is crucial to identify the industry group and sector to which a stock belongs. Stock market analysts have categorized companies into various sectors and industry groups to facilitate the monitoring, comparison, and analysis of stocks with similar characteristics. These groupings help investors understand the broader economic environment in which a stock operates, as stocks within the same group often move in tandem or share similar trends. By determining the industry group and sector of your stock, you can gain valuable insights into the broader dynamics that may influence its performance.

If your stock belongs to an underperforming industry group, it is less likely to outperform the broader market. Conversely, if your stock is part of a sector or industry group experiencing strong growth and positive trends, it may have better prospects for appreciation. Evaluating a stock within the context of its industry and sector can provide essential context for your investment analysis and decision-making.

Study the Associated Industry Group and Sector

Studying the associated industry group and sector is essential because it provides crucial insights into the broader market dynamics influencing a specific stock's performance. While it is important to thoroughly evaluate a company individually, understanding the larger context is equally significant. Each company is part of a sector and industry group, and the members of these groups often move in tandem over time. For instance, if the technology sector is experiencing a positive trend, most technology companies will benefit from this tailwind. Conversely, when a sector or industry group faces challenges or a downturn, stocks within that group may experience downward pressure. Assessing the health and performance of the sector and industry group to which a company belongs can help you make more informed investment decisions.

By examining the broader context, you can better gauge the potential for your stock's future performance. If the sector and industry group are flourishing, it can be a favorable sign for the stock's prospects. Conversely, if the broader industry is facing headwinds, it may impact the stock's performance negatively. This holistic approach to analysis ensures a more comprehensive understanding of the factors influencing your investment.

Analyze Sector and Industry Group Health and Trend

Analyzing the health and trend of the sector and industry group is a fundamental step in assessing the potential for your investment. The success or failure of a company is often closely tied to the prospects of its industry or sector. If the industry is facing stagnation, intense competition, or obsolescence, it can significantly limit the growth potential of your investment. Therefore, it is essential to choose stocks that belong to industry groups with promising growth prospects and a positive trend.

The broader industry context can have a significant impact on your stock's performance. Stocks in sectors and industry groups that are flourishing and in an uptrend are more likely to outperform the market. Conversely, stocks in sectors or groups facing challenges may struggle to deliver strong returns. By taking into account the health and trend of the industry, you can make more informed investment decisions and increase your chances of achieving favorable returns.

Analyze Industry-Specific Indicators

Industry-specific indicators provide valuable insights into the performance and health of a particular sector or industry. These indicators are tailored to the unique characteristics and dynamics of a specific industry, making them highly relevant for assessing the prospects of companies within that sector. For example, same-store sales figures in the retail industry are essential indicators because they directly reflect the consumer demand and overall health of the retail sector. Similarly, the semiconductor industry's book-to-bill ratio is a crucial metric that reveals the industry's overall health and its potential for growth. Understanding these industry-specific indicators and their implications is vital for making well-informed investment decisions.

By using these tailored indicators, investors can gain a deeper understanding of the specific factors driving a particular industry and better anticipate trends and shifts within that sector. This information allows investors to align their investment strategies with the unique dynamics of the industry, increasing their ability to make successful investment decisions and navigate the complexities of different sectors more effectively.

VERIFY TECHNICAL AND TRADING INDICATORS ARE POSITIVE

In this section, investors are introduced to key technical and trading indicators, which are essential for understanding how they can impact the performance of individual stocks as well as the stock market.

Confirm Buy Decision by Using the Moving Average Line

Fundamental analysis provides a solid foundation for making investment decisions, focusing on a company's financial health and business prospects. However, for investors who incorporate technical analysis into their strategies, it is important to confirm buy decisions using additional tools like moving average analysis. This confirmation helps ensure that both the fundamental and technical aspects align before making an investment.

One widely used technique in this context is checking whether the stock is trading above its 200-day moving average line. This moving average serves as a valuable buy signal, indicating that the stock is in an uptrend. In cases where the stock is trading below this moving average, investors may wait for the stock to cross above the line and confirm a change in direction before considering a purchase. By combining fundamental and technical analysis and using the 200-day moving average as a confirming indicator, investors can make more well-rounded and informed investment decisions, enhancing their chances of success in the stock market.

Check the Stock Price Relative to Its 50-Day Moving Average

Another valuable technical analysis tool that can provide insights for investors is the comparison of a stock's current price to its 50-day moving average. When a stock's current price is trading above its 50-day moving average, it is considered a favorable sign. This situation suggests that the stock is on an upward short-term trend, and the majority of investors who purchased the stock in the past fifty days are currently in a profitable position, reflecting a positive sentiment. In contrast, when the stock price is trading below the 50-day moving average, it signifies a more negative sentiment among recent investors. These investors are typically underwater with their positions, which can lead to a bearish sentiment. Short-term traders often use this indicator to assess the current momentum and sentiment surrounding a stock.

By analyzing the stock's relationship with its 50-day moving average, investors can gain insights into the short-term market sentiment and momentum. This information can be helpful in decision-making, especially for those who engage in shorter-term trading strategies and want to align their positions with the prevailing market sentiment.

Confirm That the Stock Is Being Accumulated

Confirming that a stock is under accumulation rather than distribution is a critical aspect of technical analysis, especially for those looking to invest based on the actions of institutional investors. The accumulation/distribution indicator serves as a valuable tool to make this determination. If the stock has an A or B rating on this scale, it is a clear indication that professionals and institutional investors, such as mutual funds and pensions funds, are actively accumulating the stock. Their buying actions can drive the stock's price higher, making it an attractive investment opportunity.

Conversely, if the accumulation rating is D or E, indicating distribution, it implies that institutional investors are offloading the stock. This trend could exert downward pressure on the stock price. A neutral rating of C indicates a balanced situation, with no clear accumulation or distribution bias. Monitoring this indicator can provide valuable insights into how institutional investors are positioning themselves with the stock, helping investors make informed decisions and potentially align their strategies with the professionals' actions in the market.

Confirm That the Stock Has Liquidity

Liquidity is a critical factor to consider when investing in stocks. Investors want to have the ability to buy or sell their positions with ease, particularly in a fast-moving and sometimes unpredictable market. Inadequate liquidity can pose significant challenges when trading a stock. A thinly traded stock with low daily trading volume may become especially problematic during times of market volatility or in the event of a broader market sell-off. In such situations, selling even a modest number of shares could be challenging, and the sale might only occur at significantly lower prices, resulting in substantial losses.

Additionally, during extreme market conditions or crashes, thinly traded stocks may not find buyers at all, leaving investors with illiquid positions that are difficult to exit. To mitigate these risks, investors should avoid stocks with insufficient liquidity, typically defined by a daily trading volume of less than 200,000 shares. Ensuring that a stock has a reasonable level of liquidity can provide a level of confidence that investors will have the flexibility to buy or sell shares as needed, even under adverse market conditions.

Evaluate Trading Risks

When evaluating a stock for investment, it is crucial to assess the trading risks associated with it. The level of institutional ownership can be a significant factor. If a large portion of the outstanding stock is held by large institutions, particularly in the case of a small company, it can limit the stock's upside price appreciation potential. High institutional ownership makes the stock more vulnerable to price swings if one or two institutions decide to sell their holdings. Such concentrated selling can lead to significant price drops, posing a risk to investors. It is important to exercise caution and thoroughly consider the implications of high institutional ownership before investing in such a stock, especially if there isn't a compelling reason to do so.

Alternatively, if the institutional ownership of a stock falls within the range of 25%–50%, it can be viewed as a positive sign. This indicates a healthy level of institutional interest without the concentrated ownership that could lead to rapid price fluctuations. Furthermore, investors should closely examine the stock's float and daily trading volume. Inadequate liquidity can result in difficulties when buying or selling shares, particularly during periods of market volatility, making it essential to assess these risks before making an investment decision.

CHAPTER 5

SELLING

WHY SELLING IS A COMMON PROBLEM

This section discusses the various challenges investors often face when deciding to sell a stock, unraveling insights to overcome common hurdles and optimize selling decisions for a successful investment journey.

Selling Strategy Is Lacking

An essential aspect of successful stock market investing is the implementation of a well-defined selling strategy. While many investors are proficient at selecting and buying stocks, they often neglect the crucial component of knowing when and how to sell. A robust selling strategy is as vital as a buying strategy, and investors should understand both aspects to thrive in the stock market. Without a clear selling strategy, selling decisions may be guided by irrational emotions, hunches, or reactions to external events, which can lead to poor outcomes.

Investors need to develop and adhere to their selling strategy to maintain a disciplined approach to managing their investments. This strategy should be based on predefined criteria that help determine when to sell a stock. Whether it involves setting specific price targets, using technical indicators, or reacting to fundamental changes in the company, having a well-thought-out selling plan can protect and optimize investment portfolios, preventing investors from making impulsive decisions that may lead to losses.

Inability to Acknowledge Mistakes

Acknowledging and addressing mistakes is a fundamental aspect of wise investing. Even the most skilled and experienced investors can make errors, and the critical difference lies in how they handle these mistakes. It is not the act of making a mistake that poses the most significant challenge but rather the inability to admit when one has picked a losing investment. Successful investing entails promptly recognizing and taking action to mitigate the impact of errors on one's portfolio. The refusal to accept a mistake and trying to rationalize it as a sound, long-term investment can lead to compounding losses, hindering overall portfolio performance.

A prudent approach involves establishing clear criteria for exiting a losing investment and adhering to these parameters. Whether it is a pre-defined stop–loss level, specific fundamental changes in the company, or a technical indicator signaling a downturn, investors must have a plan in place to cut their losses. Accepting mistakes as part of the investment process and proactively addressing them can help investors protect their capital and preserve their long-term financial goals.

Loss Definition Is Vague

Defining what constitutes a loss is a crucial aspect of an effective selling strategy. There are multiple interpretations of a loss, such as when unrealized profits turn into a loss or when there is an actual loss based on the purchase price. Investors should establish a clear and consistent method for defining losses, and this method should be outlined in their selling rules. To prevent ambiguity and emotional decision-making, these rules should be rigorously enforced. For instance, a common approach could be selling if a stock experiences a 20% pullback from its peak or if the purchase-price-based loss exceeds 8%. Regardless of the chosen basis for defining a loss, it is imperative not to procrastinate when it becomes evident that a stock has become a losing investment with dim prospects for price appreciation.

By setting unambiguous criteria and adhering to them, investors can make objective decisions about when to sell a stock, reducing the risk of emotional attachment and subjective judgments. A well-defined strategy for recognizing and addressing losses ensures that investments are managed in a disciplined and rational manner, which can lead to better portfolio outcomes over the long term.

Not Knowing When to Exit

It is essential for investors to recognize that no stock should be considered a permanent fixture in their portfolio. Every stock, whether it is performing well or poorly, should have a defined exit strategy. Knowing when to sell a stock is a vital component of an investment strategy, driven by factors like profit-taking, risk management, or the need for portfolio diversification. A fundamental rule in this regard is the practice of cutting losses, as this should be a cornerstone of the overall plan for wealth growth in the stock market. By adhering to loss-cutting rules, investors protect their capital and maintain a disciplined approach, aiming to minimize the impact of inevitable setbacks.

It is important to understand that, even in the presence of numerous small losses, a few substantial winning investments can significantly outweigh those losses, providing a net positive result. This principle reinforces the significance of a sound selling strategy that incorporates risk management measures, helping investors remain consistent and avoid making emotional decisions when it comes to selling stocks.

PLAN AND BE READY TO SELL

This section discusses how to plan and be prepared to sell a stock, so that selling is done by choice and is not a forced decision.

Avoid Forced Selling

Investors should be vigilant to avoid being pushed into a position where they are compelled to sell a stock hastily. The choice to sell should remain firmly within the control of the investor and not driven by external or reactionary factors. A well-defined strategy with established selling rules is essential in mitigating the chances of forced selling. Such a strategic approach helps in making consistent decisions rather than being subject to emotional or impulsive actions.

Investors should also be cautious not to allow external circumstances, such as immediate financial needs, to dictate their selling decisions. Allowing such external pressures to influence selling choices can lead to financial losses. Therefore, individuals should only invest in the stock market with funds they can afford to allocate for a more extended investment horizon. When financial needs or liquidity requirements are imminent, alternative financial instruments should be utilized instead of relying on stock market investments to meet those demands. This distinction helps to ensure that an investor's stock portfolio remains driven by their investment goals and strategy, rather than external urgencies.

Select a Selling Strategy

Having a well-defined selling strategy is paramount in managing a stock portfolio effectively. This strategy should encompass a comprehensive plan for various scenarios that may arise over time, covering aspects such as cutting losses, taking profits (both short-term and long-term), and the disposition of long-term winning stocks. The absence of a specific strategy can leave investors ill-prepared to respond effectively to market fluctuations and stock-specific developments. In contrast, a carefully crafted strategy equips investors with the necessary tools to make informed buy/sell decisions, whether it involves adding to existing positions or selling during unexpected price declines.

Moreover, a robust selling strategy helps investors maintain discipline and avoid emotional or hasty decisions. It acts as a compass, guiding them through turbulent market conditions and protecting them from the risks associated with sudden market swings. By adhering to a pre-established strategy, investors can navigate the stock market with greater confidence and stay focused on their long-term financial goals.

Establish and Adhere to a Price Target

Setting and adhering to price targets is a crucial aspect of any successful stock investment strategy. These price targets serve as guidelines for managing a stock position effectively and are instrumental in determining when to buy, sell, or hold. By establishing clear price targets for potential loss-selling, short-term profit-taking, and long-term profit-taking, investors can enhance their decision-making process and proactively protect their investments.

The use of limit "sell orders" is a practical means of implementing these price targets. These orders are executed only if the stock reaches a specified price, allowing investors to automate the selling process when predefined conditions are met. This not only helps maintain discipline but also mitigates the impact of emotional decision-making. Regularly evaluating a stock's performance in light of these price targets ensures that investors remain focused on the stock's fundamentals and overall market conditions. In times of bull markets, being open to raising the target price can be particularly advantageous, provided the underlying reasons for the stock's rise remain strong. However, in bear markets, investors should exercise caution and avoid hastily adjusting their price targets.

List Specific Reasons for Buying a Stock

Maintaining a record of specific reasons for buying a stock and setting performance expectations is a prudent practice that can help investors stay disciplined and methodical in their investment approach. These records serve as a reminder of the investment thesis and criteria used when purchasing the stock. Regularly reviewing this list and comparing it to the current state of the stock is a crucial step in managing one's portfolio effectively. If the initial reasons for buying the stock are no longer valid, investors should be prepared to make objective decisions and, if necessary, sell the stock. For example, if the stock was initially chosen due to its projected 25% earnings growth, but the company's earnings growth falls below that target, this disciplined approach would dictate selling the stock. This strategy ensures that investment decisions are based on realistic assessments rather than unwarranted optimism or emotions.

By establishing these clear criteria and enforcing them unemotionally, investors can protect their portfolios and make informed decisions. This practice helps avoid "hope-based" investing and emphasizes the importance of staying true to a well-defined investment strategy. It encourages investors to adhere to the principles and rationale that guided them when buying the stock, ensuring that their investments are aligned with their original objectives.

Manage Your Losers

Managing losing stocks is an integral part of investment strategy. Investors need to develop effective ways to address such situations. When faced with a losing stock, the first step is to conduct a comprehensive analysis of the reasons behind the stock's decline or lack of price appreciation. Understanding the root causes helps in making an informed decision regarding whether to sell, hold, or possibly buy more of the stock. This process should be objective and based on facts rather than emotions. If the losses are too substantial and selling the stock is unlikely to generate significant proceeds or reallocate resources efficiently, it may not be advantageous to sell. In such cases, a decision to continue holding the stock can be considered.

If the fundamentals of the company remain strong and the decline appears temporary, dollar-cost averaging is a strategy to contemplate. It involves purchasing additional shares of the stock at a lower price, thereby lowering the average cost of the investment and potentially improving the overall position as the stock's price recovers. This approach should be undertaken with a clear understanding of the company's prospects and should be a part of a well-defined investment strategy. The key is to take an objective, disciplined approach when dealing with losing stocks and ensure that every decision is driven by a thorough analysis of the situation rather than emotional reactions.

Recognize When Avoiding Selling Is Not a Mistake

While selling is a critical aspect of investment strategy, there are scenarios where avoiding or delaying selling can be a prudent decision. One such instance is when widespread pessimism surrounds a stock. Sometimes, market sentiment can become overly negative, which may lead to undervaluation of fundamentally strong companies. If an investor recognizes the pessimism as unwarranted and the stock's core fundamentals remain intact, holding the position or even accumulating more shares could be beneficial in the long term.

Another situation arises when a stock has appreciated significantly and appears "overvalued." Overvaluation can be misleading, especially if the company's earnings growth prospects and market conditions justify the high valuation. In such cases, it might be wise to reevaluate the stock's intrinsic value and hold onto it if it remains fundamentally strong. Similarly, if a stock reaches its price target, but the company's fundamentals continue to improve and support a higher valuation, it may be worthwhile to adjust the price target and maintain the position. High P/E ratios may signal overvaluation, but if the stock is a proven winner and market conditions are favorable, holding the position might lead to further gains. Other scenarios, such as institutional selling or temporary price declines that don't undermine the initial reasons for buying, can also justify avoiding hasty selling decisions and taking a more measured approach to managing the position. Ultimately, these situations require a thorough assessment of the stock's fundamentals and market dynamics to determine the best course of action.

PRIMARY REASONS FOR SELLING

This section provides strategic clarity pertaining to the key factors driving the decision to sell stocks, empowering investors with a nuanced understanding to make informed and profitable decisions pertaining to their stock portfolios.

Fundamentals Are Deteriorating

When a stock's fundamentals start to deteriorate, it is essential to prioritize this as the primary reason for selling. Fundamental analysis should guide your investment decisions, and if you observe any signs that can materially affect a company's future earnings or growth, such as a significant slowdown in earnings or revenue growth, taking immediate action is crucial. Selling a stock that exhibits signs of weakening fundamentals helps to protect your portfolio from potential losses.

In some cases, the stock price might experience a decline, but it is essential to differentiate between market-driven factors like overall market weakness, a correction, or normal fluctuations and fundamental issues within the company. If the stock's decline can be directly attributed to fundamental reasons, it is advisable to sell the stock promptly. However, it is important not to rush into selling when the stock price dips due to broader market conditions or when it follows a substantial upward move, as these situations may not necessarily indicate fundamental problems with the company. Careful assessment and discernment between market-driven fluctuations and genuine fundamental issues are vital when determining the appropriate course of action for your investment.

Interest Rate Trend Changes

Changes in the interest rate trend can have significant implications for the stock market and your investment strategy. Monitoring interest rates is essential because they can influence the overall market sentiment. If you observe a shift in the interest rate trend, particularly if it is moving upward, it is considered a negative sign for the stock market. In response to rising interest rates, it is advisable to reduce your exposure to stocks or consider reallocating your investments to favor companies that are less sensitive to interest rate fluctuations.

Specifically, keeping an eye on key interest rate indicators like the federal funds rate and the discount rate is crucial. When the Federal Reserve initiates an interest rate hike cycle by increasing these rates, it generally has a negative impact on the stock market. A widely accepted principle on Wall Street is that stock markets tend to decline after the Federal Reserve raises interest rates three times. Furthermore, if the short-term interest rates exceed long-term interest rates, it should be regarded as a significant warning sign, signaling potential economic challenges and potentially negative consequences for stocks. Staying informed and prepared to adjust your investment strategy in response to interest rate trends is essential for safeguarding your portfolio.

Financials Are Deteriorating

Assessing a company's financial health is a crucial part of your investment strategy. A company that is not financially sound faces a precarious future. Financial constraints can severely limit its ability to expand, make strategic decisions, or react to market changes effectively. In such circumstances, the company may be compelled to take on additional debt, which can lead to even more financial difficulties and pose risks to shareholders.

Therefore, if you observe that a company's financials are deteriorating or its business prospects are waning, it is prudent to consider selling the stock.

Deteriorating financials can manifest in various ways, such as declining revenues, shrinking profit margins, increasing debt levels, or decreasing cash reserves. Paying close attention to these key financial indicators is essential in your decision-making process, as it can help you avoid potential losses and make informed choices when it comes to managing your stock portfolio.

Earnings Growth Is Disappointing

Earnings growth is a fundamental driver of stock performance, and when a company consistently falls short of expectations in this regard, it should be taken as a strong warning signal. If you notice that a company's earnings have declined for two consecutive quarters or that the rate of quarterly earnings growth has slowed significantly, it is essential to investigate the underlying reasons. These can range from internal management issues to external market conditions or competitive pressures. Understanding the root causes of disappointing earnings is crucial before making a sell decision.

While disappointing earnings can trigger concerns, it's equally important to differentiate between one-time events and ongoing issues. If a thorough investigation reveals that the company's failure to meet earnings expectations is due to a specific, nonrecurring event, and there is a reasonable expectation that future growth will align with forecasts, it may be premature to sell the stock. However, if there are structural issues that indicate a continued struggle to meet earnings targets, a sell decision could be warranted. Staying vigilant and informed about a company's earnings performance is essential for making sound investment decisions.

Loss Exceeds a Predetermined Percentage

One of the most common and disciplined reasons for selling a stock is when the loss on that stock exceeds a predetermined percentage, typically a maximum allowable loss set by the investor, often around 10%. This rule helps to enforce discipline and ensures that emotions, which can lead to significant losses or delayed selling, are not allowed to influence the decision-making process. Even though there might be various reasons to justify holding onto the stock, adhering to these rules is critical to maintain a structured and rational approach to investing. While there might be instances when you decide to make exceptions to this rule, it is advisable to closely monitor the stock and place a lower mental stop, never to be violated, a few percentage points below the original predetermined number if this rule is relaxed.

In addition to the emotional aspects, setting a predetermined maximum loss also serves as a risk management tool to protect your capital. It ensures that you do not expose your portfolio to excessive risk and prevents any single stock's loss from significantly impacting your overall investment performance. Consistency in applying this rule can help you maintain discipline and mitigate the negative effects of large losses in your portfolio.

Price Action Is Negative

A declining stock price should not be a sole reason to rush into selling. In fact, it is common for stocks to experience normal pullbacks or fluctuations, and these should be approached with caution and further evaluation. When a stock declines, it is important to thoroughly assess the situation to ascertain whether the decline is due to fundamental issues or external market conditions. Fundamental weakness, deteriorating business prospects, or unexpected events should be closely examined as potential causes for the decline.

However, if the stock's price continues to fall and enters a clear downtrend, particularly if this extends beyond the maximum allowable loss set by the investor, it may be prudent to consider selling the stock. A sustained decline without any meaningful rallies can serve as a warning sign, suggesting that the stock's prospects may not be favorable. Investors should keep a close eye on the stock's price action and have predefined rules for selling in place to make rational and unemotional decisions when confronted with a stock in a prolonged downward trend. This approach can help to prevent the negative impact of significant losses and protect the overall performance of the investment portfolio.

Profit Taking

Profit taking is a common practice among both traders and long-term investors. For traders, it often involves capitalizing on short-term price increases, where they sell a stock after a quick uptick in price to secure a profit. However, even long-term investors engage in profit-taking, but their approach typically revolves around realizing capital gains after a stock has experienced substantial appreciation. In such cases, investors decide to sell stocks that have shown a significant increase in value over an extended holding period. Additionally, modest profit-taking is common among investors who have held their stocks for different time frames and decide to sell to capture moderate capital gains.

The decision to engage in profit taking can be influenced by various factors, including individual financial goals, market conditions, and the stock's performance. Whether it is realizing quick gains from trading activities or securing profits from long-term investments, profit-taking strategies can play a crucial role in managing an investment portfolio effectively.

Stock Buying Reasons No Longer Exist

Disciplined investors follow a structured approach by keeping a record of the specific reasons for buying a particular stock. This meticulous practice allows them to periodically reassess the stock's investment thesis in light of the current market conditions. If it is evident that the primary reasons behind their initial investment decision no longer hold, they make the rational choice to sell the stock. For example, if an investor initially purchased a stock with the expectation of a 30% earnings growth rate, but that rate subsequently decreases to 20%, serious consideration should be given to selling the stock.

To maintain an analytical and unemotional approach to decision-making, it is important to maintain a record of the factors that influenced the purchase of each stock at the time of acquisition. This disciplined approach helps investors avoid clinging to stocks based on outdated or irrelevant rationales and ensures that investment decisions remain grounded in reality. As market conditions evolve and stock performance fluctuates, the ability to adapt and respond based on the latest data is critical for maintaining a successful investment portfolio.

Market Is Giving a Strong Sell Signal

Recognizing market signals and the overall health of the stock market is crucial for investors to make informed decisions about their stock holdings. When the broader market starts to show signs of weakness, it is common for most stocks, including previous winners, to be negatively affected. In response to this, investors often opt to reduce their exposure to stocks as a precautionary measure. Several key sell signals can be observed in the market, which indicate that a market top or a looming bear market may be on the horizon. These include a notable change in the market's direction accompanied by heavy trading volume and the underperformance or weakening of market leaders on rising trading volume.

Another strong sell signal occurs when the market experiences distribution for several days within a two-week period, suggesting that professional investors are selling off their holdings, which should prompt investors to consider reducing their equity exposure. Furthermore, if leading stocks in the market begin to falter and many of the declining stocks maintain high relative strength, typically with RS ranks above 80, it is a negative signal for the overall market and may serve as a warning for investors to take a cautious approach. In such instances, selling stocks or lightening up on positions can help investors safeguard their portfolios from potential market downturns.

SECONDARY REASONS FOR SELLING

This section dissects additional factors influencing stock divestment, providing investors with a comprehensive toolkit to navigate the intricacies of decision-making for optimal portfolio management.

Better Prospect Is Identified

One common reason for switching stocks is the identification of a better investment opportunity. The primary goal of investing is to identify stocks that have the potential to appreciate in value over time. When an investor identifies a stock that offers significantly better price appreciation prospects compared to their current holdings, it makes sense to switch to this new opportunity. By switching to a stock with superior potential for price growth, investors can optimize their portfolio's returns and capture the benefits of a more promising investment.

Another rationale for switching stocks is to manage and reduce the level of risk in one's portfolio. There are situations where investors may need to adjust their portfolio to achieve a lower level of risk exposure. In such cases, investors can choose to switch to a comparable stock that carries less risk. This strategic shift allows them to reallocate their investments and bring their overall portfolio risk within acceptable limits. Reducing risk exposure is an essential component of managing a diversified portfolio and ensuring a balanced risk-return profile.

Stock Is a Laggard

Investors often have specific expectations and investment goals when they allocate their capital to a particular stock. These expectations may be based on a variety of factors, including the stock's financial health, earnings prospects, and market conditions. It is important to provide a stock with a reasonable amount of time, typically six to eighteen months, to perform and meet these expectations. During this period, investors assess whether the stock is achieving the anticipated results.

However, if the stock turns out to be a laggard and fails to meet the expected performance within the given time frame, it may be time to consider selling the stock. A laggard is a stock that underperforms, even in the presence of favorable factors such as strong earnings and positive news. It is a reminder of a fundamental principle known to seasoned investors: A good company does not necessarily translate into a good stock. In such cases, selling the stock allows investors to reallocate their capital to more promising opportunities and ensure that their investments align with their financial goals.

Sector Leaders Crumble

When stocks within a specific industry group or sector experience a collective decline, it is often an indicator of broader market trends. The performance of stocks within the same industry group or sector tends to be correlated, and their movements are influenced by similar macroeconomic factors. Therefore, if the sector leaders begin to falter and show signs of weakness without a substantial recovery or a clear trigger, it can be an early warning signal that other stocks within the sector may be negatively affected in the near future. Investors should closely monitor the situation to assess the reasons behind the sector's underperformance.

The severity of the decline and the cause should be carefully evaluated to determine the appropriate course of action. This may involve reassessing selling options, particularly if the downturn is significant or if it is driven by factors that could have lasting repercussions. By closely following the market and sector leaders, investors can make informed decisions to protect their investments and adjust their portfolios accordingly.

Company Is Relying on Laurels and Historical Performance

In the stock market, historical performance is important to some extent, as it can provide insights into a company's track record and management's ability to deliver results. However, investors should remember that past success does not guarantee future performance. The stock market places a significant emphasis on a company's future prospects and its ability to adapt and evolve. If a company becomes complacent and relies too heavily on its historical achievements, it may find itself struggling to meet the demands and challenges of a rapidly changing business environment.

Companies that rest on their laurels, cut back on R&D, and fail to innovate can quickly lose their competitive edge. To make informed investment decisions, focus on businesses that are forward-thinking, continuously investing in R&D, and positioning themselves for future growth. It is essential to consider a company's future potential and its capacity to adapt to evolving market conditions rather than dwelling solely on its past accomplishments.

Institutions Are Dumping

Institutional activity in the stock market carries substantial weight and can significantly influence the direction of individual stocks and market indexes. When institutions begin to offload their positions, it often signals that professional money managers with extensive resources and research capabilities see fundamental weaknesses or anticipate adverse market conditions. As an individual investor, observing institutional selling patterns can serve as a strong sell signal, especially if you witness consistent distribution days within a relatively short timeframe. A distribution day occurs when a stock or market index experiences a price decline accompanied by unusually high trading volume. Multiple distribution days within a condensed period suggest that large institutional players are unloading shares, which may lead to further price declines.

By keeping a close watch on such institutional behavior, you can make informed selling decisions to protect your investments. While not all sell-offs are driven by deteriorating fundamentals, a sudden and persistent surge in institutional selling should be regarded as a red flag, prompting you to reconsider your position and possibly take action to mitigate losses or reallocate your investment capital elsewhere.

Company Overpaid for an Acquisition

Mergers and acquisitions can be a strategic move for a company to expand its business and market share, and Wall Street often responds positively to such announcements. However, the success of an acquisition largely depends on the price paid and the impact on the acquiring company's financial health. When a company pays too much for an acquisition, it can lead to a slew of financial and operational challenges. The excessive acquisition cost can weigh on the company's financial statements, affecting its earnings, cash flow, and debt levels. Investors typically react negatively to these developments, and it can have lasting consequences for the stock.

In such cases, even if the stock's price doesn't plummet dramatically, it often experiences limited price depreciation in the aftermath of the costly acquisition. As investors become wary of the company's financial situation and management decisions, they may decide to divest their holdings, putting downward pressure on the stock. Therefore, as an investor, it is essential to monitor the impact of acquisitions on a company's financials and its stock's performance and consider selling if you believe that the acquisition was poorly executed or too expensive.

Portfolio Needs to Be Pruned

Portfolio pruning is a crucial aspect of managing your investments effectively. As stocks appreciate in value, their weighting in your portfolio can grow beyond your desired allocation. This shift can result in an unbalanced and riskier portfolio. To maintain the desired risk-reward profile, investors periodically need to prune their portfolios by selling some shares of stocks that have appreciated significantly. This action not only helps you adhere to your portfolio allocation targets but also allows you to lock in profits.

Additionally, the periodic evaluation and pruning of your portfolio are essential to enhance its overall performance. Removing underperforming or stagnant stocks from your holdings can free up capital to invest in more promising opportunities. This proactive approach can help boost the overall returns of your portfolio in the long run. When considering which stocks to prune, it is advisable to start with the losers, selling those positions that have not performed well or have declined in value. You can also sell stocks with modest profits or those that no longer meet your investment expectations to make room for more promising investments. By continuously evaluating and pruning your portfolio, you can keep it well-aligned with your financial goals and risk tolerance.

Tax Reasons

Tax considerations are often a significant factor in investment decisions, particularly at year-end. Selling underperforming or losing stocks can help offset the capital gains generated by selling winning stocks, thus reducing the overall tax liability. This strategy allows investors to maintain a more tax-efficient investment portfolio by taking advantage of capital losses to mitigate the tax consequences of capital gains. Investors typically execute this tax-loss harvesting strategy towards the end of the year when they have a clearer understanding of their tax situation.

When deciding to sell a winning stock for tax reasons at the end of the year, it can be beneficial to defer the actual sale until the beginning of the new year. This deferral allows investors to delay the tax liability associated with capital gains, taking advantage of the time value of money. By deferring the tax payment, investors can potentially earn returns on the funds they would otherwise have used to settle their tax bill, which can enhance the overall performance of their investment portfolio. It is essential to work closely with a tax advisor or accountant to ensure that your investment decisions align with your tax and financial planning goals.

TECHNICAL REASONS FOR SELLING

This section discusses how technical indicators can be used to identify stocks that need to be sold, fostering a proactive and informed approach to stock investing.

Moving Average Uptrend Turns Into a Downtrend

The moving average trend analysis is a valuable tool for investors, as it provides insights into the stock's long-term and short-term performance. A stock trading above its 200-day moving average is seen as being in a bullish long-term uptrend, signaling potential investment opportunities. Conversely, when a stock falls below its 200-day moving average, it signifies a reversal in the long-term trend, indicating a bearish phase. However, it is crucial not to act immediately on this bearish signal because stock prices can be subject to fluctuations, and a move below the moving average may not necessarily lead to a sustained downtrend. Investors should wait for confirmation and assess the stock's price movement to make an informed decision.

The 50-day moving average is another useful indicator for traders and provides insights into the stock's short-term trend. If a stock falls below its 50-day moving average, it is considered bearish, signaling potential short-term selling pressure. Just like with the 200-day moving average, investors should exercise caution when considering this signal and look for further price confirmation before making any sell decisions. These moving average trends should be incorporated into a comprehensive analysis of a stock's fundamentals and technicals to ensure well-informed investment choices.

Volume Indicator Is Negative

Analyzing trading volume is a crucial aspect of evaluating a stock or market average's price action. The relationship between price and volume can provide valuable insights into the strength or weakness of a particular move. When a stock experiences a notable price decline, and this drop occurs on heavy or abnormal volume, it is often considered a bearish signal. High-volume sell-offs indicate that significant selling pressure is in play, which can potentially lead to further price declines. Investors should closely monitor such price drops and evaluate their positions in light of this negative volume indicator.

However, when a stock achieves a new price high but does so with low trading volume, it is viewed with skepticism. This suggests that the strength behind the price advance is limited, as it lacks substantial investor participation. Furthermore, situations involving churning, where there is heavy trading activity without significant price appreciation, should raise caution. Such scenarios may indicate that traders are actively moving shares back and forth without causing substantial price movement, signaling an uncertain and potentially unsustainable market trend.

Distribution Is Recognized

Recognizing distribution, particularly when large institutions are offloading stocks, is a crucial aspect of smart investment decision-making. The actions of institutional investors, often referred to as the "smart money," can significantly impact stock prices and market trends. One effective method to identify distribution is by examining the accumulation/distribution rating, provided by many financial analysis tools. If this rating drops to D or E, it typically indicates a phase of distribution, implying that institutions are selling their holdings. This is a clear sell signal for investors who need to be attentive to these rating changes.

In addition to the accumulation/distribution rating, shifts in the number of down days versus up days in price changes can also serve as a distribution indicator. When a stock starts to decline, an increase in the number of down days can be a warning sign, suggesting that institutions may be disposing of their holdings. Furthermore, if the price drop is more significant than a typical correction (e.g., 10%–12% from a peak), it may indicate substantial selling pressure from institutions. Investors should closely monitor these distribution signs as they can provide valuable insights into market dynamics and help in making timely selling decisions.

Price Performance Is Negative

Price performance is a crucial aspect of stock analysis, and it can offer valuable insights into the stock's overall health and potential sell signals. One such signal is the breach of the stock's support level. The support level represents a price point at which the stock typically finds buying interest and reverses its downward movement. If the stock's support level fails, it's often an indication of increased selling pressure and can be interpreted as a sell signal. Investors should pay attention to this development, especially in a rising market, as it may suggest a weakening position for the stock.

Another important indicator is the relative strength rank. If the RS rank falls below 70, particularly during a period of market strength, it can be considered a sell signal. A declining RS rank indicates that the stock is underperforming compared to the broader market or its peers. This underperformance can signify reduced investor interest and potential price weakness. Additionally, assessing the group strength, or the performance of the stock's industry or sector, is crucial. If the stock appears to be moving independently and the group's strength is weak, it is a negative sign. Stocks tend to perform better when they are supported by a robust group, so a stock's ability to sustain gains may be compromised if it lacks group participation. These price performance indicators serve as important guides for investors in making well-informed sell decisions.

Stock Is Overextended

The overextension of a stock's price can be a cause for concern, particularly for those who utilize technical analysis in their trading strategies. In an ideal scenario, a stock should experience a gradual and sustainable increase in price. When a stock rises too rapidly or to a level significantly above its moving average lines, it becomes vulnerable to a potential pullback or correction. This overextension increases the probability of a price decline, which is why technical analysts often recommend considering a sell decision when a stock is overextended, typically when its approximately 70%–100% above its 200-day moving average line. This guideline serves as a warning sign that the stock may be due for a correction, and selling in this situation can help protect gains or mitigate potential losses.

Additionally, technical analysts look at the stock's relationship with its short-term moving averages, such as the 50-day moving average. If a stock closes significantly above its 50-day moving average or surges above its upper channel line, it can trigger a sell evaluation. These situations often signal that the stock's price has become stretched and may be due for a pullback or a period of consolidation. While these indicators may not always lead to immediate declines, they serve as cautionary signals to investors to reevaluate their positions and consider selling if the stock appears overextended.

SELL SIGNALS FOR SMALL COMPANIES WITH FEW OR NICHE PRODUCTS

This section navigates the unique challenges of smaller enterprises, uncovering specific indicators and signals that prompt strategic selling decisions for optimal risk management in the dynamic stock market landscape.

Earnings Growth Rate Decreases Significantly

Companies with small growth profiles are often associated with high investor expectations. These firms typically command high P/E ratios because investors anticipate rapid earnings and revenue growth. The more significant the expected growth, the higher the P/E ratio investors are willing to afford the stock. When a company's earnings growth rate decreases significantly, it can create a misalignment between the high P/E ratio and the reduced growth prospects, making the stock appear overvalued. To restore a balance between the stock's valuation and its growth outlook, its price may need to decline. Consequently, a substantial decrease in earnings growth rate serves as a potent sell signal for such companies.

A notable drop in earnings growth signifies that the company may not be living up to the previously set high expectations. This situation often leads to a reevaluation of the stock's price, with investors potentially deciding to sell. It is important to remember that stock prices are influenced by earnings performance. Therefore, when growth prospects diminish, investors tend to reassess their holdings, which can result in selling pressure as they seek to align stock prices with the new, lower growth expectations.

Business Conditions Change

The business environment in which a small, niche products company operates can be particularly sensitive to changes. The entry of a new, well-funded competitor into the market can significantly disrupt the business landscape and erode market share, leading to potential losses for the company. As a result, any change that carries the potential to impact the company's operations and future business prospects should be carefully assessed.

Rapidly losing market share over a short period or for two consecutive years should be regarded as a strong sell signal for a small growth company. This loss of market share not only threatens the company's competitive position but can also negatively affect its financial performance. Investors should be vigilant and responsive to these developments, as maintaining a proactive approach is crucial when monitoring the health and prospects of smaller companies with niche products in dynamic markets.

Financial Position Deteriorates

The financial health and stability of a company are crucial factors that underpin its long-term success. For small companies, in particular, maintaining a strong financial position is of paramount importance due to their limited resources and leverage compared to more established, larger enterprises. Small growth companies often rely on growing cash flows to fuel their expansion and development. When their financial position deteriorates and they struggle to generate the expected cash flow, it can have significant implications for their future growth and operations.

In such situations, small companies may need to explore alternative sources of financing, which often means taking on more debt. This not only introduces additional financial risk but can also have a detrimental impact on existing shareholders. For investors in small growth companies, it is essential to closely monitor the financial stability and performance of these businesses, as financial deterioration can be a potent sell signal, indicating potential trouble ahead.

Critical Product Is Delayed

Small companies often have a more concentrated product portfolio, with their success heavily reliant on just a few critical offerings. When one of these critical products faces delays or garners negative press after its introduction, it can create significant challenges for the company. In such situations, it is essential for investors to assess the reasons for the delay and how it affects the company's competitive position. If the analysis reveals that the delay or negative publicity is undermining the company's prospects, it is a clear sell signal.

Furthermore, the introduction of a formidable competing product that has the potential to substantially impact the company's market share and competitiveness is also a compelling reason to consider selling. Small companies may be more vulnerable to competition due to their limited resources and smaller market presence, making it crucial for investors to closely monitor their competitive landscape and be prepared to take action when a major competitive threat arises.

Litigation Poses a Significant Risk

Serious litigation can pose a substantial risk for any company, regardless of its size. When a small company becomes entangled in significant legal disputes, it not only drains financial resources but also diverts management's attention away from critical business operations. The potential for an adverse judgment in such litigation can be particularly devastating for smaller companies, as it can lead to severe financial losses and even threaten the company's existence. For instance, the loss of a major patent lawsuit could prevent a small company from selling its flagship or only product, seriously impairing its ability to compete in the market.

As an investor, it is prudent to establish a rule to avoid companies that are exposed to litigation with the potential to severely impact their business operations or competitive position. Conduct thorough due diligence and evaluate how ongoing or pending legal matters may affect the company's financial health and future prospects. In cases where litigation risk is high and could lead to catastrophic consequences, selling the stock may be the most prudent course of action to protect your investment.

Company Starts Wasting Money

When a company's management begins making decisions that appear irrational and resources are being squandered on nonproductive assets and expenses, it is a clear warning sign that the company may be heading in the wrong direction. If these questionable actions appear to be part of a pattern rather than isolated incidents, it becomes imperative to seriously consider selling the stock. Management's actions, such as pursuing questionable acquisitions, venturing into high-risk markets, awarding exceptionally high perks and compensations to corporate executives, and other nonstrategic financial moves, should be viewed as strong indicators that the company is making poor choices that could negatively affect its financial health and future performance.

As an investor, it is crucial to closely monitor the company's financial decisions and evaluate whether these actions align with its long-term strategy and profitability goals. If management's choices consistently appear detrimental to the company's overall health and value, selling the stock may be a prudent move to protect your investment from potential harm.

6

STOCK PRICES AND VALUATION

FACTORS CAUSING STOCK PRICES TO RISE OR FALL

This section delves into the intricate dynamics that influence stock price movements, providing investors with insight into the myriad factors that shape the volatile ebb and flow of stock prices.

Key Performance Drivers

The primary performance drivers in the stock market are closely tied to the broader economic landscape. Corporate profits are a fundamental component, as they reflect a company's ability to generate earnings for shareholders. When corporate profits are on the rise, it typically signals a healthy economic environment, and investors become more optimistic about the future, leading to stock market gains. Conversely, any factors that threaten corporate profitability, such as increased costs or decreased demand, can trigger market declines.

The overall state of the economy is another critical factor influencing stock market performance. A growing and stable economy tends to boost investor confidence and drive stock prices higher, as it implies increased consumer spending, business expansion, and job growth. Contrastingly, economic downturns or recessions can lead to investor caution and market declines. Additionally, inflation and interest rates play a signifi- cant role in stock market movements. High inflation and rising interest rates can erode the purchasing power of both companies and consumers, impacting corporate profits and reducing investor enthusiasm, leading to market declines. Conversely, low inflation and low-interest rates often create a favorable environment for stocks, as they encourage borrowing, spending, and investment. Therefore, investors closely monitor economic indicators, inflation data, and central bank policies to gauge their potential impact on the stock market.

Demand for Stock Increases

Stock prices go up when the forces of supply and demand create a favorable environment for buyers. Investors, driven by various factors, contribute to fluctuations in stock prices. When demand for a stock increase, typically due to positive developments, investor sentiment, or strong performance, its price rises. Conversely, when more investors want to sell a stock than buy it, the price tends to decline. This supply-and-demand dynamic is at the core of stock price movements.

Several key factors can drive an increase in demand for a stock. First and foremost, increased profitability or strong earnings performance often attracts investors. When a company reports robust earnings results or demonstrates a consistent track record of profitability, it creates a positive outlook, encouraging more buyers to enter the market and drive up the stock price. Additionally, expectations of future earnings growth can also spur demand, as investors anticipate higher profitability in the coming quarters or years. Moreover, a general positive trend in the broader stock market, reflected in indexes like the S&P 500 or Dow Jones Industrial Average (DJIA), can contribute to increased demand for individual stocks, leading to higher prices as well. These factors collectively influence investor behavior and contribute to the upward movement of stock prices.

Key Factors That Attract Buyers

First and foremost, an actual increase in a company's profitability, as reflected in its earnings, is a significant catalyst for driving demand and pushing the stock price higher. Strong earnings reports signal financial health and success, attracting both individual and institutional investors who seek to benefit from the company's positive performance. Such earnings growth indicates the company's ability to generate profits, which often leads to higher valuations.

Anticipation of future earnings growth is another critical factor drawing buyers to a stock. When investors expect that a company will report higher earnings in the future, they are more inclined to purchase its shares. These expectations can be based on various factors, including the company's strategic initiatives, market opportunities, and economic trends. A company with a compelling growth story is likely to attract a strong investor interest, contributing to stock price appreciation.

Additionally, a general upward trend in the stock market or a particular industry group can also boost demand for individual stocks. Investors often seek opportunities in sectors or industries that are performing well, leading to increased demand for stocks within those categories. A rising tide in the broader market or a specific industry often lifts individual stocks, resulting in price increases and attracting buyers who want to capitalize on the positive trend. These primary factors combine to create favorable conditions for stock price appreciation and act as strong magnets for potential investors.

Additional Factors That Influence Stock Performance

External and internal factors play pivotal roles in shaping a company's stock performance. External factors encompass environmental conditions beyond the company's immediate control, such as the broader economic landscape and prevailing interest rates. These external factors can significantly impact a company's operations, business outlook, and profitability. Economic conditions, for instance, can influence consumer spending, which, in turn, affects a company's sales and revenue. Likewise, interest rates can influence a company's borrowing costs and access to capital, which can directly affect its profitability. These external factors serve as a backdrop against which a company's performance is evaluated, and they can have far-reaching consequences for its stock performance.

Moreover, internal factors are directly related to the company's core business operations. These factors have a more direct influence on a company's performance, including its operations, business prospects, profitability, and even its long-term viability. Internal factors may include aspects like the company's management team, product quality, operational efficiency, and its ability to innovate and adapt to changing market conditions. A well-managed company with a strong product or service offering, efficient operations, and a robust competitive strategy is more likely to thrive and experience positive stock performance. Internal factors, in this context, represent the aspects of the company over which it has a greater degree of control and responsibility. Successful management of both external and internal factors is essential for a company to achieve and sustain strong stock performance over time.

Why Stocks Are Volatile in the Short-Term

The short-term volatility of stocks can be traced back to a complex interplay of multiple factors. Economic and business conditions are often at the forefront of investors' concerns, as they seek to gauge how these factors will impact a company's performance. Economic indicators, such as gross domestic product (GDP) growth, employment figures, and inflation rates, can spark market reactions as they provide insights into the broader economic environment. Additionally, a company's specific business conditions, including its quarterly earnings reports and guidance, can trigger substantial short-term stock price swings.

Market behavior and internal momentum are also major contributors to stock volatility. Market trends, investor sentiment, and trading patterns play a role in shaping stock price movements. Market participants may react to trends like sector rotation, which involves shifting investments among different sectors based on market conditions and expectations. Furthermore, news items, whether directly related to a company or not, can trigger significant stock price fluctuations. Information, whether accurate or speculative, often drives market reactions as investors attempt to quickly digest and react to the latest developments. The dynamic nature of these factors, combined with the constant flow of information in today's interconnected world, leads to the short-term volatility that characterizes stock markets.

What Moves Stock Prices in the Short-Term

In the short-term, stock prices are primarily influenced by investor expectations and perceptions rather than just fundamental factors. These expectations can be highly sensitive to various day-to-day factors, including news events, economic data, and market sentiment. Positive news, such as strong earnings reports or favorable economic indicators, can attract buyers and drive stock prices higher as investors become optimistic about a company's future profitability and growth prospects. Conversely, negative news or disappointing results can lead to selling pressure, causing stock prices to decline as investors react to the new information with caution or pessimism. As a result, stocks can exhibit significant volatility over short time frames, which can span from a few hours to several months.

Investor sentiment also plays a crucial role in determining short-term stock price movements. Sentiment is influenced by a variety of psychological and emotional factors, including fear, greed, and market psychology. Traders and investors often respond to changes in sentiment, and their collective actions can lead to rapid price changes. Short-term market participants, such as day traders and swing traders, frequently rely on technical analysis and momentum indicators to capture profits in this environment. Overall, the short-term dynamics of stock prices are heavily influenced by the ever-changing expectations, perceptions, and emotions of market participants, making them susceptible to rapid fluctuations and market sentiment shifts.

What Moves Stock Prices in the Long Term

In the long term, stock prices are primarily driven by sound fundamental factors that reflect the underlying financial health and performance of a company. These fundamental factors serve as the foundation for valuing individual stocks and the broader market. Some of the key factors that determine the long-term price trajectory of a stock include its earnings and dividends growth, financial condition, competitive positioning within its industry, and returns compared to alternative investment options like bonds and certificates of deposit (CDs). The growth and consistency of a company's earnings and dividends over time play a critical role in assessing its intrinsic value and its attractiveness to long-term investors.

While stock prices can experience significant short-term volatility driven by factors such as investor sentiment, news events, and market psychology, the influence of fundamental factors becomes more pronounced over longer time horizons. Investors often evaluate stocks based on their earnings potential, cash flow, balance sheet strength, and competitive advantages in the industry. These factors are more likely to exert their full impact on stock prices as investors take a longer-term perspective and consider the company's ability to generate sustainable profits and deliver value to shareholders over time. As a result, in the long term, stocks tend to be more influenced by their intrinsic worth and financial performance, making fundamental analysis a vital tool for assessing their investment potential.

Investor Perceptions Impact Stock Prices

Investor perceptions are highly dynamic and can have a substantial impact on stock prices, often leading to short-term fluctuations and even prolonged trends in either direction. These perceptions are influenced by a multitude of variables, from economic indicators and company news to market sentiment and global events. Because of the complexity and sheer number of factors involved, it can be challenging to maintain objectivity and systematically evaluate stocks. This complexity is compounded by the ever-changing values of these variables, making it inevitable that investor perceptions will shift in response to various developments, both company-specific and market-wide.

When investors' views change, stock prices may respond accordingly, either increasing, decreasing, or staying steady. If you, as an investor, identify that the prevailing perceptions of a company are negative and unlikely to change in the foreseeable future, it is important to consider whether holding onto the stock is the best course of action. Making such an evaluation and being proactive about managing your portfolio in response to changing perceptions is crucial for investors looking to maximize their returns and minimize risks in the stock market.

ADDITIONAL FACTORS INFLUENCING STOCK PRICES

This section describes additional factors, which be significant in some cases, that impact the price performance of stocks, either positively or negatively.

Traders

The Internet has revolutionized the way information is disseminated and accessed, particularly in the world of stock trading. With news and data readily available at the click of a button, traders can react swiftly to any developments in the market or specific companies. When negative news is released or a stock's price falls below key technical indicators like moving averages, it triggers a near instantaneous response from traders. The result is often a rapid influx of sell orders as numerous traders aim to offload their shares simultaneously. This surge in selling activity creates significant downward pressure on the stock's price, contributing to sharp declines.

Conversely, positive news and developments can propel a stock higher, as traders react just as promptly to capitalize on the opportunities presented. When a favorable announcement is made, such as a strong earnings report or a major partnership agreement, it can trigger a flurry of buy orders, leading to a rapid increase in the stock's price. These dynamics highlight the significant role that traders play in shaping short-term stock price movements, where market sentiment can change rapidly in response to the latest news and data.

Analyst Recommendations

Analyst recommendations provide valuable insights into the perceived prospects of specific stocks. When analysts issue a "buy" recommendation, it signifies their belief that the stock has the potential for significant price appreciation, making it an attractive investment opportunity. Conversely, a "sell" recommendation suggests that the stock is expected to underperform, and investors should consider divesting their holdings. The "hold" rating advises maintaining the current position, which implies that, while there may not be an urgent need to sell the stock, it may not present a compelling opportunity for additional buying.

Understanding these ratings is crucial for investors to make informed decisions. However, investors should not rely solely on these recommendations and should conduct their own research to make well-informed investment choices. It is also important to consider the credibility and track record of the analysts and the underlying factors influencing their recommendations.

Impact of Analyst Recommendations

Analyst recommendations hold significant sway over investor sentiment and can have a substantial impact on stock prices. When an analyst upgrades a stock, it typically leads to increased buying activity as investors perceive the stock as having improved growth potential. This increased demand can drive the stock price higher. Conversely, a downgrade recommendation can result in a sell-off as it signals that the company's prospects may have deteriorated, prompting investors to reduce or divest their holdings. The extent of this impact is influenced by various factors, including the nature of the recommendation change, the market's prior expectations for the stock, and the element of surprise. A highly unexpected upgrade or downgrade may elicit a more pronounced market response.

Monitoring the accuracy of specific analysts in predicting a stock's performance and earnings estimates is a valuable practice. If you find that a particular analyst consistently provides reliable insights, their recommendations may carry more weight in your decision-making process. It is important to stay informed about the recommendations of these trusted analysts and consider their assessments in conjunction with your own research to make well-informed investment choices. This strategy can help you navigate the stock market with greater confidence and potentially achieve more successful outcomes.

Share Buyback Announcements

Share buyback announcements by a company can have a significant positive impact on its stock price. When a company announces its intention to repurchase its own shares, it sends a strong signal to the market that it believes its stock is undervalued. This act of confidence often reassures investors and can lead to increased buying activity, causing the stock price to rise. The reduction in the total number of outstanding shares also effectively increases EPS, since earnings are divided by a smaller share count. Higher EPS is typically well received by investors as it reflects improved profitability on a per-share basis and can further contribute to the stock's upward momentum.

The effect of share buybacks is amplified by the fundamental principle of supply and demand. With fewer shares available for trading, the supply of the stock is reduced, making it relatively scarcer. In response, investors may compete to acquire the remaining shares, driving up the stock price. Consequently, share buyback announcements are often seen as a positive corporate action that can enhance shareholder value and reinforce investor confidence in the company.

Manipulation and Hype

The stock market, despite being heavily regulated, can still be vulnerable to manipulation and hype. Various tactics are employed to artificially inflate or deflate stock prices. For example, companies may issue misleading statements with the aim of temporarily boosting their stock prices. Additionally, short sellers may spread rumors to create negative sentiment and drive down stock prices, ultimately profiting from the decline. Unscrupulous analysts might release biased recommendations for personal gain, and false news releases can be distributed to mislead investors. While these manipulative practices can have short-term effects on stock prices, it is important to understand that, in the long run, a company's profitability and fundamentals remain the most crucial factors for sustainable value.

As an investor, it is essential to remain vigilant and focus on the underlying fundamentals of a company. While market manipulation and hype can lead to temporary fluctuations, a company's true value is determined by its financial health, earnings, and long-term growth prospects. By staying informed and discerning between genuine news and misleading information, you can make more informed investment decisions and avoid being swayed by short-term market dynamics.

Stock Splits

Stock splits are often misunderstood by some investors who believe that a stock split will lead to extraordinary profits. The misconception is that after a stock split, which essentially increases the number of shares while reducing the stock price per share, the stock will eventually rebound to its previous price level, resulting in substantial gains. This belief leads to a spike in the stock price upon the announcement of a stock split. However, extensive research and studies have consistently shown that stock splits have no lasting impact on a stock's long-term price performance. While short-term fluctuations may occur before and after a split, the ultimate destination for the stock price is determined by the company's underlying fundamentals. Investors should exercise caution when they observe a company engaging in excessive stock splits, as this can indicate overly optimistic sentiment and may not align with the company's true value.

In reality, stock splits are essentially cosmetic changes that do not affect a company's financial health, earnings, or intrinsic value. The number of shares an investor holds increases, but the overall ownership stake remains the same. It is the company's fundamentals and performance in the market that should guide investment decisions rather than the occurrence of a stock split.

Mergers and Acquisitions

Mergers and acquisitions (M&A) are often perceived as positive events in the stock market. When a company is acquired, its shares are typically withdrawn from the stock market, reducing the overall supply of that stock. If demand remains constant, the decrease in supply can lead to a positive impact. In many cases, the stock price of the acquired company rises, often receiving a premium over its trading price when the acquisition is announced. This increase in the stock price is seen as a benefit to the shareholders of the company being acquired.

Conversely, the stock price of the acquiring company may experience a drop upon the announcement of the acquisition. This drop is often associated with concerns that the acquiring company may have overpaid for the acquisition, which can be viewed negatively by investors. The extent of the drop in the acquiring company's stock price can vary depending on the specific terms of the deal and how well it is received by the market. It is important to note that M&A transactions are complex and involve many factors that can affect stock prices, making it essential for investors to carefully evaluate the potential impact on both the acquiring and acquired companies.

EXTERNAL FACTORS INFLUENCING STOCK PRICES

There are many external factors that can impact the business as well as the stock price of a company, which are described in this section.

Inflation

Inflation has a significant impact on the stock market. Investors often choose between various investment options, such as stocks, bonds, and money market funds. When inflation remains low, stocks are generally favored because they have the potential to offer higher returns compared to other assets. However, when inflation starts to rise and the Federal Reserve (aka "The Fed") responds by raising interest rates to combat inflation, it can negatively affect stocks. The reasoning behind this is that rising inflation reduces the real value of future earnings for companies, making it more challenging for stocks to provide adequate returns when adjusted for inflation. In essence, inflation dilutes the value of future earnings, which leads to a decrease in stock prices and causes concern among investors and financial markets.

As a result, Wall Street views inflation as a potential threat, since it can erode the purchasing power of earnings and create uncertainty in the stock market. When inflation is on the rise, investors may shift their preferences toward assets that provide better protection against inflation, such as Treasury Inflation-Protected Securities (TIPS) or commodities. Understanding the dynamics of inflation and its effects on stock prices is crucial for investors to make informed decisions and manage their portfolios effectively.

Monetary Policy

Monetary policy and its associated conditions play a pivotal role in influencing the overall trend of the stock market. Key factors, such as the prevailing interest rate trends, the state of inflation or deflation, and decisions made by the Federal Reserve, are central drivers that define the dominant direction of the stock market. Once an upward or downward trend has been established, it often persists for an extended period, typically ranging from one to three years. For investors, it is essential to closely monitor changes in monetary policy and attempt to identify any shifts in these trends. If such changes suggest a bullish or bearish pattern for the market, investors should reassess their investment strategies to ensure they are aligned with the anticipated market conditions.

The Federal Reserve, as the central bank of the United States, wields significant influence over the economy and financial markets through its monetary policy decisions. The Fed can impact the stock market by adjusting interest rates, conducting open market operations, and signaling its stance on economic conditions and inflation. Investors, therefore, need to be vigilant in following the Federal Reserve's actions and statements, as they can provide crucial insights into the future trajectory of the stock market and help them make informed decisions regarding their portfolios.

Factors Causing Interest Rates to Rise and Fall

Interest rates, which are crucial determinants of economic and financial market conditions, can be classified into two primary categories: short-term and long-term rates. Typically, stronger economic growth exerts upward pressure on short-term interest rates. The Federal Reserve Board has a significant role in regulating short-term interest rates, often using monetary policy tools to manage economic conditions and control these rates. Long-term interest rates, however, are influenced by various factors, including the outlook for inflation and the interest rate differentials between the United States and other foreign countries. Over the long term, the levels of government spending and deficit financing, in addition to fluctuations in the inflation rate, serve as key determinants of the extent to which long-term interest rates either rise or fall.

Understanding the dynamics of interest rates, both short-term and long-term, is vital for investors and market participants. These rates have a profound impact on a wide range of financial instruments, including bonds, mortgages, and lending practices, which in turn can influence investment strategies and portfolio management decisions. Therefore, staying informed about the factors that drive interest rate movements is essential for making sound investment choices in various economic environments.

Relationship Between the Stock and Bond Markets

The relationship between the stock and bond markets is a complex and interdependent one. Bonds are essentially long-term, fixed-interest securities that, like stocks, can experience price fluctuations. In general, when inflation and interest rates rise, bonds tend to be negatively affected as they erode the effective yield of fixed-rate bonds. As a result, factors that contribute to higher interest rates and inflation are typically detrimental to bonds. Therefore, if bond prices rise, leading to a lower yield (since bond prices and yields move inversely), it is often interpreted as an indication that the economy may be heading for a period of weakness, which could result in lower interest rates.

This relationship has implications for both stock and bond investors. When bonds become less attractive due to lower yields, some investors may shift their focus toward stocks, expecting better returns. Conversely, when bonds are considered more appealing due to higher yields, investors may be more inclined to allocate their funds to bonds, potentially diverting funds away from the stock market. This dynamic interaction between the stock and bond markets highlights the importance of monitoring interest rates, inflation, and economic conditions when making investment decisions involving these two asset classes.

METHODS FOR VALUING STOCKS

Buying an overvalued stock will reduce the ultimate profitability of an investment. Therefore, investors must understand the methods used to value stocks, which are described in this section.

How Stock Prices Are Determined

The determination of stock prices is a fundamental process in the stock market, and it involves the interaction of various factors and market participants. A stock represents a trading commodity, and the price is ultimately determined through the continuous matching of willing buyers and sellers. Both buyers and sellers aim to determine a price that they find favorable for their respective transactions, and the market facilitates this process.

Valuing stocks is a complex endeavor, as it requires investors to assess the relationship between price and intrinsic value. The challenge stems from the fact that the actual intrinsic value of a stock is difficult to quantify accurately. Furthermore, investors must consider the various investment options available to them, making the valuation process even more intricate. Ultimately, the stock market's dynamic nature results from the ongoing evaluation of stocks by market participants who collectively set the prices based on their perceptions and expectations, as well as external influences like economic conditions, corporate performance, and market sentiment.

Commonly Used Valuation Methods

The most commonly used valuation methods in stock analysis offer investors a range of techniques to assess a stock's worth. Among these methods, four stand out as frequently employed by investors to evaluate stocks. These techniques primarily focus on comparing the stock's value to the broader investment landscape, assessing its relative value compared to other investments, projecting its expected performance, and calculating its intrinsic value. The selection of a specific valuation method often depends on the investor's approach and preferences. For instance, value investors tend to favor the intrinsic value approach as a central component of their investment strategy, while other investors may prioritize different methods based on their investment objectives and risk tolerance.

By comparing these various methods, investors can develop a comprehensive view of a stock's potential and risks. These valuation techniques provide investors with tools to make informed decisions and effectively navigate the dynamic and complex world of the stock market.

Valuing Through Comparison With Investment Alternatives

Valuing stocks by comparing them to other investment alternatives involves a critical assessment of the stock's potential in relation to various investment options. This method aims to determine the most attractive vehicle for deploying funds. Investors consider both nonstock investments, such as bonds and CDs, as well as different sectors or industry groups within the stock market. This holistic analysis incorporates two key factors that significantly influence the valuation process: interest rates and inflation. These elements play a pivotal role in shaping the relative appeal of stocks compared to other financial instruments, such as bonds. For instance, when interest rates increase, investors tend to favor bonds over stocks due to the more predictable and secure nature of fixed-income securities.

By weighing these factors, investors can make informed decisions regarding their capital allocation and select investments that best align with their risk tolerance and financial goals. The comparative approach helps investors assess the relative merits of various investment options and adapt their strategies in response to changing market conditions.

Valuing By Comparing Relative Value

Valuing stocks by comparing their relative value involves assessing a stock's worth in relation to its competitors, which are vying for the same pool of investment capital. This method employs various criteria for comparison, such as earnings, dividends, growth rates, or other relevant investment parameters chosen by the investor. Additionally, stocks are compared to widely recognized stock market benchmarks, such as market indexes or averages, including the S&P 500 and NASDAQ. Investors can also gauge a stock's relative value by comparing it to specific industry groups or sectors within the broader market.

This method allows investors to evaluate a stock's performance and prospects within the context of its industry and the overall stock market. By comparing a stock's metrics to those of its peers and benchmark indexes, investors can gain valuable insights into whether the stock appears overvalued or undervalued. This comparative analysis assists investors in making well-informed investment decisions that consider the competitive landscape and the potential for outperformance relative to other investment options.

Valuing By Comparing Performance Expectation

Valuing stocks by comparing their performance expectations involves evaluating a stock's anticipated performance over the next six to twelve months in relation to the expected performance of other stock alternatives and the broader stock market. The primary goal is to pinpoint the stock that is poised to deliver the most favorable performance during the designated investment horizon, surpassing selected stock market indexes and averages, as well as competing stock alternatives. This method is rooted in the investor's unique investment expectations and risk tolerance, allowing for a tailored assessment of stocks in terms of their growth potential.

Investors using this method focus on the near-to-intermediate term, making it suitable for those looking for relatively short investment horizons. By comparing a stock's projected performance against that of alternative investments and the market as a whole, investors aim to select stocks with the best growth prospects, as they anticipate these stocks will outperform their peers and deliver superior returns over the specified time frame. It allows investors to strategically position their investments based on their short- to medium-term goals and market outlook.

Valuing By Intrinsic Value Determination

Valuing stocks through intrinsic value determination involves establishing a stock's true worth in isolation, without regard for how other stocks are valued in the market. The primary objective is to ascertain the market value of the company, which represents the value that shareholders would receive if the company were to be liquidated. In this approach, the focus is entirely on analyzing the company's financial health, examining factors such as its assets, liabilities, book value, earnings, dividends, and other fundamental indicators to determine its fair market value.

Investors employing this method seek to identify stocks that are trading at a substantial discount to their intrinsic or real value. By conducting a thorough analysis of the company's financials and underlying fundamentals, they aim to pinpoint stocks that are potentially undervalued, presenting opportunities for capital appreciation over the long term. This method is particularly favored by value investors who believe that markets can misprice stocks, and by identifying such discrepancies, investors can capitalize on the potential for future price corrections. It provides a more intrinsic and fundamental approach to stock valuation, often focusing on the balance between risk and reward in a more long-term investment horizon.

CHAPTER 7

PROFITABILITY AND PRICE PERFORMANCE

GENERAL

This section discusses profitability and price performance, both of which are important for investors, who need to understand their various aspects to ensure that their investments provide acceptable returns.

Importance of Earnings

Earnings play a pivotal role in determining the attractiveness of a stock as an investment. The consistency and growth of a company's earnings are crucial factors that directly influence its stock price. For investors, the ability of a company to generate profits is a fundamental indicator of its financial health and strength. Companies with a track record of increasing profits are often seen as more desirable investments because they demonstrate their ability to adapt and thrive in a competitive market environment.

Historically, stocks that have experienced robust and consistent earnings growth have been associated with better investment outcomes. Whether its established industry leaders or emerging growth companies, a pattern of increasing earnings is typically viewed positively by investors. Such companies are seen as having the potential to provide better returns and capital appreciation, which often attracts investors seeking value and growth. On the contrary, companies that consistently fail to deliver profits are usually met with skepticism and can face reduced investor interest and declining stock prices. It is essential for investors to favor companies with a strong earnings track record and, ideally, focus on those achieving annual earnings growth rates of 20% or more, as this typically indicates robust financial performance and the potential for future stock price appreciation.

How Earnings Are Reported

Quarterly earnings reports are a key event in the world of stock investing. Companies are required to report their earnings, along with financial highlights, every three months. These reports provide a comprehensive overview of a company's financial performance during the specified quarter and are eagerly awaited by investors. The timing of these reports can vary from one company to another, but many follow a calendar-based schedule. Typically, companies report their quarterly earnings in April (for the first quarter), July (for the second quarter), October (for the third quarter), and January (for the fourth quarter and full year). Investors closely monitor these quarterly earnings announcements because they have the potential to significantly impact a company's stock price.

Earnings reports are typically released through various channels, including the company's official website, official press releases, financial news websites, and major newspapers. These reports contain vital information, such as revenue, earnings per share, net income, and other financial metrics that investors and analysts use to evaluate the financial health and performance of a company. The contents of these reports, along with management's commentary and guidance for the future, can have a profound effect on investor sentiment and influence trading decisions. Consequently, investors often pay close attention to these reports as they seek to make informed investment choices and respond to market opportunities.

Learn How to Interpret Earnings

To make informed investment decisions, it is crucial to learn how to interpret reported earnings since they are a primary driver of stock prices. Start by analyzing both quarterly and annual earnings reports. Pay attention to the percentage increase in earnings year over year, which provides insights into a company's growth trajectory. When examining a specific quarter, compare it to the same quarter from the previous year to identify seasonality or any significant changes in performance. For instance, compare the third quarter of 2023 with the third quarter of 2022, as this allows for a more relevant year-over-year comparison.

It is also essential to evaluate the current quarterly earnings increase, expressed as a percentage, compared to the same quarter a year ago. Look for a consistent, upward trend in earnings per share over at least two to three quarters. Analyzing the quarterly trend is important, as it can reveal changes and potential issues that might be masked when looking at consolidated yearly figures. Additionally, consider comparing the company's earnings to those of other stocks within the same industry and group to assess its relative performance and position in the market. Favoring companies with the highest percentage increase in EPS can be a valuable strategy when selecting stocks. By following these practices, you can gain a deeper understanding of how a company's earnings performance impacts its stock price and make more informed investment decisions.

Analyze Earnings In-Depth

Earnings announcements should not be taken at face value; a thorough and critical analysis is essential to understand the true financial health of a company. It is important to look beyond the surface-level figures reported by company officials. For instance, even if the reported earnings are labeled as "record earnings," they may not present a positive picture when compared to the previous year in percentage terms. It is crucial to examine whether the company's earnings growth is genuinely increasing or if it is actually on the decline despite higher revenues.

Pay close attention to financial anomalies such as "write-offs" and restructuring charges, as they can distort the earnings figure and misrepresent the true profitability of the company. Additionally, track the company's earnings trajectory over time to identify any signs of acceleration or deceleration. A strong trend of earnings acceleration is often a good indicator of potential gains, while deceleration can signal potential losses. By scrutinizing earnings reports and digging deeper into the financial data, you can gain a more accurate understanding of a company's performance and make more informed investment decisions.

Earnings Can Be Related to the Economic Cycle

Earnings and the economic cycle are intimately connected, significantly impacting the performance of the stock market. The overall strength and trajectory of the economy play a pivotal role in shaping the level of profits that companies can expect to generate. In times of robust economic growth, corporate profits tend to surge, leading to higher stock prices. Conversely, during periods of recession, profits may plummet or result in losses, triggering declines in stock prices. This interplay between earnings and the economic cycle provides investors with a useful tool for forecasting earnings trends. Historically, the stock market has demonstrated an ability to serve as a leading indicator of the state of the economy, often predicting economic shifts six to twelve months in advance. By monitoring stock market performance, investors can gain valuable insights into the potential direction of corporate earnings and the broader economic landscape.

Understanding the relationship between earnings and the economic cycle is crucial for informed investment decisions. Investors who grasp the correlation between these factors can more effectively navigate the stock market's ebbs and flows, strategically positioning their portfolios based on the current economic environment. Whether it's recognizing opportunities during economic upswings or adopting defensive strategies in anticipation of a downturn, a deep understanding of earnings and the economic cycle empowers investors to make more informed choices in an ever-changing market.

Why Dividends Have Lost Their Importance

In recent years, the significance of dividends has diminished compared to the past. Several factors contribute to this shift in emphasis. Many companies have opted to redirect the funds traditionally allocated for dividends toward alternative strategies aimed at increasing earnings. This includes initiatives such as reinvesting in the business, funding R&D, expanding operations, or pursuing mergers and acquisitions. These measures are designed to enhance the company's growth prospects and, subsequently, its earnings per share. In addition to corporate preferences, investors have also altered their investment priorities, increasingly favoring companies that offer the potential for capital appreciation over those providing substantial dividend payouts. As a result, many investors have shifted their focus away from dividends and toward stocks with strong growth potential.

This change in perspective underscores the evolving investment landscape, where the value of a stock is increasingly associated with its growth prospects and earnings performance rather than just its dividend yield. Companies and investors alike have adapted to these shifting dynamics, emphasizing strategies and stocks that align with these evolving preferences. Consequently, dividends, while still important, have lost some of their historical significance in comparison to other factors that drive stock market performance.

What Return on Equity Indicates

Return on equity (ROE) is a fundamental financial metric that measures the profitability and efficiency of a company in generating returns for its shareholders. ROE is calculated by taking the company's net income and dividing it by the shareholders' equity and is typically represented as a percentage. It provides insight into how effectively a company utilizes its shareholders' investments to generate profits. The higher the ROE, the more efficient the company is in generating returns on the equity investment of its shareholders.

A high ROE is often indicative of a company's ability to grow its shareholders' wealth at an accelerated rate, as it signifies that the company can generate substantial profits relative to its equity base. Generally, an ROE of 15% or higher is considered desirable as it indicates that the company is efficiently using its equity to generate substantial returns. Conversely, an ROE below 10% may be viewed as inadequate, suggesting that the company is not effectively utilizing its shareholders' capital to generate profits. In summary, ROE is a crucial metric for assessing a company's financial performance and its ability to provide a solid return on the investments made by its shareholders.

ROE Can Be Related to a Stock's Price Performance

Return on equity is closely related to a stock's price performance as it reflects a company's ability to generate profits and increase its retained earnings, which, in turn, impacts the stock's valuation and price. A higher ROE is often associated with a more significant increase in a company's book value, which can drive stock prices higher. Companies that consistently maintain high ROE levels tend to experience substantial stock price appreciation over time.

For instance, numerous companies recognized for their impressive ROE figures have witnessed significant stock price growth. In the case of some, with ROE levels as high as 30%–40%, these companies have seen their stock prices appreciate multiple times over the years. Investors often favor stocks of companies with strong ROE, as it indicates efficient utilization of shareholder equity and the potential for robust financial performance, which, in turn, can lead to substantial price appreciation in the stock market.

HOW TO ANALYZE EARNINGS

This section discusses various aspects of a company's earnings, which are the fundamental bedrock upon which stocks depend for their price appreciation.

What the Quarterly EPS Indicates

The quarterly EPS is a crucial indicator of a company's current profitability, reflecting recent earnings' magnitude and trend, forming the foundation for stock valuation. When analyzing it, investors should focus on earnings consistency and growth, ideally exhibiting a steady upward trend. A substantial percentage increase in the current quarterly EPS compared to the previous year's comparable quarter, typically approximately 20%–30% or more, is favorable. More powerful is an acceleration in earnings growth, where a company's earnings show an increasing rate, for example, from 15% to 20% and further to 30%, signifying robust growth potential for the stock price.

Consistently increasing and accelerating earnings growth makes companies more attractive to investors. Higher growth rates indicate a company's ability to generate more profits, leading to stronger stock price appreciation. These trends are closely associated with a stock's potential for significant price gains, a key focus for investors when evaluating performance.

Analyzing Quarterly EPS

When analyzing quarterly EPS, it is crucial to dig deeper and scrutinize the reported figures carefully to ensure they are not distorted for any reason. A significant aspect to consider is the context in which these earnings are reported. For instance, if a company had a loss in the previous year or reported very low earnings, the current year's earnings may appear significantly better, potentially misleading investors. It is essential to compare the earnings to historical data and industry benchmarks to gain a more accurate understanding of a company's performance.

Another factor that can distort earnings is the presence of extraordinary charges or unusual events, such as write-offs or one-time gains. These irregularities can have a substantial impact on the quarterly EPS, and investors need to assess whether these events are likely to recur or are exceptional circumstances. Additionally, changes in the number of outstanding shares, whether due to stock buybacks or dilution from employee stock options, can also affect EPS figures. Therefore, investors should delve into the financial statements and disclosures to uncover the underlying factors affecting the reported earnings and make more informed investment decisions.

Use Annual EPS to Determine Profitability Consistency

Analyzing a company's annual EPS over a five-year period is a valuable strategy to evaluate its consistency and sustainability in delivering healthy earnings. A general guideline is to look for an increasing trend in annual

EPS over this time frame. This consistency demonstrates that the company has been able to grow its earnings steadily, which is a positive sign for investors. However, it is important to be flexible in your assessment and allow for occasional fluctuations in earnings. If there was a decline in earnings in one year but the company quickly rebounded and resumed an upward earnings trajectory in the subsequent year, it may not necessarily be a cause for concern. The key is to focus on the overall trend and ensure that the company's long-term earnings performance remains strong.

By analyzing annual EPS, investors can gain insights into a company's financial health and performance over an extended period. A consistently rising EPS indicates that the company has the potential for long-term growth and may be a sound investment. However, it is essential to combine this analysis with other factors, such as the industry's economic conditions and the company's competitive position, to make a well-rounded investment decision.

Current Quarterly EPS Growth Rate Should Be Rising

When analyzing a company's earnings, it is essential to examine both the quarterly and annual EPS figures. While the raw EPS numbers per share provide valuable information, it's often more meaningful to focus on the percentage change in the quarterly EPS compared to the previous year's corresponding quarter. The growth rate in the current quarterly EPS should be noticeably higher, by a substantial percentage, than the same quarter in the previous year. This increase indicates accelerating earnings growth, which is a strong positive signal for investors. A company that exhibits a consistent pattern of rising growth rates, such as progressing from 20% to 25% to 30%, should be particularly favored, as it suggests strong and sustained performance.

In addition to the quarterly EPS growth, investors should also consider the company's annual EPS performance. A history of increasing annual EPS over several years is a vital indicator of a company's ability to deliver consistent and healthy earnings growth. This upward trajectory not only demonstrates the company's financial stability but also instills confidence in its capacity to adapt to changing market conditions and generate sustained profits. By analyzing both the quarterly and annual EPS figures, investors can gain a comprehensive view of a company's earnings performance and make more informed investment decisions.

Projected EPS Should Be in an Uptrend

When evaluating a company's earnings, it is crucial to not only focus on the historical figures but also consider the future outlook. Projected quarterly and annual EPS should display a clear upward trend, indicating that the company is expected to maintain or enhance its profitability in the coming periods. To assess this, investors should pay attention to the consensus annual earnings estimate provided by analysts, which forecasts the company's earnings for the following fiscal year. An increasing trend in these earnings estimates is a positive sign, as it reflects growing confidence in the company's financial performance. Additionally, examining quarterly earnings estimates is equally important, as they should also be on an upward trajectory. Companies with such positive earnings expectations, consistently rising and accelerating, are typically more attractive to investors as they demonstrate a strong outlook for profitability.

Earnings are a fundamental factor that directly influences a company's stock price, and their consistent growth is a clear indicator of a company's financial health. Consequently, favoring companies with a history of rising earnings and optimistic future earnings estimates can be a valuable strategy for investors seeking profitable and rewarding investment opportunities.

Use Projected Annual Earnings to Estimate Future Price Performance

The P/E ratio is a widely utilized valuation metric to assess whether a stock is overvalued or undervalued. Typically, a high P/E ratio indicates that a company is overvalued, while a low P/E ratio suggests that a stock is undervalued. In P/E ratio calculations, E represents earnings, and two types of earnings numbers can be employed: trailing earnings and projected earnings. Usually, P/E ratios available to investors are based on trailing earnings, reflecting past performance. However, for a more forward-looking approach, it is advisable to use projected earnings, as this number carries greater relevance when estimating a stock's future price performance.

Projecting earnings provides investors with a clearer insight into the potential future valuation of a stock. By considering projected earnings in P/E calculations, investors can better anticipate how a company's earnings are expected to evolve in the coming periods, enabling them to make more informed investment decisions. This approach aligns more closely with assessing a stock's future potential, as opposed to relying solely on historical data provided by trailing earnings.

Projected Long-Term Earnings Growth Rate Must Be High

The projected long-term earnings growth rate is a vital indicator used to assess the expected earnings growth a company will achieve over the next five years. This metric plays a crucial role in separating companies with sustained, robust growth potential from those with slow growth or transient success. A high long-term earnings growth rate is indicative of a company's ability to maintain a strong growth trajectory over an extended period, making it an attractive prospect for investors. This metric can also help filter out companies with hyperbolic growth rates that are unsustainable in the long term, as their growth may fizzle out after a year or two.

When considering investments, it is advisable to favor growth stocks with a historical earnings growth rate exceeding 20% and a forecasted 3–5 year growth rate of 20 to 30%. These stocks typically have a solid track record of consistent and robust earnings expansion, making them potentially lucrative opportunities. Conversely, it is prudent to be cautious of companies with historical annual earnings growth rates below 15%, unless there are specific, exceptional circumstances that warrant a closer look. Such companies may not offer the same level of growth potential as those with more impressive historical and projected growth rates.

Obtain Projected Earnings Growth Rates From Reliable Sources

Obtaining accurate and reliable projected earnings growth rates is crucial for making informed investment decisions. These growth rates are a key determinant of a company's future performance, and professional investors, with a long-term perspective, place significant importance on the company's projected 3–5 year growth rate when assessing its potential. Therefore, it is paramount to ensure that the data you use for your investment analysis is as accurate as possible.

Selecting a reputable and trustworthy source for earnings forecasts is of utmost importance. The reliability of the data can significantly impact the quality of your investment decisions. Relying on inaccurate forecasts can lead to misguided judgments when evaluating a company for potential acquisition or sale. Thoroughly vet your data sources and consider using a combination of reputable financial analysts' estimates and consensus forecasts to obtain a comprehensive view of a company's expected growth rate. By drawing on trusted sources, you can better position yourself to make well-informed investment choices based on accurate growth rate projections.

Favor Companies With Consistent Earnings Growth

Favoring companies with a history of consistent earnings growth is a prudent strategy for investors seeking long-term opportunities. When a company consistently exhibits strong earnings growth over several years, it demonstrates its ability to adapt to changing market conditions and generate sustained profits. This consistency instills confidence in investors that the company can continue to perform well in the future. A compounded annual earnings growth rate of 20% or higher over a 3- to 5-year period is indicative of a company's ability to maintain a high-growth trajectory, making it an attractive prospect for investors.

However, it is essential to remain vigilant, even with companies that have shown consistent growth. If a company's earnings growth rate begins to decelerate significantly, such as dropping from 30% to 20%, it may be a signal to reevaluate the investment. Slower earnings growth can indicate that the company is facing challenges or that its competitive advantage is eroding, which could affect its stock price. As an investor, staying attuned to these changes and adjusting your investment decisions accordingly is crucial to making informed choices in the stock market.

EARNINGS ESTIMATES AND REVISIONS

This section delves into various aspects of earnings estimates, which are available to investors from various sources and, periodically, revised as the investing environment changes.

Why Earnings Estimates Are Revised

The revision of earnings estimates is a common and essential practice in the dynamic world of stock market analysis. Investors and analysts continuously assess a company's future earnings expectations because these forecasts are deeply ingrained in the pricing of the company's stock by Wall Street. These expectations are based on the most recent information available about the company and its surrounding environment. However, this environment is highly susceptible to change, and these changes can be either favorable or detrimental to the company's profitability. Consequently, when any event unfolds that has the potential to impact a company's earnings, investors and analysts swiftly adapt by revising their earnings forecasts for that particular company.

When analysts revise their earnings forecasts, these updated expectations are quickly reflected in the stock's price. If the revision is an upward adjustment, indicating improved earnings prospects, the stock price typically experiences an increase. Conversely, if the revision is downward, signaling deteriorating earnings expectations, the stock price often declines. In essence, these revisions serve as valuable signals to investors about the expected performance of a company, influencing their buying and selling decisions and contributing to the stock's price movement.

Drill Down and Check Range of Earnings Estimates

When assessing earnings estimates, it is crucial to go beyond the consensus earnings estimate, which represents the average of the estimates provided by all reporting analysts, and delve deeper into the range of estimates. The consensus estimate offers a general overview, but it is essential to understand the degree of dispersion among the estimates. For instance, while the consensus may be $1 per share, individual estimates could vary, ranging from $0.90 per share to $1.05 per share. This dispersion reflects the diversity of opinions among analysts regarding the company's earnings potential.

After the company reports its actual earnings, it is beneficial to ascertain which analyst's estimate proved to be the most accurate. This information can guide your future evaluation of analysts' estimates, as the analyst with the closest forecast to the actual results may provide more reliable insights for your investment decisions. By considering the full range of estimates and pinpointing analysts with a track record of accurate forecasting, you can enhance the precision of your investment strategy and make more informed decisions.

Earnings Estimates Should Be Based on at Least Four Estimates

It is essential to ensure that earnings estimates are based on a substantial number of reporting analysts to minimize the risk of distortion in the consensus estimate. Typically, earnings estimates reported by sources (like Reuters, Bloomberg, MarketWatch, FactSet, and Zacks) rely on data provided by numerous analysts. To enhance the reliability of these estimates, it is advisable to look for consensus estimates derived from a minimum of four reporting analysts. This threshold provides a more robust consensus figure and reduces the vulnerability to significant distortions caused by a single outlier or erroneous estimate.

The level of confidence in earnings forecasts generally increases with a higher number of analysts covering a company. This is because a larger analyst pool can withstand the impact of an individual analyst's inaccurate estimate more effectively. Consequently, having a larger sample size of estimates contributes to a more accurate and dependable consensus estimate, making it a valuable resource for investors seeking to make well-informed decisions based on earnings projections.

Earnings Estimate Revisions Should Be Positive

Earnings estimate revisions play a pivotal role in the analysis of stock performance. These revisions are reflective of the dynamic nature of a company's business environment. Typically, earnings estimates are revised by analysts in response to various factors, including the actual earnings reports, changes in company guidance, shifts in competitive landscapes, or other significant developments. An essential aspect to consider is that upward revisions in earnings estimates are generally perceived as positive signals for a stock. Such positive revisions often drive the stock price higher, reflecting the analysts' growing optimism about the company's future earnings potential.

Conversely, when earnings estimates are revised downward, it can have a dampening effect on the stock price. Investors often respond negatively to such revisions, as they indicate potentially weaker performance expectations for the company. Therefore, it is prudent for investors to favor stocks whose earnings estimates are experiencing upward revisions, as this suggests a more optimistic outlook and better growth prospects for the company. Additionally, understanding the historical tendencies of analysts to underestimate earnings during rising trends and overestimate them during falling trends can provide valuable insights into stock performance and assist investors in making informed decisions.

EARNINGS PER SHARE (EPS) RANK

This section discusses various aspects of the earnings per share rank which many investors, especially momentum investors, analyze when evaluating a stock.

What EPS Rank Indicates

The EPS rank indicator serves as a valuable tool for investors seeking to assess a company's profitability and its relative position within the broader stock market landscape. It essentially quantifies how a company's profit growth compares to all other companies traded in the stock market. It specifically focuses on the company's earnings growth over the past five years, with particular emphasis on the last two quarters. This measure employs a numerical scale ranging from 1 to 99, where a higher rank indicates superior profit growth in relation to other companies.

A high EPS rank, typically closer to 99, signifies that the company has demonstrated robust and consistent earnings growth over time, with a strong recent performance. Investors may view this as a positive signal, indicating that the company's financial health and profitability are on an upward trajectory. Conversely, a lower EPS rank, nearing the 1 end of the scale, may indicate that the company's earnings growth has been less impressive compared to its peers. Investors may interpret this as a sign that the company is facing challenges or experiencing a decline in profitability, potentially warranting a cautious approach to investing in such a stock.

EPS Rank Is Related to a Stock's Performance

Selecting stocks with high EPS rank is a prudent strategy for investors looking to capitalize on profitable companies. High EPS rank stocks are often associated with strong earnings growth and a consistent track record of financial success. Consequently, these stocks are more likely to exhibit favorable price performance, which tends to attract positive attention from Wall Street. Investors are generally drawn to companies that can demonstrate superior earnings, and as a result, high EPS rank stocks are often seen as leaders and winners in the market. This is because they have both earnings and price momentum working in their favor, making them attractive investments.

The performance of stocks with high EPS rank is also influenced by broader market trends. In an upward-trending market, these stocks tend to shine, outperforming their counterparts with lower EPS ranks. Conversely, during a market downturn, high EPS rank stocks typically experience smaller declines compared to stocks with lower EPS ranks. This resilience in bearish conditions further solidifies their appeal to investors who seek stability and growth potential in their investment portfolios. As such, high EPS rank stocks are considered valuable assets that can contribute to a well-rounded investment strategy.

Sources Providing the EPS Rank

Investor's Business Daily is a valuable resource for investors seeking EPS rank information. It consistently offers EPS rank data for individual stocks in its daily stock tables, allowing investors to readily access this crucial metric. Additionally, in the stock tables featuring significant movers, *IBD* provides EPS ranks, aiding investors in quickly identifying stocks with outstanding earnings performance. To make informed investment decisions, it is advisable to prioritize stocks with an EPS rank of at least 80, signifying that their earnings performance surpasses that of over 80% of companies in the stock market. For those seeking the cream of the crop in terms of performance, stocks in the 90–99% range are the ones to focus on, as they represent the highest echelon of earnings success.

Investors can gain valuable insights by consistently reviewing EPS ranks in the Investor's Business Daily, as well as other reputable sources such as Zacks, Reuters, Bloomberg, Morningstar, and Yahoo Finance. These sources offer comprehensive data on EPS ranks, aiding investors in pinpointing stocks with robust earnings growth histories and consistent outperformance. Focusing on stocks with elevated EPS ranks enhances the likelihood of selecting companies poised for superior price performance in the stock market.

EPS Rank Limitations

While the EPS rank is invaluable for assessing a company's historical earnings performance, investors must recognize its limitations. Notably, the EPS rank relies on past earnings data, offering no insight into a company's future performance or potential for earnings growth beyond historical trends. Therefore, caution is essential, as investing in high EPS rank stocks involves risk due to their typically high valuations and heightened market expectations. To mitigate these risks, investors should adopt a comprehensive approach, combining fundamental analysis with a focus on the stock's future potential, rather than relying solely on the EPS rank.

To manage the risks associated with high EPS rank stocks, investors should base their decisions on sound fundamental analysis, considering both historical performance and future growth prospects. Ongoing vigilance is crucial after acquiring such stocks, allowing investors to proactively respond to changes in the company's outlook and market conditions. This approach ensures effective management of investments and the ability to navigate potential challenges related to stocks with high EPS ranks.

RELATIVE STRENGTH (RS) RANK

This section discusses various aspects of the relative strength rank which many investors, especially momentum investors, analyze when evaluating a stock.

What RS Rank Indicates

The RS rank serves as a valuable metric for investors seeking to evaluate a stock's price performance compared to its peers in the stock market. It focuses on the stock's price changes over the past year, with a greater emphasis placed on the most recent three-month period in the ranking calculations. The resulting RS rank is expressed on a scale from 1 to 99, with higher values indicating stronger price performance. This ranking system allows investors to identify stocks that have demonstrated superior relative strength in the market, showcasing their ability to outperform their peers during the given time frame.

Investors often rely on the RS rank as a key indicator of a stock's price momentum and market leadership. Stocks with higher RS ranks are considered to be more attractive, as they have consistently displayed better price performance compared to other stocks in the market. Therefore, the RS rank is a valuable tool for investors seeking to identify stocks with strong price momentum and a competitive edge over their industry peers.

Favor Stocks With High RS Rank

Investors often prefer stocks with high RS ranks as they signal robust price performance and market leadership, serving as a valuable tool to gauge a stock's potential to outperform most of its peers in terms of price momentum. The RS rank provides insights into a stock's relative strength, aiding investors in identifying opportunities for potential market outperformance.

Investors commonly favor stocks with RS ranks exceeding 90, as these stocks exhibit robust price momentum and are frequently associated with strong market performance. However, it is essential to consider other factors in addition to the RS rank, as some stocks may display impressive price performance but lack sound fundamentals, making them susceptible to sharp declines. Therefore, while a high RS rank can be a valuable indicator for stock selection, a comprehensive analysis that includes other relevant factors is advisable to make well-informed investment decisions.

Using RS Rank With Other Criteria

Combining the RS rank with other criteria, such as the EPS rank, offers a comprehensive assessment of a stock's potential. When both ranks surpass 80, it suggests robust performance on two key fronts: fundamental strength and price momentum. This blend of strong fundamental and valuation metrics, along with a history of robust price performance, indicates a stock with excellent growth potential.

Using the RS rank in conjunction with the EPS rank provides a balanced view of a stock's health. A high RS rank signifies strong price performance, while a high EPS rank reflects solid earnings growth. Considering both indicators helps identify stocks with consistent growth and market leadership, often seen as attractive investment opportunities. However, a comprehensive analysis, including other relevant factors, is crucial for a well-informed investment strategy.

RS Rank Can Be Used to Find Winners

Using the RS rank to identify winning stocks is a strategy commonly employed by momentum investors. These investors believe that stocks with high RS ranks, indicating past outperformance, are likely to continue their strong price appreciation in the near future due to their existing momentum and upward trends. As a result, they focus on finding winning stocks among those with RS ranks greater than 80, effectively filtering out underperforming or stagnant stocks. This approach is a departure from value investing, which centers on buying stocks when their prices are considered undervalued or depressed.

Momentum investors understand that the market often rewards strength and that stocks with strong recent performance tend to attract further investor interest. They leverage RS rank to identify stocks that have demonstrated this trend and aim to ride the momentum to capitalize on potential future gains. However, it is essential to remember that momentum investing can be riskier, and investors should conduct thorough research to ensure they are comfortable with the stocks they choose based on RS rank, especially given that past performance is not always indicative of future results.

Sources Providing the RS Rank

Investor's Business Daily stands out as an invaluable resource for investors, offering the RS rank for individual stocks in its daily stock tables. This proprietary RS rating provides a snapshot of a stock's relative strength compared to all other stocks in the *IBD* database. Investors can leverage this information to identify stocks with strong price performance and market leadership, aiding in their decision-making process. Beyond *IBD*, investors can explore a range of reputable sources to access RS rank data. Prominent financial websites like Yahoo Finance, Bloomberg, and Reuters routinely provide RS-related metrics, enhancing the accessibility of this critical information. Moreover, brokerage platforms and charting tools, including TradingView and Thinkorswim, offer investors the means to assess relative strength.

Additionally, online stock screeners play a pivotal role in delivering RS rank insights. These screeners, available on financial news websites, brokerage platforms, and independent stock analysis platforms, empower investors to filter and identify stocks based on their relative strength characteristics. Whether checking daily stock tables, exploring financial news websites, or utilizing advanced charting tools, investors have a wealth of options to analyze RS ranks and integrate this valuable metric into their stock evaluation strategies.

Risk With High RS Rank Stocks

While a high RS rank can be an attractive indicator of a stock's strong price performance, investors should exercise caution and conduct comprehensive due diligence. One key risk of owning a high RS rank stock is that it may have already experienced substantial price appreciation, and its best days in terms of growth may be behind it. Investors should not solely rely on RS rank and must consider other factors, such as the company's fundamentals and earnings projections, to ensure they are making a well-informed investment decision. High RS rank should ideally be accompanied by strong earnings growth and other positive fundamental factors to increase the likelihood of a successful investment.

Investors should be aware that superior historical performance, as indicated by a high RS rank, does not guarantee future success. The future performance of a stock depends on various factors, including future earnings, market conditions, and economic trends. Therefore, RS rank should be used as a screening indicator, and a more in-depth analysis of a stock's fundamental health and prospects is necessary to make a well-rounded investment decision. By considering a combination of both price momentum and strong fundamentals, investors can better position themselves for success while managing potential risks.

Monitor Your Stock's RS Rank

For momentum-oriented investors, tracking the RS rank is a crucial part of their strategy, and any decline in this indicator can serve as an early warning sign. A decreasing RS rank while a stock is moving sideways or even rising could indicate that the stock is not keeping up with the broader market's performance. This can be a signal that the stock might be entering a period of underperformance or a potential decline. However, if a stock maintains its RS rank and performs relatively well during a market decline when the RS of leading stocks is dropping, it suggests that the stock has resilience and the potential to become a winner. In such cases, when the market rebounds, these stocks may have a higher probability of outperforming.

Furthermore, when a stock's price starts to decline, which typically precedes a drop in the RS rank, it can serve as an early warning sign of a more significant decline in the future. Investors should closely investigate and monitor such stocks that exhibit price declines, especially those that persist over several months. This vigilant monitoring can help investors make timely decisions to protect their investments and potentially identify opportunities for portfolio adjustments.

Use Relative Strength (RS) Line for Comparison

The RS line is a valuable tool for investors to gauge a stock's price trend and compare its performance against broader market indexes like the S&P 500 or NASDAQ. When analyzing a stock's uptrend, the RS line can be used in conjunction with the moving average line to confirm the stock's overall performance. Once a trend line is established, it typically continues for some time, making it advisable to favor stocks with a higher-trending RS line. In cases where a stock experiences a correction, but the RS line remains unaffected and does not decline, this is generally considered a bullish sign. Contrastingly, if the rising RS line trend is broken, it is viewed as a bearish signal, potentially indicating a shift in the stock's performance relative to the broader market.

Investors often use the RS line as an additional data point in their technical analysis toolkit to make more informed decisions about stock investments. By tracking the RS line alongside other relevant indicators, they can gain insights into a stock's relative strength or weakness, helping them identify opportunities and assess the overall market environment more effectively.

CHAPTER 8

PRICE/EARNINGS (P/E) RATIO

UNDERSTANDING THE P/E RATIO INDICATOR

The significance of the P/E ratio is discussed in this section, where insights are provided to gauge the valuation of individual stocks, sectors, as well as the overall market.

Learn Valuation Techniques

Learning valuation techniques is a crucial skill for anyone participating in the stock market, whether as a buyer or a seller. When you understand how to determine the value of stocks, you can make more informed decisions, ensuring that you don't overpay when acquiring a stock. Overpaying can hinder your ability to achieve your profit objectives, so having a solid grasp of valuation techniques is essential for successful investing.

Moreover, knowing how to value stocks enables you to assess when it is the right time to sell a stock in your portfolio. You can identify overvalued stocks and make more strategic decisions about when to divest. This knowledge is invaluable in avoiding common mistakes, such as prematurely selling winning stocks, which could lead to missed opportunities for further gains. By mastering the indicators used for stock valuation, you can make more precise and profitable investment choices.

How P/E Ratio Is Calculated

The price-to-earnings ratio is a fundamental valuation tool, which provides valuable insights into a stock's relative affordability and is a crucial indicator for many investors. To calculate the P/E ratio, you simply divide the current stock price, denoted in dollars ($), by the earnings per share, which is represented as $/share. For example, if a stock is currently trading at $50 and it has earned $2 per share, the P/E ratio would be calculated as 25 (50/2). In this context, the P/E ratio is essentially a measure of how much an investor is willing to pay for each dollar of earnings generated by the company.

Investors typically aim for a lower P/E ratio, as it implies that they are paying less for each dollar of earnings. The exact range of what constitutes an acceptable P/E ratio may vary depending on the investor's strategy, risk tolerance, and the industry or sector in which the stock operates. Some investors may prefer stocks with lower P/E ratios, signifying potential value investments, while others may be willing to pay a premium for stocks with higher P/E ratios if they believe in their growth prospects.

Importance of the P/E Indicator

The P/E ratio is an essential indicator for investors, particularly for value investors who seek to find undervalued stocks in the market. It serves as one of the foundational metrics for evaluating a stock's relative worth by establishing a relationship between the stock's price and its EPS. This makes the P/E ratio a critical tool for assessing whether a stock is trading at an attractive or unattractive valuation and for comparing it to other stocks in the market. By leveraging the P/E ratio, investors can identify stocks that are reasonably priced, potentially enabling them to avoid overpaying. In doing so, they increase the prospects of achieving above-average returns as they invest in stocks with stronger potential for future price appreciation.

Nonetheless, it is crucial for investors to recognize the limitations of the P/E ratio and exercise caution when using it to select, value, or time their stock investments. The P/E ratio, while valuable, is just one piece of the puzzle in stock valuation. It does not provide a comprehensive view of a company's financial health, nor does it factor in the company's growth potential or the broader market conditions. Therefore, it should be used in conjunction with other financial metrics and qualitative analysis to form a well-rounded evaluation of a stock's investment potential.

P/E Ratios for Individual Stocks, Overall Market, and Sectors

The P/E ratio is a pivotal metric for assessing the valuation of individual stocks, which is a fundamental analysis cornerstone. Investors must discern whether the reported P/E ratio is based on trailing earnings or projected earnings, as this distinction provides essential context for evaluating the stock's current valuation. Employing the P/E ratio as a key indicator, investors can gauge whether a stock is undervalued or overvalued, potentially identifying buying opportunities or warranting caution. The analysis of individual stock P/E ratios empowers investors with valuable insights, facilitating informed decision-making and comparisons among different stocks within their portfolio.

In addition to scrutinizing individual stock P/E ratios, investors frequently compute the P/E ratio for broader market indexes, like the DJIA or the S&P 500, to gauge overall market valuation. The DJIA's P/E ratio, calculated by dividing its current value by the combined earnings of its thirty constituent companies, offers insight into the entire index's valuation relative to collective earnings. Similarly, investors assess P/E ratios for sectors by summing individual components' values. This analysis of market indexes and sectors enables investors to discern overall market conditions, identifying potential overvaluation or undervaluation. A high P/E ratio suggests a bullish sentiment and possible overvaluation, while a low ratio indicates a more conservative outlook, signaling potential undervaluation and buying opportunities. Combining these broader market P/E ratios with individual stock ratios empowers investors to make informed decisions and navigate the dynamic landscape of the stock market.

Trailing P/E Ratio Is Backward Looking

The trailing P/E ratio is based on a stock's most recently reported earnings, which means it offers a retrospective look at a company's valuation in relation to its historical earnings. This historical perspective is valuable for assessing how a company has performed in the past and understanding its current valuation relative to its earnings. It is important to note that the trailing P/E ratio primarily reflects past performance and does not inherently provide insights into a company's future growth potential or expected earnings.

For a more comprehensive view of a stock's investment potential, investors should consider a forward-looking perspective as well. Combining trailing P/E ratios with forward-looking indicators, such as projected earnings growth rates, can help paint a more complete picture. This dual approach allows investors to evaluate a company's past performance while considering its future growth prospects, ultimately making more informed investment decisions. In summary, while trailing P/E ratios are valuable for historical context, they should be used alongside other metrics and analysis for a more holistic assessment of a stock's investment attractiveness.

Use Projected P/E Ratio to Determine Future Prospects

To gauge a stock's future prospects more accurately, investors often turn to the projected P/E ratio, which is calculated by dividing the current stock price by estimated future earnings per share. This valuation metric is considered more valuable for assessing a stock's potential performance than the trailing P/E ratio because it better aligns with the stock's anticipated future earnings. Long-term investors, who tend to have a forward-looking approach, frequently rely on projected earnings to guide their valuations and predict future price appreciation. The use of the P/E ratio based on projected earnings is common in many analyses.

Utilizing the projected P/E ratio for stock valuation can help investors make more informed decisions and anticipate potential price movements. Nevertheless, it's vital to remember that projections are based on estimates and can be subject to change, so a well-rounded assessment should also consider other fundamental and market-related factors when evaluating a stock's future prospects.

Relative P/E Indicates Historical Range

The relative P/E ratio, which is a stock's current P/E ratio compared to its historical range over a period of months or years, plays a crucial role in stock valuation. Value investors, in particular, find this indicator valuable in assessing a stock's valuation. When a stock trades near the lower end of its historical P/E range, it is often seen as fairly valued or even undervalued, making it a potential buy candidate. Conversely, when the P/E ratio reaches the upper end of its historical range, it signals that the stock might be overvalued. It is important to note that buying or selling decisions should not be based solely on this indicator, as other fundamental factors should be considered in conjunction with the relative P/E.

Using the relative P/E provides investors with valuable insights into a stock's valuation compared to its historical performance. But it is crucial to avoid making investment decisions based solely on the historical range of the P/E ratio. Careful fundamental analysis and consideration of current market conditions are essential to make well-informed investment choices.

UNDERSTANDING P/E RATIO VARIATIONS

There are many factors at play in the investment world which impact earnings and prices. Therefore, when they change, which can happen quite frequently, they lead to variations in the P/E ratio. These factors are discussed in this section.

Factors Causing the P/E Ratio to Fluctuate

The P/E ratio is a dynamic valuation tool that reflects the interaction of two key variables: a stock's price and its earnings. These variables contribute to the numerator and denominator of the P/E ratio, respectively. The stock price undergoes frequent fluctuations, often on a daily basis, leading to corresponding changes in the numerator. Consequently, the P/E ratio can change rapidly, reflecting the dynamic nature of the stock market.

The second variable, earnings, forms the denominator of the P/E ratio. Earnings are reported on a quarterly basis, and these periodic updates affect the P/E ratio, either increasing or decreasing depending on the earnings performance. As a long-term investor, it is crucial to focus on the broader picture and not be swayed by daily fluctuations. Over the long term, a stock's price tends to align with its earnings and overall financial health. By maintaining a long-term perspective, you can better navigate the daily noise and fluctuations in the P/E ratio, allowing you to make more informed investment decisions.

Factors Causing the P/E Ratio to Expand

A significant driver of P/E ratio expansion is the positive perception by investors that a stock's future earnings will grow. When investors anticipate such growth, it generates heightened interest and attracts new capital into the stock. As a result, the stock price rises, causing the P/E ratio to expand as the numerator (stock price) increases. This increase reflects the market's optimism about the company's potential for higher earnings in the future.

Another factor contributing to P/E ratio expansion is an improvement in the return on equity. A higher ROE captures the attention of investors seeking superior returns on their investments, making them willing to pay a premium for stocks with a stronger ROE. This elevated interest from investors further drives the expansion of the P/E ratio. Additionally, an increase in institutional ownership can also push the P/E ratio higher. As more institutional investors acquire shares of the stock, it indicates their confidence in the company's growth potential, leading to an upward movement in the P/E ratio as institutional ownership increases.

P/E Ratios Vary in a Wide Range Across Industries

P/E ratios exhibit significant variability across different industries and sectors, reflecting varying expectations related to industry growth, earnings projections, and risk factors. Optimism about a company's or industry's future earnings potential plays a pivotal role in determining its P/E ratio. In industries or sectors with strong growth prospects, P/E ratios tend to be higher as investors are willing to pay a premium for a piece of that growth. A stock's P/E ratio depends on its industry and individual growth rate. Higher growth rates are often linked to increased risk and, consequently, a higher P/E ratio, as investors are willing to pay more for companies showing superior growth prospects.

It is essential to assess and compare your stock's P/E ratio against industry benchmarks to better understand its valuation within the context of its sector. Analyzing P/E ratios within an industry context can help investors identify stocks that are trading above or below the sector's average. This comparison can be useful for discerning relative valuations and potential investment opportunities. A P/E ratio that significantly deviates from industry norms might signal either an overvalued or undervalued stock, depending on whether it is trading at a premium or discount to its peers within the same sector. While comparing P/E ratios, investors should also consider other relevant factors, such as the company's growth prospects, competitive positioning, and its capacity to generate consistent earnings.

Avoid Extreme P/E Ratios

Investors are generally advised to steer clear of stocks with extreme P/E ratio values, as both very low P/E (below 5) and very high P/E (over 35) can be problematic. Extremely low P/E ratios may suggest that the company is facing significant challenges, experiencing declining earnings, or is in financial distress. Such stocks may be perceived as having a higher level of risk, and investors should be cautious when considering investments with very low P/E ratios. Contrastingly, extremely high P/E ratios often require justifications in the form of exceptional revenue and earnings growth rates. High-growth stocks might have P/E ratios within the range of 20–40 without being considered overvalued. Nevertheless, it is crucial for investors to be aware of the inherent risks associated with high P/E ratio stocks, particularly when they are unable to meet market expectations. These stocks can be highly volatile and may experience substantial price declines if they fail to deliver on their anticipated growth.

Investors should exercise caution when dealing with extreme P/E ratios, as they may signal the need for thorough due diligence. It is essential to carefully assess the underlying reasons for the stock's P/E ratio, including whether it aligns with the company's earnings, growth prospects, and overall financial health. While high-growth stocks with high P/E ratios can be rewarding, they also come with heightened risks. Therefore, a balanced approach that considers both potential returns and associated risks is advisable when investing in stocks with extreme P/E ratios.

Economic Cycle Impacts the P/E Ratio

The economic cycle exerts a significant influence on the P/E ratio, reflecting the relationship between a company's earnings and the broader economic environment. In periods of slow economic growth, companies, especially large corporations, may struggle to increase their earnings, making it challenging for them to achieve substantial P/E multiples. During these times, investors tend to favor companies that are still capable of delivering above-average earnings, which results in these companies receiving higher P/E ratios as investors value their potential for growth. In contrast, economic recessions often result in sharp declines in earnings, leading to a significant increase in P/E ratios. As earnings decline, stock prices also decrease until P/E ratios align with the lower earnings. This alignment is considered a more reasonable valuation level, especially during challenging economic periods.

Conversely, when the economy emerges from a recession, stock prices tend to rebound rapidly, outpacing the growth in earnings. This leads to an increase in P/E ratios, as the stock market anticipates brighter earnings prospects. As companies begin to report higher earnings, P/E ratios may eventually decrease to more sustainable levels. Understanding the cyclical nature of the P/E ratio and its relationship with economic conditions is crucial for investors, as it can help them make more informed decisions about when to buy or sell stocks based on the prevailing economic environment.

Inflation and Interest Rates Impact the P/E Ratio

Inflation and interest rates play a vital role in shaping the P/E ratio and are closely monitored by investors. The relationship between these factors and the P/E ratio is interconnected. During periods of high inflation, interest rates tend to rise to counter the impact of rising prices on the economy. As interest rates increase, the P/E ratios often decline. This is because higher interest rates lead to higher borrowing costs for businesses, which can reduce their profitability and potentially hinder earnings growth. As a result, investors may be less willing to pay a premium for stocks, causing P/E ratios to contract.

Conversely, in environments characterized by low and controlled inflation, market valuations typically soar, leading to higher P/E ratios. When inflation is subdued, interest rates tend to remain low, which reduces borrowing costs for companies, supports profitability, and encourages investors to pay more for stocks. These conditions can result in elevated P/E ratios as investors express optimism about the future earnings prospects of companies. Therefore, the interplay between inflation, interest rates, and the P/E ratio is a critical factor for investors to consider when assessing stock market valuations.

USING THE P/E INDICATOR

This section discusses the importance of P/E for various investment approaches and, also, various ways in which it can be used, such as using it as a comparison tool or for checking valuations.

P/E Ratio Usage Is Determined by Investment Approach

The utilization of the P/E ratio as a valuation indicator varies depending on the investment approach. Investors should understand that the P/E ratio is just one piece of the puzzle and must be considered in the context of their overall strategy. For momentum investors who prioritize price performance over valuation, the P/E ratio may hold little relevance, as they focus on trends and market sentiment. Value investors, however, rely on the P/E ratio as a screening tool to identify potentially undervalued stocks that have low P/E ratios.

Growth investors incorporate the P/E ratio into their analysis, but their primary concern is the company's future earnings growth rate. They may be more lenient with higher P/E ratios if a company has a strong growth outlook. Generally, they consider a stock to be overvalued only if its P/E ratio exceeds its projected earnings growth rate. In summary, the P/E ratio is a versatile tool, and its application should align with the specific investment strategy and objectives of the investor. It is important to use the P/E ratio in conjunction with other financial metrics and fundamental analysis to make informed investment decisions.

Use P/E Ratio as a Comparison Tool

The P/E ratio is most effective when used as a comparison tool rather than being treated as a standalone number. When evaluating a stock, it is essential to compare its P/E ratio to those of similar companies within the same industry. P/E ratios can vary significantly across industries due to differences in growth expectations, earnings potential, and risk profiles. By comparing a stock's P/E ratio to industry peers, you can gain valuable insights into whether it is overvalued, undervalued, or in line with market expectations.

Additionally, comparing the current P/E ratio to its historical P/E ratio is a crucial step in assessing a stock's valuation. Understanding whether the P/E ratio is at the high or low end of its historical range can provide context and help identify potential investment opportunities or red flags. It is essential to note that comparing a stock's P/E ratio to the market's collective P/E ratio, as represented by indexes like the DJIA or S&P 500, can lead to misleading conclusions since individual stocks and industries often have unique dynamics that differ from the broader market trends.

Favor Stocks at the Low End of Their Historical P/E Range

The relative P/E ratio is a valuable tool for investors seeking to make informed decisions about stocks based on their historical valuation. This indicator compares the current P/E ratio of a stock to its own historical P/E range. When analyzing the relative P/E ratio, it is important to consider a stock's historical trading range, as it can vary over time due to changes in earnings and stock prices. For example, if a stock has historically traded with a P/E ratio ranging from 20 to 45, a relative P/E ratio of 100 would indicate that it is currently trading at the upper end of its historical valuation range.

Investors, particularly value and growth investors, tend to favor stocks with a relative P/E ratio at the lower end of their historical range. This preference arises from the belief that buying a stock with a relatively low P/E compared to its historical norm offers reduced downside risk, as it implies a more reasonable valuation. It is important to note that momentum investors, who focus on short-term price trends, do not typically consider the relative P/E ratio when making investment decisions.

What a Consistently High P/E Ratio Means

A consistently high P/E ratio for a stock can be an indicator of investors' strong expectations for continued rapid earnings growth. In many cases, stocks with P/E ratios that remain higher than what is considered normal for an extended period, quarter after quarter, are seen as potential winners and leaders in their respective sectors. Investors' confidence in the growth prospects of these companies typically leads to elevated P/E ratios. It is common for these leaders to have P/E ratios above the market's average P/E ratio at the beginning of a significant upward move. This is because investors are willing to pay a premium for companies that they anticipate will experience strong earnings growth.

These stocks may not meet the criteria for value investors who adhere to stringent P/E screening standards. Value investors typically seek stocks with lower P/E ratios, and they may be hesitant to invest in companies with P/E ratios that are significantly higher than the market's average. They often focus on stocks that are perceived as undervalued and trading at lower multiples relative to their earnings. Consequently, the suitability of stocks with consistently high P/E ratios depends on the investor's specific strategy and preferences.

Use P/E-to-Projected Growth Rate Indicator to Check Valuation

The P/E-to-projected growth rate (P/E-to-PGR) indicator is a valuable tool for evaluating the valuation of growth stocks. To calculate this indicator, you divide the stock's current P/E ratio by its expected annual earnings growth rate. For example, if a stock has a P/E ratio of 30 and is projected to have an annual earnings growth rate of 40%, the P/E-to-projected growth ratio would be 0.75 (30/40). Ideally, the ratio should be below 1.0, suggesting an appealing investment. When the ratio is less than 0.75, it suggests that the stock is particularly appealing from a valuation perspective. Conversely, if the ratio exceeds 1.25, it implies that the stock may be overvalued and associated with higher risk.

This indicator is helpful in assessing whether a growth stock's current valuation aligns with its expected future earnings growth. An attractive P/E-to-PGR ratio suggests that investors are not paying an excessive premium for future growth potential, making the stock more appealing. Conversely, a high P/E-to-PGR ratio may indicate that the stock's price already reflects aggressive growth expectations, potentially posing greater downside risk if those expectations are not met.

P/E RATIO RISKS

The P/E ratio is a useful tool that needs to be used carefully, as there are some risks associated with its use, which are discussed in this section.

Be Aware of Distortions

It is essential to be aware of potential distortions in the P/E ratio, particularly when dealing with projected P/E ratios. Inaccurate or overly optimistic projected earnings can lead to misleading valuations. These projections are inherently uncertain, making it crucial to approach them with caution when relying on the P/E-to-PGR indicator. Additionally, unusual accounting events, such as reported losses or one-time charges, can distort earnings figures, affecting the accuracy of the P/E ratio. When assessing a stock's value, it is essential to consider the context of such events and their impact on earnings.

Another important consideration is the P/E ratio for young companies experiencing rapid earnings growth. While a high P/E ratio may suggest overvaluation, it is crucial to assess whether this growth is sustainable or a result of short-term factors. In such cases, it is wise to look beyond the P/E ratio and conduct a thorough analysis of the company's fundamentals and growth prospects to avoid making decisions based solely on potentially misleading valuations. By recognizing the limitations of the P/E indicator and employing it alongside other fundamental and valuation tools, investors can make more informed and well-rounded investment choices.

High P/E Stocks Can Be Risky

Investing in high P/E stocks can be inherently risky, as these stocks are often priced for perfection. The market expects these companies to continue delivering exceptional growth and profitability, and any deviation from this can lead to sharp and sometimes brutal corrections in the stock price. The magnitude of the price decline tends to be more significant for stocks with higher P/E ratios, reflecting the heightened investor expectations and the disappointment that can ensue when those expectations are not met.

While high P/E stocks can offer substantial returns when everything goes as anticipated, investors should be aware of the potential downside and be prepared for increased volatility and risk. Due diligence and careful analysis of a high P/E stock's fundamentals, growth prospects, and the sustainability of its earnings are essential to make informed investment decisions and mitigate the risks associated with such investments.

Low P/E Stocks Can Be Risky

Low P/E stocks can be deceptive, and investors should exercise caution when interpreting their valuations. A low P/E ratio may indeed signal an undervalued stock, but it can also be an indicator of underlying issues or negative market sentiment surrounding the company. In some cases, a low P/E ratio might be justified due to concerns about the company's earnings potential, financial stability, or competitive pressures, making it a value trap rather than an attractive investment opportunity.

When considering low P/E stocks, it is crucial to conduct thorough due diligence and understand the reasons behind the low valuation. Investors should evaluate the company's fundamentals, assess its potential for earnings growth or decline, and consider whether the low P/E is justified or if it represents an opportunity for value investing. Simply buying a stock with the lowest P/E ratio within its industry or sector can be risky without a comprehensive understanding of the factors driving that low valuation.

CHAPTER 9

MARKET BEHAVIOR

GENERAL

Individual stocks operate in the stock market, not in an isolated environment. This section discusses market behavior and analyzes it from different perspectives.

Learn How to Interpret Market Behavior

Understanding the dynamics of the market is an essential skill for investors. The market's condition and trends, whether it is in a bull or bear phase, have a direct and significant impact on the performance of most stocks. As such, investors cannot afford to ignore the prevailing market sentiment and direction. To make informed investment decisions, it is crucial to interpret market behavior accurately.

Recognizing the difference between bull and bear markets, as well as understanding how to navigate each scenario, is fundamental for investors. In a bull market, investors aim to maximize their exposure to stocks, while in a bear market, they often reduce their stock holdings to mitigate potential losses. Being able to adapt your investment strategy and tactics in response to the market's health is crucial for long-term success as an investor. Additionally, recognizing and preparing for different market conditions, such as choppy or volatile markets, allows investors to make more informed choices regarding their portfolios.

The Stock Market Has a Discounting Mechanism

The stock market operates as a forward-looking discounting mechanism. It evaluates and processes information with a focus on its potential impact on individual stocks and the market as a whole, often looking ahead 6–9 months. This forward-looking approach allows the market to anticipate future events and adjust stock prices accordingly. For instance, when the Federal Open Market Committee (FOMC) announces a reduction in the federal funds interest rate, even though its actual economic stimulus effects may take several months to materialize, the stock market reacts positively immediately. This rapid reaction reflects Wall Street's emphasis on pricing in future prospects and expected impacts well ahead of time.

Similarly, the stock market's behavior regarding individual companies is forward focused. If a company announces record earnings but also signals an anticipated slowdown in future growth, investors react promptly by selling off the stock. This is because, on Wall Street, historical performance is given less importance compared to future earnings expectations. Therefore, when analyzing a stock, it becomes essential to gauge how much of its future earnings are already factored into its current price, as this can significantly influence investment decisions.

Learn How to Determine Market Trend

Understanding market trends is essential for investors because the overall market behavior significantly impacts individual stocks. Approximately 75% of the time in the long term, the market typically trends in a bullish direction. During bullish periods, the overall positive sentiment sets a favorable tone for most stocks. Investors tend to be more optimistic, leading to higher stock prices and increased trading volumes. This positive sentiment can fuel an upward momentum that benefits the majority of stocks. It is important to remember that while most stocks may rise during a bullish market, not all stocks perform equally, and careful stock selection is still necessary to maximize potential returns.

Conversely, when the market is in a bearish trend or experiencing a decline, it tends to drag most stocks down with it. In bear markets, investors often become more risk-averse, leading to declining stock prices, lower trading volumes, and a generally pessimistic sentiment. Even though some individual stocks may display temporary resilience or outperformance during a bear market, the broader negative sentiment can create challenges for stock valuations and price appreciation. Therefore, investors need to recognize the prevailing market trends and make well-informed investment decisions that align with the market's overall direction. This may involve adjusting their investment strategies, portfolio allocation, or risk management approaches to navigate the ever-changing market conditions.

Learn How to Identify Market Tops and Bottoms

Identifying market tops and bottoms is a crucial skill for investors who aim to maximize their returns and manage their risk effectively. Market tops usually occur when the stock market becomes significantly overvalued, often due to excessive speculation and optimism. During these periods, there are fewer buyers left, and stock prices may have risen to unsustainable levels. Recognizing a market top can be beneficial for investors, as it provides an opportunity to assess their portfolios and consider reducing their exposure to stocks. This proactive approach may help them avoid significant losses when the market inevitably experiences a correction or bear market.

Significantly, market bottoms are characterized by an oversold condition where there are few sellers left, causing the market to stabilize. Identifying a market bottom can provide investors with a chance to accumulate undervalued stocks at attractive prices, as stocks are expected to rebound from these low levels. Successful timing of market bottoms can lead to substantial gains when the market begins to recover. It is important to note that accurately pinpointing market tops and bottoms is challenging and often requires experience, market analysis, and an understanding of market sentiment. It is essential for investors to use a combination of technical and fundamental analysis, as well as risk management strategies, to make well-informed decisions during these critical market junctures.

Use Market Declines as Buying Opportunities

Bear markets and corrections can indeed be challenging and unsettling for investors, but they also offer significant potential for long-term gains for those who are prepared and proactive. While market declines can lead to short-term losses, they present excellent buying opportunities for investors with a longer-term perspective. History has shown that the most substantial profits, in terms of percentage gains, are often realized when the market begins to rebound from a bear market or a correction. These rebounds can be powerful, and investors who are well-prepared and positioned to take advantage of them can benefit greatly from the subsequent recovery.

To make the most of these opportunities, it is crucial to have a well-thought-out investment strategy that includes plans for capital allocation and risk management. During bear markets and corrections, having a portion of your portfolio in cash or liquid assets can provide you with the flexibility to purchase undervalued assets when market sentiment is at its most pessimistic. Being able to buy stocks at attractive prices when others are selling can lead to substantial gains when the market eventually recovers. Additionally, it is essential to remain patient and maintain a long-term perspective, as bear markets and corrections can be followed by periods of strong market growth and upward trends.

Be Aware of Limitations in Forecasting Market Levels Accurately

Forecasting the future state of the economy and the stock market is a challenging task, and it is fraught with uncertainties. Economic forecasts are influenced by various complex factors, making it difficult to predict with precision. Economic indicators such as inflation, interest rates, consumer sentiment, and geopolitical events can all have a significant impact on economic growth and stock market performance. Even seasoned professionals may face challenges in making accurate predictions, given the dynamic and interconnected nature of these factors.

It is important for investors to be aware of the limitations in forecasting economic and market levels accurately. Instead of relying solely on economic forecasts, it is advisable to focus on creating a diversified and resilient investment portfolio that can weather different market conditions. Diversification can help mitigate risk, as it involves spreading investments across various asset classes and sectors, reducing the impact of adverse market movements. Additionally, maintaining a long-term perspective and regularly reviewing and adjusting your investment strategy can help you navigate the uncertainties of economic forecasting and adapt to changing market conditions.

BULL AND BEAR MARKET CHARACTERISTICS

The stock market is characterized by two stock price trends, rising and declining. The characteristics of these trends, better known as bull and bear markets, are described in this section.

What Is a Bull Market?

A bull market is a prolonged period in which the stock market experiences an overall uptrend, characterized by rising stock prices and a positive investor sentiment. It is a period of optimism and economic growth, where investors have confidence in the future and are willing to buy and hold stocks. Typically, a bull market lasts for an extended period, often several years, during which stock prices steadily climb higher. This upward trend is not without minor setbacks or pullbacks, but the overall trajectory is positive, and these pullbacks are seen as temporary corrections rather than signs of a market reversal.

The duration of a bull market can vary, but it is generally characterized as such when the market experiences a price increase of over 20%. Investors actively participate in a bull market, and it is often associated with strong economic fundamentals, increasing corporate earnings, and a positive outlook for various sectors of the economy. During a bull market, investors are more inclined to take on risk, and there is a general belief that stock prices will continue to rise, which can create a self-fulfilling prophecy as demand for stocks drives their prices higher. This positive sentiment encourages investment and stimulates economic growth.

What Is a Bear Market?

A bear market is a period of declining stock prices, characterized by pessimism, economic uncertainty, and general negative sentiment among investors. It follows a period of bullishness and signifies a significant and sustained downturn in the stock market. While the downward movement is not always a continuous decline and may include short-term rallies or upward movements, the overall trend is one of falling stock prices. A bear market is typically characterized by a decrease of approximately 20% or more in the value of a broad market index, such as the S&P 500. These periods can last for several months to over a year, and investors may experience significant losses during this time.

During a bear market, economic conditions are often challenging, and investors become more risk averse. Factors such as economic recessions, geopolitical instability, high inflation, rising interest rates, or corporate earnings declines can contribute to the onset of a bear market. Investor sentiment turns negative, and there is a general lack of confidence in the future direction of the market. As a result, investors may sell stocks and move their investments to safer assets, like bonds or cash, to protect their portfolios from further losses. Bear markets can be a challenging time for investors, and it is important to have a strategy in place to navigate these periods and minimize potential losses.

How a Bull Market Starts

Bull markets typically begin when extreme fear and pessimism dominate the market landscape after a significant decline. At the bottom of the market cycle, when investors are most fearful and uncertainty abounds, the stage is set for a potential bull market. As the market starts to recover and climb, fear gradually diminishes. Investors begin to cautiously reenter the market, often driven by bargain-hunting and the belief that prices have hit attractive levels. As the recovery continues and gains momentum, caution transitions into optimism.

The bull market gains further traction as investors gain confidence and become increasingly euphoric, believing that the upward trend will persist indefinitely. During this phase, speculative behavior becomes more pronounced, and investors may disregard or forget the challenges of the preceding bear market. As a result, stock prices rise more rapidly as demand surges, and the optimism reinforces itself. This cycle of sentiment changes from extreme fear to optimism and, eventually, euphoria characterizes the beginning and early stages of a bull market. While it can be a rewarding period for investors, it is essential to exercise caution and maintain a disciplined approach to avoid the pitfalls of excessive speculation and overconfidence.

How a Bear Market Start

Bear markets typically begin when investors exhibit extreme confidence and euphoria, often driven by an extended period of market success. During the late stages of a bull market, investors become increasingly complacent and dismissive of risk. This exuberance leads to excessive valuations and speculative behavior, creating a market top. As the market reaches this zenith, the optimism becomes unsustainable, and the first signs of trouble emerge. When a catalyst triggers a downturn or economic concerns intensify, the optimistic sentiment begins to unravel.

As the market starts its descent, investor emotions reverse, transitioning from confidence to caution and, ultimately, fear. The declines are often marked by significant selloffs and increasing volatility. During this period, investors grapple with uncertainty and mounting losses, leading to widespread pessimism. The bottom of the bear market is characterized by extreme fear and a belief that the market will continue its descent indefinitely. At this point, the bear market is exhausted, and the groundwork is laid for the eventual start of a new bull market. Recognizing these emotional shifts is crucial for investors to navigate market cycles effectively and make informed decisions.

Why Many Bull Markets Start During Recessions

Bull markets often find their roots in the midst of a recession because economic conditions and investor sentiment are at their most pessimistic. During a recession, corporate profits decline, unemployment rates rise, and consumers tighten their spending. As a result, the stock market reflects these low expectations, causing prices to drop. To counter this economic downturn and promote recovery, central banks, like the Federal Reserve, employ monetary policy tools, primarily lowering interest rates. By lowering interest rates, borrowing becomes more affordable for businesses and consumers, encouraging spending, investment, and economic growth. This policy creates a favorable environment for corporations to improve their profitability, as lower borrowing costs can enhance their earnings.

As the economy stabilizes and corporate profits begin to show signs of improvement, investor sentiment gradually shifts from pessimism to optimism. The perceived potential for higher profits encourages renewed interest in the stock market, leading to increased buying activity and subsequent price gains. This combination of positive sentiment and improved economic conditions contributes to the development of a new bull market. Bull markets often start during recessions as they represent a turning point, where negative expectations give way to a more positive outlook, sparking the recovery and eventual growth of the market.

Why Bear Markets Are Feared

Bear markets are dreaded by investors for two main reasons. First, they can cause substantial losses, potentially erasing years of accumulated profits quickly. This loss of wealth can significantly impact investors' financial security and retirement plans, emphasizing the importance of understanding bear market characteristics and warning signs for portfolio protection.

Second, bear markets pose psychological challenges for investors due to prolonged periods of declining stock prices, economic uncertainty, and negative sentiment. This can trigger emotions like anxiety, fear, and frustration, making it difficult for investors to stay disciplined. During bull markets, overconfidence may lead investors to ignore warning signs, leaving them overly exposed to stocks even when a bear market looms. Recognizing signs of an impending bear market and taking defensive actions, such as reducing stock exposure and increasing allocations to less volatile assets, can help investors navigate turbulent times and safeguard their portfolios.

How to Recognize Bullish Signs

Recognizing bullish signs in the stock market is crucial for investors seeking favorable investment opportunities. Key indicators and characteristics can aid investors in identifying periods of bullish sentiment and potential market upswings. A lower trending inflation and interest rate environment is often viewed as bullish, fostering a favorable investment climate with reduced borrowing costs and increased interest in equities. Additionally, moderate and sustainable economic growth is a positive indicator, signaling enhanced corporate profits and market stability, instilling confidence among investors.

Fiscal responsibility in government management is another positive sign contributing to economic stability and investor confidence. Extreme investor pessimism serves as a contrarian indicator, suggesting that market sentiment has reached maximum negativity, potentially creating buying opportunities. High cash holdings in mutual funds indicate the capacity for increased stock investments, boosting market demand. A decrease in initial public offerings (IPOs) may signify increased confidence in the current economic environment, as companies focus on expanding existing businesses rather than going public. Finally, market highs without widespread bullishness suggest room for further gains as optimism grows over time. Recognizing these bullish signs helps investors make informed decisions and potentially benefit from favorable market conditions.

Bullish Technical Indicators

In addition to fundamental indicators, technical analysis plays a vital role in recognizing bullish signs in the stock market. Intensive selling on heavy volume can indicate a potential market bottom, as it suggests that extreme pessimism and fear have gripped the market, and a reversal may be imminent. Successive lows on decreasing volume can be seen as a sign that the downward momentum is weakening, which can pave the way for a market recovery. Market rallies accompanied by price increases on increasingly heavy volume during successive rally days are a strong indicator of bullish sentiment, as they suggest that investors are becoming more confident and are actively participating in the upward move.

Other technical indicators can provide further confirmation of bullish signs. When there are a small number of stocks on the New York Stock Exchange (NYSE) making new lows, it is a positive sign, indicating that a limited number of companies are experiencing significant declines, while the majority remain stable or are showing strength. The NYSE advance/decline indicator trending upward can also be a sign of growing market strength, as it reflects the number of advancing stocks outweighing decliners. Additionally, indications of institutional accumulation, as shown by the accumulation/distribution indicator, can reinforce bullish signals, as it suggests that large, professional investors are actively buying stocks. Overall, these technical indicators offer investors valuable tools for recognizing bullish market conditions and making informed investment decisions.

How to Recognize Bearish Signs

Recognizing bearish signs is vital for investors in preparing for potential market downturns. One common bearish indicator involves similarities to historically weak periods, particularly after a sharp market run-up, signaling a potential correction or bear market. Rising interest rates are often considered bearish, as they can increase borrowing costs and impact corporate profits. An impending recession can also forewarn challenges for the market. When reported earnings fall below expectations, and stocks no longer respond positively to robust earnings reports, it may indicate waning market enthusiasm. High valuations with elevated P/E ratios are another bearish sign, suggesting potential overpricing of stocks. Excessive bullishness, widespread speculation, and rising margin interest levels can all signify an overheated market due for a correction.

Shifts in market sentiment become evident if small-cap stocks falter and investors turn their focus to conservative, blue-chip stocks. Changes in market leadership, such as breakdowns or distribution among current bull market leaders or a shift to defensive or speculative stocks, can strongly indicate potential market trouble. Recognizing these bearish signs is essential for investors to take protective measures and make well-informed decisions about their investments.

Bearish Technical Signs

To effectively recognize bearish signs in the stock market, technical indicators offer valuable insights. One such bearish indicator is the comparison of trading volume between the NASDAQ and the NYSE. When the NASDAQ experiences increased trading volume compared to the NYSE, it can indicate that the speculative or high-growth stocks on the NASDAQ are facing selling pressure, which is a negative signal for the overall market. The advance/decline (A/D) line trending lower is another significant bearish sign, suggesting that more stocks are declining than advancing, reflecting a weakening market breadth.

Moreover, a surge in the number of stocks hitting new lows compared to new highs is a clear bearish indicator. When more than forty stocks hit new lows, it can signal widespread weakness in the market. A churning market, characterized by heavy trading volume but a lack of significant upward progress, can also be a bearish sign, as it indicates that despite high activity, the market is struggling to make substantial gains. Heavy trading volume on days when the market declines, contrasted with light volume on up days, is another concerning bearish indicator. This suggests that investors may be more active when the market is falling, potentially reflecting a shift in sentiment. Rallies on light volume that ultimately fail to sustain themselves can further confirm bearish sentiment in the market. Collectively, these technical indicators offer investors insights into potential bearish market conditions and help inform their investment decisions.

CORRECTIONS

Individual stocks as well as the overall stock market periodically undergo a short-term price decline, known as a correction. This section discusses various correction aspects, including how to recognize them as well as how to benefit from them.

What Is a Correction?

A correction occurs when the price of an individual stock or the stock market experiences an interruption in its upward trajectory, typically taking place within the context of a bull market. These interruptions are characterized by declines exceeding 5% in magnitude, and they can extend up to 10%. While it is common to observe multiple corrections ranging from 5% to 10% during the course of a bull market's lifespan, some corrections may even reach as high as 15%. Despite the decline, the distinguishing feature of a correction is that it is followed by a reversal in market direction, with the stock or market resuming its upward trend.

During a correction, investors often witness a short-term pullback, which can trigger a sense of uncertainty and volatility in the market. Corrections serve as a means of recalibrating stock or market valuations and providing opportunities for both investors and traders. While corrections can be seen as temporary setbacks within the broader context of a bull market, their significance lies in the fact that they help prevent markets from overheating, ensure a healthy balance between supply and demand, and set the stage for renewed upward movement following the correction's conclusion.

Corrections: Cause and Effect

Corrections can be initiated by a variety of factors, and each of these triggers can have a distinct impact on the market. Rising interest rates, for instance, can lead to a correction as they make other fixed-income investments more attractive compared to equities, prompting investors to reallocate their capital. High market valuations can cause a correction because overvalued stocks can result in profit-taking, leading to price declines. Stock group rotations can occur when investors move their investments from one sector to another, which can affect the prices of stocks in the respective sectors. Additionally, external factors and news events can trigger corrections, as they often bring uncertainty and volatility into the market, causing investors to reassess their positions.

Despite the initial unease that a correction may bring, it is crucial to understand that these market phenomena play a vital role in maintaining a balanced and sustainable market environment. They serve as a mechanism to temper excessive speculation and bring stock prices in line with their true valuation, making it an essential part of the market's long-term health. Corrections offer opportunities for investors to reassess their portfolios, enter the market at more favorable prices, and enhance the overall stability and resilience of the financial markets.

Rolling Correction Phenomenon

The rolling correction phenomenon can be quite complex to navigate for investors, as it often involves a dynamic reshuffling of strengths and weaknesses across different sectors and groups. While the overall market may appear stable, hidden beneath the surface, some sectors may be facing significant headwinds and corrections, while others thrive. This phenomenon underscores the importance of conducting a thorough analysis of individual groups and sectors, as it may reveal valuable insights into where opportunities and risks lie.

Recognizing sector rotation is a crucial aspect of investment strategy, as it allows investors to adapt to changing market conditions and allocate their capital wisely. When one sector experiences a correction, it can provide opportunities for investors to rebalance their portfolios by shifting their investments to areas that show stronger performance and resilience, thereby capitalizing on the market's ever-evolving dynamics.

Learn How to Recognize Rolling Corrections

Recognizing rolling corrections and sector rotations is paramount for investors to make informed decisions in an ever-changing market landscape. These phenomena may not always be apparent when observing the overall market averages, which could remain relatively stable or even show modest gains. Nevertheless, beneath this seemingly calm exterior, certain market sectors or industry groups may be undergoing significant corrections, highlighting the need for a more nuanced analysis.

Sector rotation occurs when corrections are concentrated in specific sectors or groups, rather than affecting the entire stock market. This can lead to substantial fluctuations within these sectors, sometimes to the extent of resembling a bear market. Identifying such rotations can offer investors a competitive advantage by allowing them to reposition their portfolios strategically. By reallocating investments from underperforming sectors to those exhibiting strength, investors can optimize their risk–reward profiles and capitalize on the changing dynamics of the market.

Why Sector Rotation Takes Place

Sector rotation is a strategic approach employed by investors to optimize their portfolios and navigate the ever-changing market conditions. In recent years, this phenomenon has become increasingly prevalent due to investors' reluctance to entirely exit the stock market. Their conviction that stocks remain one of the most attractive investment vehicles, combined with the fear of missing out on potential market upswings, has led them to implement sector rotation strategies.

The process of sector rotation typically begins with investors identifying sectors that are likely to underperform in the broader market. Once these underperforming sectors are identified, investors start divesting stocks within those sectors, thereby triggering a correction. The capital generated from these divestments is then reallocated to sectors expected to outperform the overall market. This approach allows investors to remain engaged in the market while actively managing their investments, aiming to benefit from the relative strength of different sectors over time. Sector rotation strategies can be highly effective, enabling investors to adapt to shifting market dynamics and capitalize on opportunities for growth and stability.

Take Advantage of Corrections

Stock market corrections, although accompanied by investor fear and uncertainty, can provide savvy investors with valuable opportunities. Being prepared for these market downturns allows you to take advantage of favorable conditions, particularly when others are selling off their stocks. It is during corrections that significant bargains may arise, and the change in market leadership offers a chance to identify potential leaders for the upcoming market recovery. These emerging leaders often exhibit high EPS and RS rankings, making them well-positioned for substantial gains as the market rebounds.

It is essential to approach corrections with caution and avoid favoring fallen leaders whose declines have been more pronounced than average. Such companies may struggle to regain their former status as leaders. Additionally, corrections present an opportunity to review your investment portfolio and make strategic adjustments. By weeding out underperforming or weak stocks during these periods, you can enhance the overall quality and resilience of your investment holdings, positioning your portfolio for stronger long-term performance.

Learn How to Pick Leaders During Corrections

During market corrections, investors can strategically identify potential leaders that are likely to outperform when the market recovers. One key indicator to consider is RS, which measures a stock price performance relative to the broader market. Stocks with high RS rankings, despite a correction, indicate their resilience and potential for leadership. It is essential to recognize that high RS stocks may experience smaller declines than the market average during downturns, positioning them as strong contenders for leadership roles in the subsequent market rally.

When seeking out emerging leaders during corrections, pay attention to stocks achieving new highs despite the challenging market conditions. These stocks display remarkable strength, reflecting their ability to weather the storm and stand out among their peers. Additionally, consider companies with improving or strengthening fundamentals, as these are more likely to continue their upward trajectory when the market recovers. By identifying these characteristics during corrections, investors can strategically position themselves to capitalize on the next market upswing.

Avoid Market Timing to Avoid Corrections

Market timing, or attempting to predict corrections and reentries with precision, is an arduous task fraught with challenges. Even seasoned professionals often struggle to consistently time the market accurately. Typically, by the time most investors recognize that a correction is underway, it is already too late to implement effective defensive strategies. The timing of reentry into the market poses another challenge, as pinpointing the ideal moment can be equally challenging. Investors who attempt to move in and out of the market may risk missing the short and powerful upward moves that characterize the market's unpredictable nature.

As a result, unless you are an experienced trader well-versed in market timing, it is generally advisable to avoid such tactics in order to mitigate the impact of a market correction. Instead, it is more effective to focus on a long-term investment strategy based on your financial goals, risk tolerance, and diversification. This approach can help you weather market fluctuations, corrections, and overall volatility without the stress of trying to time the market effectively.

TECHNICAL ANALYSIS

BASIS AND LIMITATIONS OF TECHNICAL ANALYSIS

Besides fundamental analysis, technical analysis is used by many stock market investors. This section discusses various aspects of technical analysis, including concept and usage.

Learn Basic Technical Analysis Concepts

In addition to practicing fundamental analysis, a significant number of investors, estimated to be approximately 10–15%, employ technical analysis in their decision-making process, particularly with the increasing ease of online trading. Given the growing popularity of this approach, it is valuable for all investors to have a basic understanding of the fundamental tenets of technical analysis. This knowledge will enable investors to interpret and make sense of the sometimes inexplicable behavior of stocks, such as the occurrence of abnormally heavy buying or selling, often driven by signals derived from technical analysis tools like moving average crossovers. This ability to comprehend technical signals and market dynamics is akin to defensive driving. Just as a skilled driver remains vigilant of other drivers' actions on the road, investors should be equipped to take defensive action, when necessary, particularly in response to sudden market moves that may potentially affect their investments.

Moreover, technical analysis can be a valuable tool for spotting trends, potential entry or exit points, and identifying support and resistance levels. It involves the examination of historical price and volume data to forecast future price movements. By understanding the basics of technical analysis, investors can gain insights into the market's collective psychology and behavior, which can help in making informed decisions.

It is important to note that while technical analysis can provide valuable insights, it should be used in conjunction with other forms of analysis and not be the sole basis for investment decisions.

What Technical Analysis Is Based On

Technical analysis is fundamentally based on the examination of stock price behavior and trading volume. It aims to forecast future price movements by closely scrutinizing these two main variables. Technical analysts utilize tools such as stock price charts and a range of technical indicators in their analysis. At the core of technical analysis lies the principle that the behavior of a stock or of the broader stock market can be meaningfully linked to the price direction or trend that develops over time. The central belief is that price movements are not random occurrences; rather, they unfold in patterns that can be systematically analyzed to make predictions about the future price movements of the stock or market.

This approach hinges on the assumption that historical price and volume data contain valuable information, and that patterns, trends, and price levels exhibit repetitive tendencies. By recognizing these patterns and trends, analysts aim to gain insights into potential future price movements, thus enabling investors to make more informed decisions. While technical analysis is a well-established method, it is essential to remember that it should be used in conjunction with other forms of analysis, as its effectiveness can vary across different market conditions and circumstances.

What Technical Analysis Indicates

Technical analysis serves as a valuable tool for several key aspects of stock market analysis. First, it helps identify resistance and support levels in stock prices, as these are critical for determining potential turning points in a stock's performance. By recognizing these levels, investors can make informed decisions regarding entry and exit points. Second, technical analysis is instrumental in shedding light on the reasons behind price swings and the behavior of stocks or the market as a whole. Understanding the underlying factors driving market movements is essential for strategic investment choices. Additionally, it is a useful method for analyzing both short-term and long-term trends, enabling investors to anticipate potential future price movements.

It is important to note that technical analysis is most effective when used in conjunction with fundamental analysis. By confirming fundamental insights with technical indicators, investors can make more well-rounded and informed decisions. For instance, if technical analysis signals a potential market top, investors may consider reducing their overall stock holdings. Conversely, when technical indicators suggest a reversal in direction, investors can seize opportunities to position themselves advantageously in the market. This illustrates the complementary role of technical analysis in investment strategies, acting as a supplementary tool alongside fundamental analysis to enhance decision-making.

Use Technical Analysis for Entry Point Determination

Fundamental analysis lays the foundation for stock selection by assessing a company's financial health and performance. Importantly, when it comes to deciding the right time to enter a position, technical analysis plays a crucial role. Investors often utilize technical indicators to identify favorable entry points and confirm that a stock is currently in an uptrend. One common practice is examining the stock's relationship with its 200-day moving average. If the stock is trading above this moving average, it generates a bullish signal, signifying that it is on a long-term uptrend. Conversely, when a stock crosses below its 200-day moving average, it may trigger a bearish signal, indicating a potential exit point. This approach provides a clear and straightforward way to time your investments based on long-term trends.

For shorter-term strategies or for traders with a preference for holding stocks over brief intervals, the 50-day moving average is employed as a short-term signal for entering or exiting positions. By monitoring this indicator, traders can make nimble decisions that align with the stock's more immediate price dynamics. These moving averages serve as essential tools in technical analysis, guiding investors on when to buy and sell, ensuring their actions are in harmony with the stock's prevailing trend, whether short-term or long-term.

Limitations of Technical Analysis

While technical analysis provides valuable insights into a stock's price movements, it falls short in evaluating the underlying fundamentals of a company. It cannot offer information about a stock's business conditions, future growth prospects, or financial health. As such, it is not a suitable substitute for fundamental analysis, which remains an essential component for selecting stocks for long-term investments. Fundamental analysis delves into a company's financial statements, competitive positioning, industry trends, and management quality, offering a comprehensive understanding of its intrinsic value and growth potential.

Limitations of technical analysis become apparent when investors seek a deeper understanding of a company's overall health and viability. Unlike fundamental analysis, technical analysis focuses solely on historical price and volume data. Consequently, technical analysis has inherent limitations in providing a comprehensive perspective on a company's intrinsic value and growth potential. Relying solely on technical analysis may cause investors to overlook crucial aspects essential for making well-informed and strategic long-term investment decisions.

UNDERSTANDING MOVING AVERAGES

This section discusses moving averages, which play a crucial role in technical analysis by smoothing out price data over a specified period, helping traders identify trends, potential reversals, and overall market momentum.

What Is a Moving Average

A moving average is a fundamental technical analysis tool used to assess the overall trend of a stock, index, or market average. It calculates the average price of the asset over a specified period, helping to smooth out short-term fluctuations and highlight the prevailing direction of the trend. Moving averages are versatile and can be applied to various time frames, ranging from short-term to long-term perspectives, making them valuable for different trading and investment strategies.

By plotting a moving average on a price chart, traders and investors can gain valuable insights into the asset's trend behavior. When the moving average line is rising, it indicates an uptrend, suggesting that the asset's prices are generally increasing over the chosen time frame. Conversely, a declining moving average line signals a downtrend, indicating a general decline in prices. Traders often use moving averages to identify potential entry and exit points based on crossovers or divergences with price movements, making this a key tool for technical analysis in the stock market.

Most Popular Moving Averages

Among the most popular moving averages used in technical analysis, the 200-day moving average stands out as one of the most widely monitored. This moving average is calculated by summing up the closing prices of a stock over the past 200 days and then dividing that sum by two hundred. The 200-day moving average is considered a long-term indicator that helps investors identify the long-term trend of a stock or market. When a stock's price is above the 200-day moving average, it typically suggests a bullish sentiment and an upward trend. In contrast, when the stock's price falls below the 200-day moving average, it may indicate a bearish sentiment and a potential downward trend.

In addition to the 200-day moving average, the 30-day and 50-day moving averages are also commonly used in technical analysis. These moving averages offer shorter-term insights into price trends. The 30-day moving average and 50-day moving average calculate the average closing prices over their respective time frames, helping traders and investors identify intermediate-term trends and potential trading opportunities. By closely monitoring these moving averages, market participants can make informed decisions about when to enter or exit positions in response to market trends and price movements.

Significance of Moving Averages

Moving averages are widely used in technical analysis because they offer valuable insights into a stock's or a market's trend direction and potential momentum. The basic premise is that when a stock or index crosses above its moving average line, it signifies a shift in trend direction, indicating a bullish sentiment. This crossing above the moving average is seen as a buy signal, suggesting that the asset is expected to continue moving upward for some time. Conversely, when the stock or index falls below its moving average line, it is perceived as a sell signal, signaling a shift toward a bearish sentiment and an anticipated decline in price.

The significance of moving averages lies in their ability to help traders and investors identify and confirm trends in stock prices. They serve as dynamic support and resistance levels that guide market participants in making decisions about buying or selling assets. By incorporating moving averages into their technical analysis, traders can better understand the underlying sentiment in the market and make informed decisions on when to enter or exit positions, maximizing the potential for profitability.

Moving Averages Can Give Mixed Signals

Moving averages are valuable tools in technical analysis, but their reliability can vary depending on the specific time frame and the moving average used. While the 200-day moving average is generally regarded as a reliable indicator for long-term trend analysis, the shorter-term moving averages, like the 30-day or 50-day, can produce mixed signals due to their sensitivity to shorter period price fluctuations. It is essential for investors and traders to understand the limitations of these shorter-term moving averages.

The 30-day and 50-day moving averages, being shorter in duration, are more responsive to short-term price movements and can lead to frequent crossings over a short period. This frequent crossing can generate false signals, making it challenging to determine a clear and consistent trend direction. Therefore, when using shorter-term moving averages, investors should exercise caution and consider additional technical or fundamental analysis to filter out noise and ensure a more accurate interpretation of market trends.

Moving Averages Can Be Related to Investor Sentiment

Moving averages provide insights into investor sentiment and can offer a valuable perspective on market dynamics. When a stock is trading above its moving average, it signals that the recent buyers, within the chosen time frame of the moving average, are experiencing gains, creating a positive sentiment among those holding the stock. This uptrend suggests that investors are optimistic and confident about the stock's performance.

Conversely, if a stock is trading below its moving average, it signifies that recent buyers are holding positions with losses that can lead to a bearish sentiment. This trend implies that investors may be less optimistic and more cautious about the stock's prospects. By examining moving averages, investors can gauge the collective sentiment of market participants and make more informed decisions based on these insights.

Influence on Momentum Investors

Moving averages can have a significant influence on the behavior of momentum investors and traders. These market participants are highly attuned to technical indicators, especially moving averages, to guide their trading decisions. When a stock is trading above its moving average line, indicating an uptrend, it is seen as an attractive buying opportunity by momentum investors, who aim to ride the momentum and capitalize on upward price movements. Conversely, when a stock falls below its moving average, signaling a downtrend, these investors may interpret it as a signal to sell, aiming to profit from the expected downward price movement.

The widespread adoption of this strategy by momentum investors means that it can become self-fulfilling in the market. As more traders react to signals generated by moving averages, they contribute to reinforcing the trend, causing a bandwagon effect. This phenomenon underscores the significance of moving averages as a tool for understanding market sentiment and behavior, as well as the potential impact of trading strategies on stock price movements.

Which Moving Average to Use

The choice of which moving average to use largely hinges on the investor's specific time horizon and trading style. Long-term investors typically rely on the 200-day moving average, as it provides a broader perspective on a stock's price trend. Some long-term investors may also consider the 50-day moving average for additional insights into intermediate trends. In contrast, intermediate, short-term, and day traders often turn to shorter moving averages, such as the 50-day or even the 5-day moving average. The 50-day moving average is particularly popular due to its common usage in the trading community, and price movements crossing this average can trigger significant trading activity and sentiment shifts among traders.

The stock's inherent volatility also plays a role in the selection of a moving average. More volatile stocks with sharp price swings may benefit from the use of longer time frame moving averages to provide a smoother trend line. In contrast, less volatile stocks may be analyzed using shorter-term moving averages to capture more immediate price changes. The choice of moving average is therefore a nuanced decision that takes into account the investor's investment horizon, trading objectives, and the specific characteristics of the stock in question.

Understand the Concept of Trend Lines

Trend lines are fundamental tools used in technical analysis to gauge a stock's price movement and predict its future direction. When it comes to drawing trend lines, two primary types are essential: rising trend lines, which connect low or bottom points in a price chart to represent an ascending trend, and falling trend lines, which connect high or top points for a descending trend. By analyzing how a stock behaves relative to these trend lines, technical analysts aim to make predictions about the stock's future price movement. The underlying concept is rooted in the idea that established trends, whether rising or falling, tend to persist over a certain period before a potential weakening or reversal occurs.

Trend lines help analysts determine whether a trend is losing strength or potentially undergoing a change. For instance, a rising trend line that was providing support to a stock's price may weaken or break, signaling a potential trend reversal. Conversely, a falling trend line that had been acting as resistance may be breached, suggesting a change in the stock's direction. By examining the interaction between a stock's price and these trend lines, analysts can make informed decisions about trading or investing based on the likelihood of a trend continuation or reversal.

Analyze Charts With Moving Averages and Trend Lines

The combined analysis of moving averages and trend lines is a powerful approach used by technical analysts to confirm and interpret stock price charts effectively. While these tools can be employed individually, they often yield stronger insights when used in conjunction, providing dual confirmation of the stock's trend. When a rising moving average line aligns with an uptrend line, it offers robust confirmation of an uptrend in the stock. Conversely, if both the moving average line and the uptrend line are violated on the downside, it serves as a strong signal that the uptrend has likely come to an end.

This combined analysis is valuable for traders and investors in identifying key entry and exit points in the market. It helps them distinguish between the continuation of an existing trend and the potential reversal of that trend, guiding their decision-making and risk management strategies. By examining moving averages and trend lines in tandem, market participants can gain a clearer perspective on a stock's price movements, thereby enhancing their ability to make well-informed trading and investment choices.

Limitation of Moving Averages

Moving averages are primarily lagging indicators, especially the 200-day moving average, which is considered a long-term trend indicator. One of the main limitations of moving averages is their delayed signals. By the time a stock crosses its 200-day moving average, the trend reversal or continuation is often quite apparent in the price action. This means that if moving averages are used as the primary tool for generating buy and sell signals, their signals may come after a substantial price move has already occurred. Consequently, relying solely on moving averages for timing decisions can be less effective and, in some cases, result in missed opportunities or unfavorable outcomes.

To mitigate the moving average limitation, investors and traders should integrate them into a comprehensive analysis that considers various technical and fundamental factors. This approach provides a more accurate and timely assessment of market conditions, helping navigate potential pitfalls associated with the delayed signals of moving averages and ensuring well-informed decision-making.

How to Monitor Moving Averages

Monitoring moving averages is crucial for investors and traders to gauge the direction and trends of stocks and market indexes. There are numerous sources available for tracking moving averages, both for individual stocks and broader market indexes. Many websites offer stock price charts with moving averages, which can be accessed in both delayed and real-time modes. Some of the popular websites for monitoring moving averages include stockmaster.com, stockcharts.com, bigcharts.com, tradingview.com, and Yahoo Finance. Some of these sites provide free access to basic charting tools, while others may offer premium or subscription-based services with advanced features.

Brokerage account holders typically have access to comprehensive charting tools, including moving averages, on their trading platforms, enabling them to monitor stock trends. For those who prefer traditional media, several newspapers, such as The Wall Street Journal and Investor's Business Daily, also publish stock and market charts, making moving average data readily available to a wide range of investors and traders.

200-DAY MOVING AVERAGE CHARACTERISTICS

Various aspects of the 200-day moving average, which is a long-term trend indicator widely used by stock market investors, are discussed in this section.

200-Day Moving Average as a Trend Indicator

The 200-day moving average serves as a critical long-term trend indicator for stocks and the overall market. Its primary function is to determine the prevailing trend direction. When a stock is trading above its 200-day moving average line, it is widely recognized as being in an uptrend, which is viewed as a bullish signal. Conversely, if a stock is trading below its 200-day moving average, it is considered to be in a downtrend, signaling a bearish sentiment. Investors, especially professional ones, tend to prefer buying stocks that are trading above a rising 200-day moving average line as it indicates a strong uptrend.

Due to the lagging nature of the 200-day moving average, many professional investors opt to take preemptive action by selling a stock before it even crosses below this moving average, particularly if they anticipate a forthcoming decline. The same principles of trend identification apply to the 200-day moving average when analyzing the broader stock market. By closely monitoring the 200-day moving average, investors and traders can gain valuable insights into the long-term trends of individual stocks and market indexes, which can be crucial for informed decision-making.

200-Day Moving Average as a Market Direction Change Indicator

Market analysts closely monitor the 200-day moving average not only for individual stocks but also for various market indexes and averages to gauge their overall trend direction and to detect signals of potential market shifts. Among these indicators, the DJIA is regarded as a particularly valuable one for assessing the broader market's future behavior. When the DJIA rises above its 200-day moving average, it sends a bullish signal for the entire market, signifying a change in trend that is expected to result in upward momentum. Conversely, when the DJIA crosses below its 200-day moving average in a downward trajectory, it generates a bearish signal, indicating a potential shift in market sentiment toward a more pessimistic outlook.

The 200-day moving average, especially when applied to well-established market indexes like the DJIA, can be an invaluable tool for market analysts and investors in predicting and reacting to overall market trends. By keeping a watchful eye on these trends, they can make more informed decisions regarding their investment strategies and the timing of buying or selling stocks and other financial assets.

200-Day Moving Average Can Give a False Signal

The 200-day moving average is a valuable tool for investors, but it is not infallible, and false signals can occur. When a stock or market index crosses below its 200-day moving average, it does not necessarily guarantee a long-term trend change. Sometimes, the decline below this moving average is short-lived, and the stock might experience a swift rebound or trade in a choppy manner around the moving average line. In such cases, investors should exercise caution because the initial decline may not signify a substantial shift in trend direction.

In these situations, the validity of the signal depends on whether the stock can sustain its rebound or if it falls back below the moving average. A failed rebound could be an indicator of a more prolonged bearish trend, suggesting that the stock might encounter difficulties. To avoid falling victim to false signals, investors should use the 200-day moving average in conjunction with other technical and fundamental analysis tools to make well-informed investment decisions.

Tips for Individual Stocks

When analyzing individual stocks, the 200-day moving average plays a significant role in signaling potential buy or sell opportunities. Decisively crossing above the 200-day moving average is often interpreted as a buy signal, indicating that the stock might be in an uptrend. It is essential to be cautious about overextended situations. If a stock is trading 50% or more above its moving average line, it could be considered overextended, which makes it vulnerable to a correction. When a stock extends even further, reaching 70%–100% above the moving average, profit-taking is often advisable to lock in gains.

Conversely, if a stock falls below its moving average line on heavy volume or experiences a gap-down, which is a sudden sharp price drop, it is a negative development that usually results in a sell signal. These conditions are often accompanied by strong indications of bearish sentiment. On the flip side, if a stock experiences a breakout to the upside with significant volume support, it generates a buy signal.

It is crucial to consider the stock's fundamentals in conjunction with these technical signals. A stock that rises above its 50-day moving average while also trading above its 200-day moving average is typically seen as a bullish sign, while a move in the opposite direction is considered bearish. This integration of technical and fundamental analysis provides a more comprehensive view for investors when making decisions about individual stocks.

Tips for the Market

When assessing the overall market, the behavior of major market averages and indexes, such as the DJIA or NASDAQ, in relation to their 200-day moving average lines plays a crucial role in determining the market's trend and sentiment. If a major index crosses above its 200-day moving average line after a prolonged period of trading below it, this shift is typically seen as a bullish signal, indicating a positive trend change. As long as the index maintains its position above the 200-day moving average, it suggests the continuation of an uptrend. Conversely, if a major index crosses below its 200-day moving average line after an extended period of trading above it, it signals a trend change and is viewed bearishly.

The slope of the moving average is also important in interpreting market direction. When the moving average line is rising sharply, even if it is situated below the index, it is considered a bullish sign. Conversely, if the moving average is rapidly declining and positioned above the index, it sends a bearish signal. Additionally, it is essential to keep an eye on divergences between key market indexes and their respective moving averages. For instance, when major indexes are above their 200-day moving averages, and one suddenly drops below this level, it can serve as a leading indicator for other indexes to potentially follow suit. Determining which index is leading in an upward or downward direction is key to understanding market dynamics and trend changes.

Relating the 200-Day Moving Average to the Market Health

The market's health and its prevailing trend can be effectively assessed by examining the percentage of stocks that are trading above their 200-day moving average line. When the majority of stocks are trading above this threshold, it is indicative of an uptrend in the market, signifying a bullish sentiment. Conversely, if most stocks are trading below their 200-day moving average, it suggests that the market is in a downtrend, reflecting a bearish tone.

The percentage of stocks that are trading above their 200-day moving average is a valuable gauge of the overall market health. A higher percentage of stocks above this threshold is associated with a healthier market condition, indicating robust underlying strength and more widespread investor confidence. In contrast, a lower percentage can signal market weakness and increased caution among investors, highlighting the potential for a bearish trend.

Relating Stocks Trading Over Their 200-Day Moving Average to Market Health

The percentage of stocks trading over their 200-day moving average serves as a valuable market health indicator with important implications for investors. In the context of a bull market, this percentage tends to be notably high or trending higher, reflecting a robust and optimistic market environment. It is important to note that when bear markets or corrections are underway, this percentage typically experiences a significant decline.

A noteworthy occurrence is when the percentage surpasses the 90% mark and maintains that level. This situation indicates the presence of a powerful and resilient market, capable of making substantial upward moves. Historically, the percentage of NYSE-listed stocks trading above their 200-day moving average has fluctuated within a broad range. At market tops, this percentage has been known to reach as high as 80%–90%, signaling elevated market exuberance. Conversely, during market bottoms, the percentage has dwindled to as low as 10%–20%, illustrating a market plagued by pessimism and extreme caution. Daily reporting of this number by the *IBD* and various online sources offers investors valuable insights into market conditions.

SUPPORT, RESISTANCE, AND BASING

In this section, investors will be introduced to the concepts of support, resistance, and basing, which form the foundation of technical analysis, enabling them to understand how identifying key levels can guide strategic decision-making.

Be Familiar With the Stock Price Cycle and Its Current Phase

Understanding the stock price cycle is essential for effective stock market investing. A typical stock price cycle encompasses four primary phases: basing, rising, topping, and declining. The most favorable phase for investors is the rising phase, characterized by an uptrend in stock prices, making it an opportune time for buying. Conversely, the declining phase signifies a downtrend in stock prices, making it advisable to consider selling rather than buying. Recognizing and identifying these phases in a timely manner can enhance profit potential or help mitigate significant losses.

The application of technical analysis principles and techniques is instrumental in discerning these phases within the stock price cycle. By analyzing key technical indicators and patterns, investors can make informed decisions, navigating the stock market with greater confidence and increasing their chances of financial success.

What Is a Support Line?

In technical analysis, the concept of a support line is fundamental for understanding price dynamics and making informed investment decisions. A support line represents the price level at which a stock stabilizes following a significant price drop or decline. At this juncture, the stock's descent comes to a halt as the selling pressure subsides, and the number of buyers equals or exceeds that of sellers. The emergence of this support level can be identified by distinct markers, such as a sharp sell-off characterized by heavy trading volume or a series of price lows occurring on progressively diminishing volume. These support levels are critical for market participants as they represent crucial reference points for assessing potential future price movements.

To visualize a support line, technical analysts connect the low points or bottoms on a stock price chart, effectively creating a line that underscores the price levels at which the stock's descent found support. It is important to recognize that a single stock may have multiple support levels, each denoting a distinct price range at which the stock encountered support during its price decline. In the context of technical analysis, breaching a support level to the downside is viewed as a bearish signal, indicating potential downward pressure on the stock's price. Moreover, if this breach occurs decisively, investors may anticipate that the next support level will serve as the next potential support threshold, with implications for future trading decisions.

Moving Average as a Support Line

Moving averages play a pivotal role in technical analysis, particularly as support lines for stocks. They represent a stock's average price over a specific time frame, such as 30 days, 50 days, or 200 days. Among these, the 50-day and 200-day moving average lines are widely recognized as robust support levels for stocks due to their ability to reflect the underlying trend. When a stock's price approaches or descends near these moving average lines, the dynamics of supply and demand come into play. Selling pressure tends to wane, and buying interest increases, contributing to a potential rebound in the stock's price. This phenomenon is driven, in part, by the fact that major institutional investors frequently use these moving averages as predetermined levels at which they initiate positions. Consequently, a breach of a moving average line to the downside is often interpreted as a bearish signal, suggesting potential weakness in the stock's price trajectory.

In practice, these moving average lines act as dynamic support levels, helping traders and investors gauge the strength of a stock's trend and make informed decisions. The proximity of a stock's price to its moving average lines can serve as an important reference point for assessing whether the stock is trading in alignment with its longer-term or shorter-term trends, thereby guiding buying and selling strategies. By offering consistent support levels based on historical price data, moving averages provide valuable insights into a stock's price dynamics, making them a key tool in the technical analyst's toolkit.

How Solid Is a Support Line?

The solidity of a support line depends on the historical price action and how often it has been tested and validated by the stock. The more frequently a stock approaches a support line and successfully rebounds from it, the more solid and dependable that support line is considered to be. This recurring validation instills confidence in traders and investors, making the support line an attractive entry point. Essentially, the support line is seen as a price floor that the stock is reluctant to breach, and from which a rebound can be anticipated. This reassures traders who use it as a reference point for their buying decisions, believing that the support line will act as a buffer against further declines.

It is important to remember that if a support line is decisively breached, it can transform into a resistance level. This reversal of roles signifies a significant change in the stock's price dynamics and is closely monitored by traders and investors. Not only traders but also long-term investors are keen on watching support lines, as they offer valuable insights into the stock's price behavior and its potential resilience during market fluctuations. In summary, a well-established and frequently tested support line is an important aspect of technical analysis, providing traders and investors with key reference points for their trading and investment decisions.

What Is a Resistance Line?

A resistance line is an important concept in technical analysis, representing a price level at which a stock or security tends to encounter selling pressure and struggles to move beyond. This occurs after a period of price appreciation, when the stock reaches a peak or resistance level. At this point, the number of buyers diminishes, and sellers become more prominent, leading to a halt in the stock's ascent. A resistance line is depicted on a price chart by connecting the high points or peaks, beyond which the stock has previously struggled to progress.

In contrast to a support level, which acts as a floor for the stock's price and provides a rebounding point, a resistance line serves as a price ceiling that a stock has difficulty breaking through during an upward move. Traders and investors closely monitor resistance levels, as they offer insights into potential obstacles a stock might encounter in its journey higher. A stock can have multiple resistance levels, and traders often use these lines as reference points for their trading decisions. If a resistance line is decisively breached, indicating that the stock has successfully moved above it, this is interpreted as a bullish sign. Such a breakthrough suggests that the stock has the potential for further upward movement.

How Solid Is a Resistance Line?

The strength and significance of a resistance line are closely related to the frequency with which a stock approaches it and retreats from it. The more often a stock's price approaches a resistance line and fails to break through it, the more psychologically important that line becomes to traders. As a result, traders are cautious about buying near resistance levels since they are aware of the historical tendency for stocks to struggle at these points. Instead, traders often look for opportunities to sell near resistance levels, expecting the stock's price to retreat after another unsuccessful attempt to break through the resistance line.

A powerful breakout through a resistance level on heavy trading volume can be a highly attractive entry point for traders who believe that the stock has the potential for significant upward movement. Once a resistance level is successfully breached, it often transforms into a support level, offering a floor beneath which the stock's price is less likely to fall easily and from which rebounds are expected. This change in role from resistance to support is significant because it reflects a shift in market sentiment and expectations for the stock.

Effect of Overhead Supply on Rebounding Stocks

When a stock makes a recovery after a period of decline or corrects from a sharp pullback, it has to contend with the concept of overhead supply. For instance, if a stock has recently experienced a decline from $75 to $50 through a series of steps (e.g., $70, $62, $55, and $50) and subsequently reverses direction to move up to $55 after consolidating around the $50 level, many investors who initially purchased the stock at $55 will often look to sell once the price returns to their breakeven point. A similar pattern of selling pressure emerges as the stock progresses back up to the previous trading levels, such as $62, $70, and $75, as more investors look to offload their shares. This phenomenon, where stocks that were previously purchased at specific levels are offered for sale once the price returns to those levels, is termed overhead supply. When a stock has remained at a certain price level for an extended period before declining, it will encounter a substantial volume of overhead supply when it embarks on a recovery. Consequently, it may face formidable resistance when attempting to break through this supply level.

Overhead supply can create hurdles for a rebounding stock, making it more challenging to surpass these levels and continue its upward trajectory. The presence of many willing sellers who previously bought the stock at these levels can lead to increased selling pressure as the price approaches these points, potentially slowing down the stock's ascent. Investors and traders often closely monitor overhead supply levels to gauge the likelihood of a stock successfully breaking through these price points or facing resistance. Understanding the dynamics of overhead supply is crucial when analyzing stocks that have experienced recent declines and are attempting to recover, as it can provide valuable insights into potential price movements and decision-making.

What Is Basing?

In technical analysis, basing refers to a specific phase in a stock's price cycle characterized by trading activity occurring within a confined price range and on relatively low volume. During this phase, the stock's resistance and support levels are in close proximity to each other, often leading to a prolonged period of equilibrium between buyers and sellers. Basing phases can extend for several weeks, months, or, in some cases, even longer, depending on market conditions and stock-specific factors. This phase can manifest in various scenarios, including during an ongoing uptrend when the stock needs to consolidate and absorb prior gains. Alternatively, it can emerge following a gradual price decline or a sudden, substantial drop in the stock's value, marking a period of stabilization and indecision in the market.

Basing is a critical technical analysis concept as it indicates a temporary pause or consolidation in the stock's price movement. This phase can offer valuable insights for traders and investors, allowing them to anticipate potential future price trends based on the stock's behavior during this period. Understanding basing patterns is essential for those seeking to make informed decisions about entering, exiting, or holding positions in stocks, as it can help in assessing the stock's readiness to resume its upward or downward trajectory.

What Is a Breakout

In technical analysis, a "breakout" is a pivotal event that transpires after a stock has spent a significant period basing or trading within a confined price range. This phase of consolidation can persist for months, signifying a temporary equilibrium where buyers and sellers are more or less evenly matched. During a breakout, the stock moves out from this trading range by making a decisive move, either upward or downward. An upside breakout materializes when fresh buyers enter the market and the number of available sellers diminishes, causing buying pressure to dominate. Conversely, a downside breakout unfolds when new sellers emerge, leading to a predominant selling trend. Identifying and monitoring breakouts are of particular interest to technical analysts because these events often foreshadow the potential for rapid and substantial price movements in a relatively short time frame.

Breakouts hold a significant place in the toolkit of traders and investors, as they can present lucrative opportunities for capitalizing on price changes. Traders often leverage breakouts to initiate positions or make quick trading decisions, aiming to ride the momentum generated by the breakout in the direction of the prevailing trend. By identifying breakouts early and correctly, market participants can position themselves to seize the potential gains or manage risk, which can be particularly advantageous when market conditions align with their strategies and objectives.

Understanding the Breakout Strategy

The breakout strategy is a fundamental approach employed by momentum traders to pinpoint stocks displaying promising price momentum characteristics. Nonetheless, not all breakouts guarantee success, as a stock that breaks out may subsequently retreat or fail to register a significant upward move. To enhance the probability of a successful breakout, it is crucial to scrutinize certain key factors. First and foremost, assess the stock's fundamentals, such as its earnings. Stocks with strong earnings performance tend to be more resilient and are better poised for sustained upward momentum. Additionally, pay heed to relative strength, aiming for stocks with relative strength scores that exceed 70 and preferably exceed 90, indicating strong price performance compared to the broader market.

Furthermore, consider the stock's overall trend, as a major uptrend can amplify the impact of a breakout. An extended basing period is also a valuable criterion, with a preferred duration of three to five months, as it reflects the stock's resilience and its ability to absorb selling pressure during the consolidation phase. Stocks that are based above the 50-day moving average line are often considered stronger, suggesting solid investor interest. Longer basing periods, combined with a significant rise or a surge in trading volume during the breakout, contribute to a more powerful expected breakout. Finally, a breakout that propels the stock into new high territory, free from overhead supply, is particularly favorable, as it minimizes the risk associated with encountering resistance and potentially strengthens the stock's long-term prospects.

TRADING VOLUME AND PRICE PERFORMANCE

This section explores the intricate relationship between market activity and stock price movements, uncovering the significance of trading volume as a key indicator to analyze and interpret price trends.

Volume Can Be Related to Trend Changes or Turning Points

Trading volume is a critical indicator in the realm of stock analysis, closely examined by traders and investors in tandem with the price movements of individual stocks and the overall market. Elevated trading volume often signals the occurrence of something extraordinary or the anticipation of significant forthcoming developments. It serves as a notable barometer for potential news and events, catching the attention of investors who closely follow volume levels. Investors and traders are astute in monitoring trading volume, recognizing its association with substantial price fluctuations, whether upward or downward. One well-established principle is the direct correlation between rising volume and price, indicating the likelihood of further price appreciation. In essence, simultaneous increases in both volume and price momentum are typically interpreted as precursors to the commencement of a new trend.

By observing the interplay between volume and price movements, market participants endeavor to decipher pivotal turning points and shifts in market dynamics. Heightened trading volume can signify the onset of a significant trend and serve as a harbinger of notable price movements. Conversely, dwindling or irregular volume may herald a potential market shift or signal that the prevailing trend is losing momentum. In essence, trading volume provides valuable insights into market sentiment, helping traders and investors navigate their decisions and identify potential trend changes.

Analyze Trading Volume

Interpreting trading volume is an essential aspect of stock analysis, providing valuable insights into market sentiment. When daily trading volume surpasses the average daily trading volume, it indicates heightened investor interest and activity, which can be driven by various factors. A notable scenario unfolds when a stock experiences a breakout from its established trading range, whether to the upside or downside, and is accompanied by increased trading volume. An upside breakout with heavy volume is often viewed as a robust buy signal, suggesting significant buying activity, particularly from institutional investors. This surge in trading volume reflects the strong interest in the stock, which can propel it to new heights. In contrast, when a stock registers an increase in price while trading volume remains stagnant or declines, it is considered a bullish indicator, indicating a lack of selling pressure.

On the flip side, when a stock experiences a downside breakout, it is typically regarded as a sell signal, regardless of whether trading volume rises or not. A price decline associated with heavy volume is a particularly bearish signal, signifying robust selling activity and potential market weakness. This is particularly concerning when it occurs in a strong and rising market. In contrast, a price decline on low volume following a period of significant selling may suggest that the selling pressure has waned or is nearing its conclusion. Generally, trading volume tends to be above average during uptrends and below average during downtrends, offering valuable cues to market dynamics and potential trend reversals. Additionally, reaching new highs on low volume can raise concerns and serve as a warning sign, indicating a potential lack of commitment among buyers.

Focus on Percentage Change in Volume

When analyzing trading volume, it is crucial to focus on the percentage change in volume rather than simply comparing the absolute volume numbers. Stocks can have vastly different average daily trading volumes, and evaluating their volume changes using a percentage-based approach ensures that the analysis is meaningful and applicable across a broad spectrum of stocks. By focusing on the percentage change, you can pinpoint stocks with the most substantial volume changes, even if they do not have the highest daily trading volume. This approach allows investors to identify stocks experiencing significant shifts in market interest, which can be indicative of noteworthy news or developments affecting those particular stocks.

To illustrate, consider two stocks where both experience a one million share increase on a particular day. The first stock has an average daily trading volume of two hundred thousand shares, while the second stock has a daily trading volume of five million shares. By concentrating on the percentage change, it becomes evident that the first stock has a 500% rise in volume, while the second stock has a 20% increase, which is not as significant. Such percentage-based analysis is invaluable for investors seeking early insights into potential news or developments that could impact their stock investments.

11

MONITORING THE ECONOMY

GENERAL

Economic indicators reflect the health of the economy and, therefore, have a significant impact on the stock market. This section discusses the importance of monitoring the economy, as well as the indicators that can be used for that purpose.

Why the Economy Should Be Monitored

Monitoring the economy is crucial for investors because it provides valuable insights into the factors that influence a company's profitability and, consequently, the stock price performance. The state of the economy and the stage of the business cycle have a significant bearing on a company's earnings, as consumer spending, business investment, and overall economic health directly affect corporate revenues and profitability. Therefore, investors need to keep a watchful eye on economic indicators and variables that are closely linked to the financial health of companies and the broader stock market. These economic variables are typically released through periodic reports by government agencies and various organizations, and the data is promptly disseminated by newspapers and websites, allowing investors to stay informed and make informed decisions about their investments.

Investors must pay attention to a wide range of economic indicators and reports that include, but are not limited to, GDP growth, employment statistics, consumer sentiment, inflation rates, and interest rates. By closely following these economic metrics, investors can gauge the overall economic health and direction, which is a vital factor in determining the potential future performance of individual stocks and the broader stock market. Economic data can signal changes in the business cycle, helping investors make informed decisions about their portfolios and respond to shifting economic conditions, ultimately maximizing their investment outcomes.

Key Indicators Used to Monitor the Economy's Performance

Investors rely on a variety of indicators to assess the health of the economy and its potential for future growth, both of which play a crucial role in determining the level of earnings and the price performance of the stock market as well as individual companies. These indicators include inflation, employment, GDP, Institute for Supply Management (ISM) Purchasing Managers' Index (PMI), factory orders, housing and construction spending, consumer confidence index, retail sales, personal income and consumption expenditures, industrial production and capacity utilization, housing starts, stock market indexes, and money supply.

By closely monitoring these economic indicators, investors can make informed decisions about their investments and better position themselves to navigate the complexities of the financial markets.

Interest Rates and Fiscal Policy

In addition to economic indicators, investors keep a close watch on the policies and actions of the Federal Reserve when it comes to interest rates. Short-term and long-term interest rate trends are of particular interest, with the thirty-year bond rate and the prime-lending rate being commonly monitored indicators. These interest rates have a significant impact on various aspects of the financial markets, including the cost of borrowing for businesses and consumers, which in turn affects spending, investments, and economic growth.

Furthermore, fiscal policy, as represented by government spending and the budget deficit, is a crucial area of concern for investors. These factors can influence interest rates, as the level of government borrowing required to fund deficits can place upward pressure on interest rates. Therefore, investors closely follow government fiscal decisions, as they play a pivotal role in shaping the economic landscape and can have direct implications for both the bond and equity markets. By staying informed about interest rates and fiscal policy, investors aim to make more informed decisions in their investment strategies and understand the potential risks and opportunities in the financial markets.

PRIMARY INDICATORS

This section discusses the most important economic indicators, such as inflation and unemployment, used by investors for analyzing the state of the economy.

Inflation

Inflation holds a significant place in the minds of Wall Street investors, primarily due to its potential to erode the purchasing power of money. The relationship between inflation and stocks is particularly crucial, as stock prices tend to respond to inflationary pressures within the economy. Investors closely follow inflation-related news, especially indicators pointing to an uptick in inflation. When inflation is on the rise, it suggests that interest rates may increase to combat it, and this anticipation negatively impacts stocks. Conversely, when inflation appears to be under control, it tends to have a positive effect on stocks. The dynamics of inflation and interest rates play a role in asset allocation decisions as investors seek to optimize their portfolios. In times of rising inflation and interest rates, they may choose to shift their investments from stocks to bonds, and vice versa when interest rates are declining.

Two of the most prominent inflation indicators that investors pay close attention to are the producer price index (PPI) and the consumer price index (CPI). These metrics provide insights into the changing prices of goods and services, which are fundamental to gauging inflation trends. Additionally, the Commodity Research Bureau (CRB) index serves as a valuable tool for investors to assess potential inflationary pressures by tracking the trends in commodity prices. A rising CRB index can indicate increasing costs of raw materials, which often translate into higher prices for finished goods and services, contributing to inflation concerns. Therefore, monitoring these inflation indicators becomes an essential part of investors' strategies to navigate the effects of inflation on stock prices and asset allocation decisions.

Producer Price Index

The producer price index (PPI) plays a pivotal role in assessing inflation trends at the producer or wholesale level of the economy. It tracks and measures the price changes of various categories of goods, including crude, intermediate, and finished products, providing insights into inflationary pressures at different stages of the production process. The PPI comprises two key components: the overall rate and the core rate. The core rate, which holds greater significance, is calculated by excluding the more volatile elements of the overall rate, such as food and energy prices. Investors typically place greater emphasis on the core rate to get a clearer picture of underlying inflationary trends.

The PPI's movements and trends are of considerable importance to the financial markets, especially the stock market. Investors closely monitor the PPI, and any report indicating a rise in this index is often viewed as negative for the stock market. This sentiment stems from the fact that both the PPI and the CPI hold considerable influence over Federal Reserve policies, interest rates, and other financial metrics, such as consumer and auto loan rates. When the PPI remains low or trends downward, it is generally seen as a positive development in the market. This is because lower producer prices are indicative of a benign inflationary environment, which is often conducive to investment and economic growth. Consequently, investors are advised to scrutinize any changes in the PPI rate, as they can provide crucial insights into the potential impacts on inflation and the financial markets.

Consumer Price Index

The consumer price index (CPI) is a fundamental gauge of inflation, specifically focusing on the retail level, where it assesses changes in the prices of consumer goods and services. Much like the PPI, the CPI comprises two crucial components: the overall rate and the core rate, with the latter being of higher significance to investors. The core rate is calculated after excluding the prices of food and energy, making it a more stable and reliable measure of underlying inflation trends.

The CPI serves as an essential indicator for the financial markets, and its movements hold the potential to impact both stocks and bonds. When the CPI rate experiences an increase, it generally exerts a negative influence on these markets. Conversely, when the CPI is stable or shows signs of decreasing, it is viewed as a positive development for the stock market. The rationale behind this is that a rising CPI signifies an increase in the cost of living, which can potentially lead to reduced purchasing power and affect consumer sentiment, which in turn can affect stock market performance. Due to the monthly volatility of CPI data, it is advisable for investors to consider the CPI average over several months to gain a more accurate understanding of the inflation trend and its potential impact on the financial markets.

Commodity Research Bureau Index

The Commodity Research Bureau (CRB) index is a critical tool for assessing the trend in commodity prices, which are often the first indicators of inflationary pressures in the economy. The movement of commodity prices is of great importance to analysts and investors, as it directly impacts the prices of finished goods and services. When commodity prices remain low, it tends to keep inflation and interest rates at manageable levels, ultimately benefiting both individual consumers and the broader economy. In turn, the stock market benefits from this scenario, as it thrives in an environment of stable prices and low interest rates.

It is important to note that the CRB index does not wield the same direct influence over the stock market as indicators like the CPI or the PPI. While fluctuations in the CRB index are closely monitored for signs of inflation, the stock market's reaction to these changes may be more nuanced and influenced by a broader range of factors. Nonetheless, keeping an eye on the CRB index remains an integral part of financial analysis for investors seeking a comprehensive understanding of market conditions and potential influences on stock prices.

Employment

The monthly employment report from the Labor Department is a highly anticipated and closely watched indicator, with significant implications for investors and economists alike. This report serves as a key barometer for assessing the overall health and performance of the economy. Of all the components within the employment report, one that holds particular importance is the number of new jobs created during the reporting month. This figure provides critical insight into the trajectory of the economy, as job creation is typically associated with a thriving economy.

Another vital component of the employment report is the unemployment rate, which investors look at closely. A steady or declining unemployment rate is seen as a positive sign, indicating a labor market that is becoming increasingly robust. The reaction of investors to the employment report is contingent upon their expectations, which can vary widely depending on the current state of the economy. High expectations may lead to bullish sentiment in the stock market if the report exceeds them, while low expectations could have the opposite effect.

The employment report plays a pivotal role in shaping investor sentiment and influencing market performance. For this reason, it is imperative to closely track and interpret the data presented in this report, as it can provide critical insights into the economy's trajectory, job market stability, and overall market conditions. A strong employment report, characterized by robust job creation and a declining unemployment rate, is typically interpreted as a bullish signal for the stock market, while a weak report may raise concerns about the broader economy and trigger a bearish market sentiment.

Jobs Growth

The level of job growth holds paramount significance in assessing the economy's health and its potential impact on the stock market. In a steadily growing economy, the creation of two hundred thousand to three hundred thousand jobs per month is generally regarded as a positive indicator, signifying a healthy economy, and typically met with optimism by investors. Any figure above or below this range can convey distinct messages about the pace and vigor of economic growth. Job creation figures exceeding this range may indicate a rapidly expanding economy, raising concerns about inflationary pressures. Conversely, job growth numbers falling below this range might signal a more sluggish or slowly growing economy, influenced by the phase of the business cycle, whether the economy is emerging from a recession, currently in a recession, or has been in an extended expansion period.

Excessive job growth can be viewed as inflationary, often leading to a negative response in the stock market. The correlation between job growth and stock market performance depends on various factors, including the specific conditions of the economy and the central bank's monetary policy. Investors closely monitor job creation statistics as a barometer of economic health and potential inflationary pressures. It is essential to interpret job growth data within the broader context of economic conditions and factors influencing the stock market to make informed investment decisions.

SECONDARY INDICATORS

In addition to the primary indicators, there are many additional indicators monitored by stock market investors, which are discussed in this section.

Gross Domestic Product

Gross domestic product (GDP) is a fundamental economic indicator that offers valuable insights into the health and growth of the economy. Reported quarterly, it represents the total value of goods and services produced within a country during a specific period. The GDP's significance lies in its ability to reflect the pace of economic expansion or contraction over the reporting period. Steady GDP growth is a positive indicator for the stock market, as it signifies a growing economy, which tends to translate into higher corporate profits. Investors typically view a report indicating strong and steady GDP growth as favorable, which can contribute to positive stock market performance. Conversely, a weak or negative GDP report is viewed negatively by the stock market, as it implies economic stagnation or contraction, which can undermine corporate earnings.

It is worth noting that the market's reaction to GDP reports is often relatively muted. This is because many of the components used to calculate the GDP are known well in advance when the report is released, reducing the likelihood of significant surprises. If the actual GDP figures significantly deviate from the advance estimates made by economists, it can trigger a more substantial market reaction, leading to either optimism or pessimism among investors, depending on the nature of the surprise.

Institute for Supply Management Purchasing Managers' Index

The Institute for Supply Management (ISM) Purchasing Managers' Index (PMI) is a critical economic indicator that provides valuable insights into the state of economic growth, particularly within the manufacturing sector. The overall PMI number is a crucial element, and it serves as a clear indicator of whether the manufacturing sector is expanding or contracting. A number above 50 suggests that the manufacturing sector is in an expansion phase, which is indicative of a healthy and growing economy. Such expansion is generally viewed positively by the stock market, as it suggests a favorable economic environment with potential benefits for corporate profits. Conversely, a PMI number below 50 signifies a contracting manufacturing sector, which is perceived negatively by the stock market as it implies economic slowdown or decline.

While the overall PMI index is the headline figure, it is important to note that it comprises several components, each providing unique insights into specific areas of the manufacturing sector. These components include new orders, order backlog, supplier deliveries, inventories, prices paid, and more. Monitoring these components can provide a more comprehensive understanding of economic trends. When analyzing PMI data, investors often focus not only on the specific index number but also on the steadiness and trend of these numbers over time. A consistent trend, whether upward or downward, can offer additional context and predictability regarding the future state of the economy.

Housing

The housing sector plays a pivotal role in the broader economy, and its condition often mirrors the overall health of the economy. Investors closely monitor the housing sector as a leading indicator to anticipate the direction of the economy. Housing tends to be an early signal of economic trends; it is usually the first sector to show signs of weakening when the economy is heading into a recession, and conversely, it is often the first to recover when the economy is on an upswing. This sensitivity to economic shifts makes the housing sector a crucial barometer for forecasting economic trends.

One of the primary factors influencing the health of the housing sector is mortgage rates. The housing market is acutely responsive to fluctuations in mortgage rates, which, in turn, are influenced by changes in inflation and interest rates. When interest rates rise, mortgage rates tend to follow suit, making borrowing more expensive and potentially dampening the demand for homes. Conversely, when interest rates fall, mortgage rates also decrease, making home purchases more affordable and potentially driving an increase in housing demand. As a result, housing data and trends can provide valuable insights into broader economic conditions and can serve as a useful early warning system for investors seeking to navigate economic cycles.

Housing Starts and Building Permits

In the realm of housing data, two vital metrics take center stage as leading indicators: housing starts and building permits. These indicators are particularly important because they foreshadow future construction and spending in the housing sector, often by several months. Housing starts representing the number of new residential construction projects that have begun during a given time period. Building permits, however, are official authorizations issued by local governments to commence new construction. Both metrics serve as valuable tools for gauging the health of the housing sector and its impact on the broader economy.

An increase in either housing starts or building permits is seen as a positive sign for the economy. This is because they trigger construction spending and building activity, which, in turn, propels economic growth. When housing sector indicators reveal a healthy and robust upward trend, it typically spurs optimism in the stock market. These indicators offer investors insights into the future trajectory of the housing sector, which plays a crucial role in the overall economy, thus making them essential tools for economic forecasting and investment decision-making.

Sales of New and Existing Homes

The sales of new and existing homes are critical factors in stimulating economic activity, as they initiate a cascade of purchases for items such as furniture, appliances, and other durable goods. These sales, whether new or existing homes, are key indicators of strength in the housing sector. Consequently, robust home sales are viewed as a positive sign for the stock market. It is worth noting that the performance of the housing market can be significantly impacted by fluctuations in mortgage rates. When mortgage rates rise, it tends to put downward pressure on both new and existing home sales, which can slow down this vital sector of the economy.

Of the two, existing home sales hold a particular significance as they make up a substantial 80% of the total housing market. As a result, they are considered to be a more accurate and reliable indicator of the housing market's performance compared to housing starts, which can represent merely expected or planned construction activity. Existing home sales provide insights into the actual transactions taking place in the market, which is a vital aspect of the housing sector's health. Therefore, they play a crucial role in assessing the housing market's status and its potential impact on the broader economy, making them important reference points for investors and analysts.

Construction Spending

Construction spending serves as an essential indicator, encompassing various aspects of construction activity, including residential and nonresidential new construction, as well as public construction spending. These expenditure levels are particularly sensitive to factors such as changes in mortgage rates, which can impact the overall health of the construction industry. When construction spending data is released, it typically does not produce a significant immediate effect on the stock market. The reason for this muted response is that construction spending figures can exhibit considerable monthly volatility due to fluctuations in construction projects. To better understand the trend and the overall health of this sector, it is advisable to analyze the data over a more extended period, such as a three-month span, rather than reacting to short-term variations.

By looking at the data over a more extended time frame, investors and analysts can gain a clearer picture of the prevailing trends in construction spending. This approach allows for the identification of any overarching patterns or shifts in construction activity, which may provide more substantial insights into the state of the economy and its potential effects on the stock market. Overall, construction spending serves as an important barometer of economic health and can provide valuable guidance for investment decisions, especially when considered in conjunction with other relevant economic indicators and market data.

Retail Sales

Retail sales data is a critical economic indicator that provides valuable insights into consumer behavior. With consumers accounting for approximately two-thirds of the overall US economy, the monthly retail sales report plays a pivotal role in assessing the health of the economy. By tracking consumer spending patterns, this report offers a direct indication of whether consumer spending, which significantly impacts economic performance, is robust or weakening. Investors and analysts pay close attention to this report, as it can influence the market due to its potential to impact the broader economic landscape. When retail sales are on the rise, they are typically received positively by the market, signifying strong consumer spending and, in turn, potential economic strength. Conversely, declining retail sales are viewed negatively, indicating a potential slowdown in consumer spending, which can have adverse implications for the economy.

The Commerce Department's retail sales data report provides a clear and up-to-date snapshot of consumer spending, which is a cornerstone of economic activity. Investors react to these figures as they reflect the present state of consumer sentiment and economic health. A rise in retail sales suggests that consumers are confident and actively spending, which can contribute to an overall boost in economic growth and corporate earnings. Conversely, a drop in retail sales can signal potential challenges for both the economy and the stock market, prompting market participants to adjust their investment strategies in response to shifts in consumer behavior. Therefore, monitoring retail sales data is a fundamental practice for investors looking to make informed decisions.

Factory Orders

This comprehensive report encompasses new factory orders, which are further categorized into durable and nondurable goods, along with data on inventories, factory shipments, and unfilled orders. Each of these components contributes to a holistic understanding of economic activity. New factory orders serve as a direct measure of demand for goods, encompassing both long-lasting items (durable goods) and those with a shorter lifespan (nondurable goods). Inventories indicate the supply of goods held by manufacturers, while factory shipments provide a real-time measure of current demand in the economy. Additionally, unfilled orders reflect a longer-term perspective, indicating pent-up demand and backlogs that manufacturers need to address.

Due to the complex nature of the economy and the ever-evolving dynamics of supply and demand, factory orders can exhibit notable volatility on a month-to-month basis. Consequently, investors and analysts often analyze data spanning about three months to identify trends that provide a more stable and insightful perspective. The factory orders report is essential for tracking economic activity and assessing how various sectors are performing. It plays a pivotal role in enabling investors to gauge the overall health of the economy, as the trends in factory orders and their components reflect the level of demand for goods and services. A positive trend in factory orders may indicate a growing and robust economy, which is usually met with positive sentiment from investors. Conversely, a negative or declining trend may raise concerns about the state of the economy and its potential impact on corporate earnings and the stock market. As such, factory orders data is a valuable tool for making informed investment decisions, especially for those who recognize its importance in assessing the broader economic landscape.

Durable Goods

Durable goods orders represent a particularly vital component of factory orders, which provide a key insight into the state of the economy. Durable goods are significant investments that are expected to remain in use for an extended period, typically three years or longer. They include items like automobiles, appliances, machinery, and aircraft, among others. The measurement of new orders for durable goods serves as an indicator of future manufacturing activity. Because durable goods are often more expensive and require substantial consumer and business investment, their orders are highly sensitive to economic conditions and trends. As such, durable goods orders serve as an advance indicator, offering insights into how the economy is likely to perform in the coming months.

Durable goods orders are especially valuable in forecasting economic trends because they typically reflect changes in demand for significant capital expenditures. As a leading indicator of future economic activity, durable goods orders tend to signal turning points in the business cycle. When new orders for durable goods increase, it is seen as a sign of economic strengthening and potential growth on the horizon. Conversely, a decline in durable goods orders may suggest economic slowdown or contraction. This sensitivity to economic shifts means that changes in durable goods orders can impact the stock market. When orders for durable goods rise, indicating increased demand for long-lasting products, it tends to contribute to a positive sentiment in the market and can drive stock prices higher. Conversely, a decline in durable goods orders can raise concerns among investors about the state of the economy and its potential impact on corporate profits and, in turn, stock market performance. Therefore, monitoring durable goods orders is a valuable practice for investors to assess the broader economic outlook and make informed investment decisions.

Inventories

Inventories are a crucial economic indicator because they reflect the balance between supply and demand in the market. Businesses closely monitor their inventories to ensure they can meet customer demand without overstocking or facing shortages. The level of inventories, in particular, whether they are rising or falling, can have significant implications for future business operations and economic conditions. Investors pay attention to inventories as they offer insights into a company's management of its resources and its production and sales strategies.

When inventories are on the rise, it can suggest various scenarios. If inventories are increasing while sales remain sluggish, it could indicate that products are not moving off the shelves as expected, potentially signaling weak consumer demand or oversaturation in the market. There are times when a company may intentionally increase its inventories in anticipation of a future uptick in sales, such as during a holiday season or a product launch. In such cases, rising inventories may actually be viewed positively as a strategic preparation for higher demand. Nevertheless, for investors, the key is to interpret inventory data in conjunction with other relevant variables, such as sales figures, to gain a comprehensive understanding of a company's operational health and its positioning in the market. If rising inventories are accompanied by declining sales, it can be a red flag that a company is not effectively managing its supply chain and may be vulnerable to losses.

Personal Income and Consumption Expenditures

Personal income and consumption expenditures are essential economic indicators, reflecting individuals' financial health and spending patterns, with a significant impact on the overall economy. Personal income represents the total compensation received by individuals from various sources, such as wages, salaries, investments, and government assistance. When personal income rises, it implies that individuals have more disposable income to spend, save, or invest. This is seen as a positive sign for the economy since increased personal income can lead to higher consumer spending, which is a major driver of economic growth.

Consumption expenditures encompass the total market value of all goods and services purchased by individuals. When consumers increase their expenditures, it indicates growing confidence and willingness to spend, which can stimulate economic activity. Since consumer spending accounts for a significant portion of the overall economic activity, an uptick in consumption expenditures is viewed positively by the stock market. It suggests that a key component of the economy is strong, which can contribute to higher corporate earnings and, in turn, drive stock prices higher. Therefore, investors closely monitor personal income and consumption expenditures data to gain insights into the financial well-being of consumers and the potential direction of the economy. Rising personal income and increased consumer spending are generally seen as positive signals for both the economy and the stock market.

Industrial Production Index

The industrial production index (IPI) is an economic indicator that measures the real output of the manufacturing, mining, and electric and gas utilities sectors of the economy. It provides insight into the overall level of industrial activity, reflecting changes in production levels over time. The index is typically expressed as a percentage and is calculated based on the relative weights of different industries in the economy. It provides valuable insights into the health of the manufacturing sector, which plays a significant role in economic growth.

When the industrial production index is on the rise, it signals increased manufacturing activity and production capacity utilization, suggesting a growing and robust economy. This positive momentum is generally well received by the stock market, as it implies the potential for higher corporate earnings and increased demand for goods and services. Conversely, a decline in the industrial production index can be a cause for concern, indicating a slowdown in economic activity. A decrease in industrial production implies reduced manufacturing output, which can lead to lower corporate profits and weaker economic performance. Investors closely watch this indicator to gauge the state of the manufacturing sector and anticipate its potential implications for the broader economy and stock market. A declining industrial production index may be viewed as a bearish signal for stocks, as it suggests economic challenges and reduced demand.

Capacity Utilization

Capacity utilization is a critical indicator that provides insights into how efficiently the country's manufacturing capacity is being used. This metric is closely monitored by investors and economists because it can signal potential economic issues and inflationary pressures. When capacity utilization is excessively high, it indicates that manufacturing facilities are operating close to their maximum capacity. This can lead to bottlenecks in the production process, potentially causing inflationary pressures as demand outstrips supply. Economists often identify a utilization rate of approximately 85% as a potential threshold where inflationary concerns may arise.

When capacity utilization is on the decline, it suggests that there is reduced demand and slower economic activity, leading to lower inflationary pressures. A declining utilization rate can indicate a slackening in the economy and reduced stress on resources. In such cases, stocks tend to respond positively, as there are fewer concerns about inflationary overheating. If the utilization rate drops to very low levels, approximately 80% or less, it can signal excess capacity, which may lead to reduced capital investment in manufacturing, potentially harming economic growth. Investors generally react positively to rising capacity utilization, as it indicates a strong economy, but excessive levels can have a negative impact on stocks due to concerns of inflation and economic imbalances.

Index of Leading Economic Indicators

The index of leading economic indicators (LEI) is a vital tool used by investors to gauge the future direction of the economy. This monthly composite index consists of ten different indicators and is highly regarded for its ability to forecast the economic direction six to nine months in advance. The LEI is often considered a leading indicator because it tends to peak and trough earlier than the overall economy. Investors closely monitor this index as a change in the LEI's direction for three consecutive months can signal a turning point for the economy.

It is important to note that while the LEI is generally reliable, it can occasionally fail to provide an accurate outlook. When the LEI is released, it does not typically have a significant impact on the stock market. This is because the individual components of the LEI are released before the overall index, reducing the element of surprise. Investors generally use the LEI as a part of their broader economic analysis and decision-making process, rather than relying solely on this indicator for immediate trading decisions.

Money Supply

The money supply, a crucial economic indicator, represents the total amount of cash and checking account balances within the country's banking system, excluding government and interbank holdings. Investors keep a close eye on the money supply because it provides insights into the overall liquidity in the economy. A steadily growing money supply is generally preferred by investors as it often accompanies economic growth and stability. When the money supply is increasing at a sustainable rate and inflation remains steady or rises modestly, this is considered positive for the stock market.

Stocks tend to be negatively impacted if either inflation starts to rise significantly or if the money supply decreases. Inflation erodes the purchasing power of money, and a rapid increase in inflation can erode stock returns in real terms. Likewise, a decrease in the money supply can lead to reduced liquidity in the financial markets, potentially causing stock prices to fall. Therefore, investors pay close attention to the relationship between the money supply, inflation, and their implications for the overall economy and stock market performance.

12

MONITORING STOCKS, GROUPS, AND SECTORS

GENERAL

Serious investors must systemically monitor and analyze their individual stocks, as well as their associated groups and sectors. This will ensure that they identify opportunities, trends, and risks in a timely manner, which will enable them to become successful investors.

Monitor Everything That Can Impact Your Stock

Monitoring your stock investments requires comprehensive attention to a wide range of factors that can influence their performance. Beyond tracking the market averages and individual stock prices, you should maintain a watchful eye on any elements that can affect a company's fundamentals and its business environment. This holistic approach to monitoring involves regularly observing the broader stock market trends, analyzing the industry or sector to which your stock belongs, and assessing the prevailing business conditions, including the competitive landscape and market dynamics. Stay attuned to economic indicators, interest rates, and their trends, as they can impact the broader investing environment.

One of the most critical aspects of your monitoring routine should focus on the stock's fundamentals, with a specific emphasis on earnings. Regularly reviewing and interpreting earnings reports and financial statements can provide valuable insights into the health of the company and its potential for growth. Additionally, keeping an eye on relevant news items related to the stock and its industry is crucial to stay informed and make well-informed investment decisions. Staying vigilant about these factors helps you adapt to changing circumstances, seize opportunities, and mitigate risks as you manage your stock portfolio.

Monitor Factors That Reduce Stock Supply

Monitoring factors that influence the supply of available stock is crucial for investors. Various events can impact on the stock supply, creating situations where there is increased demand but a reduced number of shares available for trading, leading to upward price pressure. Key events include mergers, acquisitions, and stock buybacks, which can decrease the available stock supply. An expansion in supply can occur when companies issue additional shares, either through secondary stock offerings or as incentive shares to employees and management, which increases the number of outstanding shares. Additionally, stocks might become more available for trading once the lockup period for an IPO expires or if there is an increase in the stock's float. Since the stock's supply is a function of its total issued shares and daily trading volume, vigilant attention to factors that alter the stock's float is crucial for investors to make informed decisions.

By tracking these factors, investors can anticipate how changes in the stock's supply may affect its price and make more informed investment decisions. A reduced supply often creates favorable conditions for stock price appreciation, while an increased supply can lead to downward pressure on stock prices. Understanding these dynamics allows investors to adapt their strategies, take advantage of potential opportunities, and navigate potential risks in the stock market.

Monitor Factors That Increase Demand

Monitoring factors that impact stock demand is essential for investors as it provides valuable insights into potential price movements. Demand for a stock is influenced by a multitude of factors that fluctuate continuously, and these factors can exert their effects rapidly or over an extended period. Fundamental aspects, including earnings, dividends, P/E ratio, and other valuation criteria, are significant drivers of stock demand. An increase in these fundamentals, such as a boost in earnings or dividends, can attract more investors and subsequently elevate demand for the stock. Conversely, a decrease or poor performance in these fundamentals may lead to reduced demand.

Apart from fundamentals, demand is also shaped by external factors such as acquisitions, economic conditions, the behavior of the overall market or specific industry groups, investor sentiment, analyst recommendations, political developments, and other extraneous influences. For example, a positive economic outlook may boost demand for stocks, while a recession might dampen it. Similarly, favorable recommendations from analysts or positive news about an acquisition can stimulate investor interest and elevate demand. Investors should remain vigilant and continuously monitor these factors to stay informed about potential changes in stock demand that could impact their investment decisions and overall portfolio performance.

Learn to Recognize if Good or Bad News Has Been Discounted

Understanding how a stock reacts to news is crucial for investors, as it can provide valuable insights into market sentiment and help determine whether the news has already been factored into the stock's price. When assessing a stock's response to news, several factors come into play, including the timing of the news release, the magnitude of the news (whether its exceptionally good or bad), and the prevailing market conditions.

If a stock exhibits minimal or no reaction to very bad news, it suggests that the news was likely anticipated or already priced into the stock. This is known as "discounting" or discounting the news. In such cases, investors had already adjusted their expectations and positions based on the negative information, rendering any subsequent downward movement less pronounced. Conversely, if a stock does not respond significantly to good news, it implies that the market may have already priced in the positive developments, limiting the upward momentum.

The same principle can be applied to broader market movements. When extraordinary good or bad news fails to significantly impact the overall market, it can be indicative of a market top or bottom. In these instances, the market may have already factored in the extreme news, suggesting that a reversal in trend could be on the horizon. Recognizing these subtleties in stock and market reactions to news is a valuable skill for investors, helping them make informed decisions and anticipate potential turning points.

Observe How Stocks and the Market Respond to News

Observing how stocks and the market respond to news is a crucial aspect of strategic investment analysis. The market's reaction to specific news events can provide valuable insights into the underlying sentiments and expectations of investors. For instance, if a piece of news that would typically be perceived as negative for a particular stock has little to no impact on its price, it suggests that the market had already priced in this unfavorable information. This phenomenon is indicative of a mature understanding among investors, as the stock appears resilient in the face of anticipated challenges.

Conversely, analyzing the market's response to bad earnings news can offer essential clues about the overall market sentiment. If negative earnings do not result in a significant downturn, particularly following a recent market decline, it may suggest that selling pressures are waning, potentially signaling that the market has reached a bottom. Effectively observing how the stock market responds to both positive and negative news can offer investors valuable insights into anticipated or unexpected developments, facilitating more informed decision-making.

MONITORING INDIVIDUAL STOCKS

Monitoring individual stocks is a critical task that every investor needs to undertake. This section discusses how investors can systemically analyze and track individual stocks, so that they stay well-informed and become successful investors.

Key Indicators That Are Widely Monitored

When navigating the vast array of available indicators, the challenge lies in choosing the most essential ones to monitor. To streamline this process, it is advisable to begin by identifying the indicators that are most commonly utilized by investors who align with your chosen investment strategy. By doing so, you can focus on the metrics that are most relevant to your approach and better guide your decision-making in the complex world of investing.

A comprehensive approach to monitoring and analyzing stocks begins with considering a range of fundamental indicators. EPS, both on a quarterly and annual basis, provides insight into a company's profitability, while growth rates in earnings and revenue offer crucial metrics for evaluating its financial trajectory. Keeping an eye on earnings estimate revisions helps anticipate a company's future performance. The EPS rank and RS rank assess a stock's standing in the market, considering its earnings performance and relative strength against peers. Valuation metrics, such as the P/E ratio, relative P/E ratio, and P/E-to-growth ratio, provide insights into a stock's affordability and growth potential. Moving averages offer a smoothed trend line, and metrics like accumulation and distribution gauge buying and selling pressures. Other fundamental indicators include daily trading volume, institutional presence percentage, insider trading activities, and cash flow growth rate, collectively forming a robust foundation for comprehensive stock analysis.

Determine Reasons for Price Moves

Closely monitoring the stock prices of your individual holdings, as well as those of their competitors and the broader industry, is crucial in your investment journey. To gain a comprehensive understanding of how your stocks are performing within the context of their sector, you can employ industry-specific indexes like the semiconductor (SOX) index for the semiconductor sector. By tracking such an index, you can discern whether your individual stock's movement aligns with that of the industry, whether it is being influenced by the sector, or if it is a response to competition dynamics. It is important to maintain a measured approach and not react hastily to minor price fluctuations that can occur on a daily basis. Should there be any unusual or significant price movement, or if daily trading volume experiences notable shifts, it is essential to promptly investigate the underlying reasons and take appropriate action, especially when the catalyst is adverse fundamental news.

By staying vigilant and conducting thorough assessments, you can effectively gauge whether these price moves are driven by specific factors or are part of broader market trends. This level of scrutiny ensures you make informed decisions, enhance your ability to seize opportunities, and safeguard your investments in the face of potential challenges.

Monitor Earnings Releases

Staying vigilant about earnings releases is a fundamental aspect of managing your investment portfolio. It is crucial to keep a close eye on all earnings news and announcements for every stock in your portfolio. Understanding both the quarterly and annual earnings estimates is essential, as it provides insight into what the market and analysts anticipate for the company's performance. Analysts often make periodic adjustments to these estimates, so it is important to keep track of these changes and stay informed about the consensus earnings estimates, revisiting them at least once a month. Be prepared for price fluctuations, especially if the quarterly earnings reported fall short of the consensus estimates. It is important to recognize that even if a company posts excellent earnings, the stock might experience a decline, particularly if the stock had witnessed a significant price run-up leading to the earnings release. This phenomenon is often encapsulated by the Wall Street adage "Buy on the rumor and sell on the news."

By closely monitoring earnings reports, you can make more informed investment decisions. Understanding the impact of these reports, whether they meet, exceed, or fall short of expectations, is crucial in navigating the volatile post-earnings market reactions. Additionally, assessing the broader market sentiment helps you formulate a well-rounded strategy to mitigate risks and seize opportunities.

Sources for Earnings Releases

In today's digital age, accessing earnings releases and estimates has become more convenient than ever, thanks to the plethora of online sources dedicated to providing this crucial financial information. Several reputable platforms are available, such as finance.yahoo.com, investing.com, investors.com, cnbc.com, and marketwatch.com. These platforms offer a wealth of comprehensive data, allowing investors to select the one that aligns with their preferences and needs. They play a pivotal role in equipping investors with insights into predicted earnings, allowing them to anticipate financial outcomes before companies officially announce their results. Moreover, these platforms are instrumental in delivering real-time earnings data as soon as it is released by the respective companies.

The online accessibility of such platforms not only simplifies the process of staying updated on the financial performance of various companies but also enables investors to monitor market reactions to earnings releases promptly. Investors can leverage these online resources to make informed decisions, strategize their portfolio management, and adapt swiftly to the dynamic landscape of the stock market. The ease of online access empowers investors with the timely information needed to efficiently navigate the complexities of financial markets.

Investigate Earnings Surprises

Earnings surprises can be a make-or-break factor for stocks, and they often lead to significant price movements. When a company's quarterly earnings significantly deviate from the consensus estimates, higher or lower, it is considered an "earnings surprise." A positive earnings surprise, when a company outperforms estimates, can propel the stock's price upward as investors react to the unexpected strong performance. Conversely, a negative earnings surprise, often resulting from a substantial earnings shortfall, can have a devastating impact on a stock, causing its price to plummet.

To assess the significance of an earnings surprise, it is essential to investigate not only whether the company met the estimated EPS figure but also the percentage change compared to the previous year's comparable quarter. Understanding the factors contributing to the surprise, whether positive or negative, can provide crucial insights for investors looking to make informed decisions about their portfolios. Earnings surprises are closely watched by the market, and they can be a critical driver of stock price movements.

Monitor Volume Signals

Monitoring trading volume is essential for investors, as it can provide valuable insights into market sentiment and stock price movements. When volume surges to unusually high levels, whether for an individual stock or the overall market, it signifies heightened interest and activity. Abnormal trading volume can be triggered by various factors, including significant news, technical signals like moving average crossovers, market trends, or correlation with the performance of another stock. It is important to recognize that substantial price shifts, whether upward or downward, often coincide with increased trading volume. In general, higher trading volume indicates greater strength in the price move, reinforcing its significance.

Many websites, including investors.com, can be used to identify stocks that experience the "largest percentage increase in volume" compared to their average daily trading volume. By monitoring volume signals, investors can gain a better understanding of market dynamics and potentially identify stocks that are experiencing increased interest, which could lead to significant price moves. This information can be a valuable tool in making informed investment decisions.

Observe Changes in Trading Volume

Observing changes in trading volume is crucial for investors to stay informed about market developments and potential opportunities or risks. When a stock experiences a significant shift in its daily trading volume, especially when coupled with a sharp price movement, it serves as a valuable indicator of unusual activity that warrants investigation. For instance, a substantial increase in a stock's price accompanied by heavy trading volume is generally considered bullish, suggesting strong investor interest and positive sentiment. If a stock's price declines significantly on heavy trading volume, it is typically regarded as bearish, indicating potential negative sentiment and selling pressure.

Conversely, when trading volume dwindles, it can signal a potential bottom for a stock that has experienced a significant decline. Decreased trading activity may indicate that most of the selling pressure has been exhausted, potentially creating an opportunity for a price rebound.

As an investor, staying vigilant and monitoring volume patterns is essential for interpreting market dynamics and making informed decisions based on changes in trading volume, which can provide valuable insights into market sentiment and potential price movements.

Monitor What Institutions Are Doing

Observing the actions of large institutional investors is a crucial aspect of tracking stock market trends and potential price movements. Institutional investors wield substantial buying power, capable of significantly influencing a stock's direction. When institutions start accumulating a particular stock, their substantial purchases can drive the stock's price considerably higher. Conversely, if institutions begin selling a stock, their selling pressure can lead to a sharp decline in its value. As an individual investor, it is essential to monitor institutional activity to gain insights into the potential movements of stocks.

Two primary methods can be employed to keep tabs on institutional activity. First, you can utilize the accumulation/distribution indicator, which provides valuable insights into the actions of major institutional players. This indicator offers a clear perspective on whether institutions are actively accumulating or distributing a specific stock. Additionally, it can help discern the overall sentiment among institutional investors. Second, you can periodically check the percentage of outstanding stock held by institutions. This metric enables you to assess whether institutional holdings in a company are increasing or decreasing over time. This information is provided by various online sources, such as investors.com. By closely monitoring these institutional actions, individual investors can better understand the dynamics of the stock market and make informed decisions based on the activities of major players in the market.

Monitor Stock Buybacks Announcements

It is important for investors to pay close attention to stock buyback announcements made by companies. When a company believes that its shares are trading at an undervalued price, it may decide to initiate a stock buyback program. In this context, the company purchases its own shares from the open market, effectively reducing the overall number of outstanding shares in circulation. As a result, this reduction in the number of shares has the potential to enhance the EPS since it lowers the denominator used in the EPS calculation. The announcement of a share buyback program is generally viewed as a positive development by investors, as it signals that the company has confidence in its stock's future performance and is willing to allocate resources to repurchase shares. This typically leads to increased demand for the stock and, consequently, a rise in its price.

Investors should closely monitor such buyback announcements as they can offer valuable insights into a company's outlook and its belief in the current undervaluation of its shares. Moreover, stock buybacks have the potential to benefit existing shareholders by enhancing the value of their holdings through the reduction of the share count. As such, buyback announcements are often regarded as a favorable signal for investors and can contribute to positive price movements in the stock.

Monitor Revenue (Sales) Growth Trend

Monitoring the trend of a company's revenue or sales growth is crucial for assessing its overall health and financial performance. Consistent and steady revenue growth is a strong indicator of a company's well-being, as it is often a precursor to sustained profitability. A company that is able to consistently increase its revenues over time is likely experiencing strong demand for its products and services. This growth in sales is indicative of a healthy business environment, and it provides a foundation for generating consistent profits.

It is essential for investors to delve deeper into the sales figures to gain a comprehensive understanding of the company's performance. Simply observing robust sales growth is not sufficient. It is equally important to scrutinize whether the revenue growth is effectively translating into earnings at the bottom line. If revenue growth is not positively impacting earnings, it is essential to identify the reasons behind this disconnect. Additionally, while sales figures are generally less volatile than earnings, investors should closely analyze trends in sales growth. If there is a noticeable decline in the rate of increase in sales, it should serve as a warning sign that merits further investigation. Such a slowdown may indicate shifts in market dynamics or competition that could potentially affect the company's long-term growth prospects.

Monitor How Margins Are Trending

Monitoring a company's margin trend is essential for assessing its financial efficiency and competitiveness within its industry. Margins represent the percentage of sales that a company successfully converts into profits, and they play a significant role in determining overall profitability. Higher margins signify that the company is adept at converting its sales into net income and effectively managing its business operations. To evaluate a company's performance accurately, it is important to compare its margins with those of other companies in the same industry or sector.

To make informed comparisons, it is advisable to refer to company research reports that provide comprehensive data on performance metrics, financial ratios, and margins for similar businesses. Examining various types of margins, such as operating profit, pretax profit, and net profit margins, can offer valuable insights into different aspects of a company's financial performance. For example, an improvement in operating margins indicates that the company is gaining a stronger foothold in its industry by effectively managing its operating expenses and boosting profitability. Monitoring these margin trends allows investors to gauge how well the company is adapting to market dynamics, managing its costs, and ultimately generating profits, helping them make more informed investment decisions.

MONITOR THE INSIDERS

An "insider," is an individual who has access to confidential and non-public information about a company because of their position within the company. This section discusses various aspects of monitoring insiders, whose actions can influence future stock price movements.

Monitor Insider Trading

Monitoring insider trading activities can provide valuable insights into a company's potential future performance. Historically, insider selling has been more prevalent than insider buying, but it may not necessarily indicate a negative signal on its own. It is essential to be familiar with the typical insider trading patterns within your specific stock to be able to identify any unusual or significant activity. If insiders are selling shares at a rate lower than the standard behavior, it can be interpreted as a bullish sign, suggesting their confidence in the company's future prospects.

Conversely, when you notice a conspicuous or substantial volume of insider selling, especially if multiple insiders are involved, it should be regarded as a potential warning flag. This could signal that those with an intimate knowledge of the company's operations and financial health have concerns about its outlook. Insider buying is often considered a more reliable indicator of a stock's future performance compared to selling. Investors tend to view insider purchases as a vote of confidence in the company's potential for growth and financial strength. It is worth noting, however, that insider trading data is available to ordinary investors only after a certain time delay, which should be taken into account when interpreting these activities.

Monitor Insider Selling

Monitoring insider selling can indeed provide valuable insights, but it is crucial to consider the various reasons behind such sales. Insiders may sell shares for reasons unrelated to the company's business prospects, such as exercising stock options, covering personal expenses, funding their children's education, or diversifying their investment portfolio. As a result, analyzing insider selling can be multifaceted, and it is essential to understand the context of these sales.

It becomes more concerning if insider selling is unusually heavy, occurs after a rapid increase in the stock's price, or deviates from the company's typical insider trading patterns. Additionally, if you notice a situation where only insider selling is taking place without corresponding insider buying, it should raise a red flag. In such cases, it is advisable to exercise caution and carefully evaluate the stock's outlook. Historically, insider selling has often acted as a leading rather than coincidental indicator of market tops, making it a factor to watch for investors seeking to make informed decisions about their stock investments.

Monitor Insider Buying

Monitoring insider buying can offer valuable insights into a company's future prospects. The primary reason insiders purchase their own company's stock is their strong belief in the company's performance and stock's potential. Such conviction is usually grounded in positive expectations, like anticipation of robust earnings, upcoming product launches, the start of a profitable cycle, the perception that the stock is undervalued, or other factors that favor the company's business and fundamentals. Therefore, when you observe instances of insider buying, especially if it's substantial, widespread throughout the company's leadership, or conducted on the open market rather than through options exercises, it serves as a bullish signal.

Insider buying serves as an indicator that those with the most intimate knowledge of the company's operations and future prospects have faith in its success. For investors, tracking insider buying activity can provide an early indication of where the stock might be headed. When considering your own stock purchases, aiming to buy at prices close to those at which insiders have made their acquisitions can be a prudent strategy, aligning your investments with the confidence expressed by the company's leadership.

MONITORING INDUSTRY GROUPS AND SECTORS

The behavior and performance of industry groups and sectors impact their individual members and, therefore, they must be analyzed by every serious investor. This section discusses various aspects of monitoring these groups and sectors.

Monitor Stock's Sector and Industry Group Performance

Closely tracking your stock's sector and industry group performance is vital for making well-informed investment decisions. Stocks within the same sector often move in tandem, responding to similar market forces and news events. Corrections or unfavorable news affecting a leading stock in the group can significantly impact all associated stocks. Therefore, it is essential to maintain constant awareness of your stock's industry group, staying informed about its trading patterns, business prospects, and overall performance.

Assessing and monitoring industry group performance provides crucial insights into expected stock performance. By observing signs of potential deterioration or positive outlook within the group, you can adjust your investments proactively. When signs suggest sector-wide weakness or a downturn in your stock's industry group, consider reducing exposure to those areas. Conversely, in times of sector or industry strength, you can confidently increase investments to capitalize on positive market dynamics. This strategic approach allows you to adapt to changing market conditions, thus optimizing your portfolio's performance.

Identify Group Leaders

Identifying the leaders within various sectors and industry groups is a crucial aspect of successful stock market analysis. Market leaders are typically found in sectors and groups that are at the forefront of market trends and drive overall market performance. To pinpoint these leaders, it is essential to closely analyze the performance of different sectors and industry groups. By tracking how various sectors and groups are faring in the market, you can more easily narrow down potential leaders.

One valuable resource for assessing the performance of sectors and groups is the Investor's Business Daily (*IBD*), which comprehensively tracks 197 industry groups. By utilizing this source, you can identify groups with the highest percentage of stocks making new highs. Stocks in groups exhibiting this pattern are generally considered outperformers. By identifying these industry leaders, you can focus your attention on the sectors and groups with the most potential for strong returns, helping you make well-informed investment decisions and potentially enhancing the performance of your portfolio.

Monitor Industry Group's Rank and Trend

Monitoring the rank and trend of your stock's industry group is essential for making informed investment decisions. *IBD* ranks the price performance for 197 industry groups on a daily and weekly basis. Additionally, it provides historical data on their performance over the prior six months. By using the industry group table in the *IBD*, you can easily determine the rank and trend of your stock's industry group.

This information can be invaluable in helping you identify potential warning signs or positive signals. For instance, if your stock is declining while its industry group is on the rise, this divergence can serve as a warning sign. If the group has a high rank or is trending upward, it is a positive indicator. When the signals based on the industry group's rank are negative, you might consider reducing your exposure to that particular group. In contrast, when the signals are positive, you can have more confidence in your stock's potential for strong performance, making it easier to make strategic investment decisions.

Monitor Industry Specific Index and/or Report

Monitoring industry-specific indexes and reports is crucial for investors who want to stay informed about the performance and trends within specific sectors of the economy. Various indexes have been created to track and represent different sectors, such as high-tech, junior growth, senior growth, consumer, gold, and defensive sectors. Each of these indexes provides valuable insights into their respective areas, allowing investors to gauge the health and performance of specific industries. You can easily access information on these sectors through various online trading and investment websites such as investors.com.

For instance, if you have investments in the semiconductor sector, it is essential to monitor the performance of the semiconductor sector index (SOX), also known as the PHLX Semiconductor Sector Index, which includes approximately thirty semiconductor-related companies. However, the specific number of companies in the index may change over time due to adjustments or updates by the index provider. By tracking the SOX index or other relevant sector-specific indexes, you can stay updated on how your investments within that sector are likely to perform. Additionally, periodic industry-specific reports, like retail sales data, are important for investors who have holdings in those particular sectors. These reports provide valuable information on consumer spending, market trends, and the overall health of the industry, helping investors make well-informed decisions based on the latest data.

Monitor Other Groups and Sectors

In addition to keeping a close eye on your stock's industry group and sector, it is important to monitor the performance of other sectors in the market as well. The performance of various sectors can offer valuable insights and clues about the future direction of both the overall market and your specific industry group. For example, certain sectors like cyclical stocks, such as basic chemicals, tend to advance when a recession is ending, as their profits are closely tied to the state of the economy. Alternatively, defensive stocks become more attractive when economic growth starts to slow down at the end of an economic cycle, as investors seek safety and stability. These sector-related patterns can help investors make informed decisions about where to allocate their funds based on the broader economic and market conditions.

It is important to note that sector behavior should not be solely relied upon as a forecasting tool, as assumptions and predictions made by investors and market participants can sometimes be incorrect. The market is influenced by a complex interplay of factors, and sector performance may not always conform to the expected trends. Therefore, it is crucial to use sector performance as one of several tools in your investment analysis and remain flexible in adapting to changing market conditions.

CHAPTER 13

MONITORING MARKET AND PSYCHOLOGICAL INDICATORS

HOW TO MONITOR THE MARKET

Individual stocks, operating within the stock market, are not immune to its health and dynamics. Therefore, every investor needs to monitor the stock market, and various aspects of this monitoring are discussed in this section.

Monitor the Market Trend

Monitoring the overall market trend is a fundamental aspect of successful investing. The market's direction, whether it is in an uptrend or downtrend, has a significant influence on your investment strategy and the performance of your portfolio. In a declining market, it is common for the majority of stocks to be pulled down, whereas an advancing market tends to lift most stocks. While exceptional stocks can sometimes defy the trend, it is generally safer to align your investment approach with the broader market direction. As a result, understanding the health and direction of the market is crucial for making informed investment decisions.

Market trends don't change overnight, and it is essential to maintain a consistent monitoring effort to stay updated on any shifts in market conditions. Regularly analyzing market indicators, preferably at least once a week, ensures that you remain well informed and prepared to adapt your investment strategy to changing circumstances. Staying attuned to market trends allows you to adjust your portfolio positioning, whether it is adopting a more defensive posture in a bear market or capitalizing on opportunities in a bull market, all with the goal of optimizing your investment outcomes.

Monitor Market Behavior

Monitoring the market's behavior and trend is crucial for successful investing. You can gauge market behavior by closely tracking major stock market averages and indexes. These groupings, which can range from a few to thousands of stocks, provide valuable insights into the behavior of the overall market and specific sectors, helping to identify their underlying trends. Market averages and indexes are not only essential for benchmarking the performance of individual stocks but are also instrumental in assessing the overall health of the market. Investors utilize these indicators to detect signs of market extremes, such as tops and bottoms, anticipate trend reversals, analyze trading patterns, and make informed investment decisions.

For monitoring market behavior, several well-known indexes are widely used by investors. These include the DJIA, S&P 500, NASDAQ Composite, and the Russell 2000. These indexes provide a snapshot of how the broader market and specific sectors are performing, allowing investors to stay informed about market trends, which is essential for making strategic investment choices and optimizing portfolio outcomes. By consistently analyzing market behavior through these indexes, you can adapt your investment strategy to align with the prevailing market conditions and make more effective investment decisions.

Monitor Market Averages and Indexes

Monitoring market averages is fundamental for tracking the collective movement of stocks and understanding broader market dynamics. The DJIA and NASDAQ are widely recognized benchmarks, with the DJIA, consisting of the thirty largest US companies, serving as a crucial indicator of the overall market's long-term behavior and economic health. It is important to note that the DJIA has limitations, not providing a comprehensive view of the entire stock market, necessitating the monitoring of other market indexes for a more holistic perspective. Key market averages, like the S&P 500 and the technology-focused NASDAQ index, offer diversified insights into different sectors, aiding investors in making well-informed decisions and adapting strategies to changing market conditions.

Major market indexes, including the S&P 500, NASDAQ, and those related to the NYSE, play a pivotal role in assessing overall market performance. The NYSE composite index reflects the collective market value of all NYSE-listed stocks, providing a broad perspective on their performance. The S&P 500, tracking the 500 largest U.S. companies, acts as a widely accepted benchmark for US equities. The NASDAQ index, focusing on technology and innovation, showcases smaller and innovative firms, making it essential for understanding growth dynamics. By monitoring these major market indexes alongside market averages, investors gain a diverse view of the overall market's health, enabling more informed investment decisions.

Monitor Market Sector Indexes

For a more nuanced and short-term analysis of market dynamics, investors often leverage various market sector indexes to gain a detailed perspective on specific industries and segments within the broader market. These sector-specific indexes provide a granular view, allowing investors to assess the performance of distinct market segments and complementing the insights derived from more general market indexes. By examining sector-specific trends, investors can make more informed decisions based on the specific dynamics influencing industries of interest.

In addition to sector indexes, investors often turn to broader market benchmarks such as the Russell 2000 and the Wilshire 5000 for a comprehensive overview of the market landscape. The Russell 2000 index specializes in tracking the performance of small-cap stocks, offering insights into a segment of the market known for its potential volatility and responsiveness to short-term market fluctuations. Conversely, the Wilshire 5000, with its extensive coverage of the overall market, serves as a robust indicator, reflecting the collective wealth encompassed by a broad spectrum of stocks. Together, these indexes provide investors with a multifaceted toolkit for navigating the complexities of the financial markets.

USING MARKET INDICATORS

To ensure that they are well informed and on top of their investments, investors need to analyze the stock market from different perspectives, using a range of indicators, which are discussed in this section.

Select the Appropriate Average/Index

Selecting the appropriate market average or index to monitor is a key aspect of effective investment analysis. The choice should align with your investment strategy and goals. For instance, if you are a growth or momentum investor, it makes sense to compare your stock performance to indexes relevant to your investment approach, such as technology or small-cap indexes. Conversely, conservative investors who primarily invest in well-established, large-cap companies listed on the DJIA or S&P 500 would not find the Russell 2000 index a suitable benchmark for assessing their portfolio's performance. This targeted approach ensures that you are tracking indexes that are directly comparable and can provide valuable insights for your specific investment strategy.

Moreover, for those interested in gaining a comprehensive view of the market, focusing solely on a single index, such as the DJIA, may lead to missing significant market movements. Instead, it is prudent to monitor broader market measures like the S&P 500 and the NASDAQ, which encompass a wider spectrum of stocks and industries. By considering your investment objectives and the relevance of specific indexes to your strategy, you can make informed decisions about which averages or indexes to track and effectively gauge the performance of your investments.

Use Market Averages and Indexes for Comparing Performance

Market averages and indexes are invaluable tools for assessing the performance of individual stocks and portfolios. They serve as benchmarks against which you can measure the success of your investments and overall strategy. For instance, if you have invested in semiconductor stocks, it is crucial to compare their performance to the semiconductor index. This comparison provides a clear picture of how your stocks are faring within the context of their respective industry, allowing you to make informed decisions about your investment strategy.

Similarly, when evaluating your entire portfolio, you can compare its performance to an appropriate market index or average. For instance, if you are a growth investor focused on smaller companies, the NASDAQ is a suitable benchmark. By analyzing how your portfolio stacks up against these benchmarks, you gain insights into the effectiveness of your investment choices and can make necessary adjustments to refine your strategy or tactics. Performance data for various indexes and averages is readily available from numerous online resources, ensuring you have access to the information needed to assess and optimize your investment performance.

Do Not Be Misled by the DJIA

While the DJIA is widely reported in daily news bulletins, it is essential not to conflate its performance with the overall health of the stock market. Ordinary investors often mistakenly associate the DJIA with the entire stock market's well-being. To accurately assess the market's condition, it is vital to examine the actions of other indexes and indicators that may paint a different picture. For example, the DJIA could be reaching new highs while the NASDAQ, S&P 500, and the advance/decline line show a downward trend. Such discrepancies can signal the end of a bull market, as DJIA stocks are typically the last to decline. To gain a comprehensive understanding of the market, it is crucial to monitor multiple major market averages and indexes beyond just the DJIA.

By taking a more holistic approach to analyzing market indicators and indexes, investors can better identify broader trends and potential shifts in market sentiment. Relying solely on the DJIA could lead to incomplete or even misleading insights into the overall market's performance and trajectory.

Divergence Is a Warning Sign

Divergence in the movements of different market indexes, such as the DJIA and the NASDAQ, can serve as a crucial warning sign for investors. This phenomenon occurs when these indexes are heading in opposing directions, indicating a potential shift in market dynamics. Divergence often precedes changes in market direction and trends, making it an early indicator that investors should be vigilant about. It is essential to continually monitor the major market averages for any signs of divergence, as it can offer insights into the future direction of the market.

When you detect divergence between indexes, the next step is to assess whether the DJIA will ultimately follow the lead of the other index or vice versa. This interpretation may require experience and a deep understanding of market dynamics. By identifying and understanding divergence, investors can better position themselves to respond to market shifts and make informed investment decisions.

Monitor Market Averages and Indexes but Retain Perspective

While monitoring market averages and indexes is a valuable aspect of your investment strategy, it is crucial not to become overly fixated on these indicators. The primary focus of your monitoring efforts should always be the individual stocks within your portfolio. Investing success hinges on the performance of your specific holdings, so your primary concern should be getting your stock selections right. You could be accurate in predicting the market's direction but still not achieve significant profits if your stock choices are flawed.

A critical piece of advice for investors is to avoid basing stock-picking decisions on market forecasts. Instead, your stock selections should be grounded in a thorough and comprehensive analysis of individual companies' fundamentals. By conducting in-depth research on each company in your portfolio and closely monitoring their performance, you can make more informed decisions that will ultimately determine your success as an investor.

Be Aware of Factors Causing Volatility

Investors should always be aware of the factors that can cause market volatility. Volatility can arise for various reasons and can significantly impact both the broader market and individual stocks. For instance, a sudden change in market direction, marking the onset of a correction or bear market, can lead to increased volatility as investors react to changing conditions. Additionally, external events, such as negative political developments or economic news, can create uncertainty and fear in the market, causing abrupt and unpredictable price swings.

Other factors contributing to short-term volatility include major index changes, like a stock being added or removed from the S&P 500, options expiration days, triple witching day (when stock index futures, stock index options, and stock options all expire simultaneously), and end-of-quarter "window dressing" by money managers. During the latter, portfolio managers may adjust their holdings to make them appear more successful by removing underperforming assets and increasing their holdings in winners. All these factors can lead to temporary turbulence in the market, making it crucial for investors to stay informed and vigilant in their monitoring efforts to make sound investment decisions during volatile periods.

Monitor New Daily Lows to Determine Market Health

Analyzing the number of new daily lows on the NYSE is a valuable technique for evaluating the market's health and potential issues. This metric measures the total number of stocks whose prices have reached new lows over the past year (prior fifty two weeks). A low number of new lows, typically less than forty, is a positive sign of a healthy market, indicating that a majority of stocks are performing well. It should be noted that when the number of new lows exceeds this threshold, it serves as a warning signal that the market might be encountering difficulties.

A persistent trend of more than forty new lows for five consecutive days is an even more severe concern. This condition suggests a deeper issue within the market, potentially indicating broader weakness in the performance of various stocks. Investors and analysts use this information to make decisions about their portfolio and adjust their strategies accordingly, especially when the number of new lows on the NYSE surpasses the critical threshold, as it may indicate a troubled market environment.

Monitor Indicators Spanning a Broad Spectrum

Monitoring a wide range of indicators is essential to comprehensively understand the market and make informed investment decisions. These indicators span various categories, including economic, psychological, technical, and performance factors. The importance and relevance of each indicator may vary depending on your investment approach and strategy. Nevertheless, ignoring any one of these indicators entirely can expose you to unnecessary risk as the market can be influenced by each of them.

For instance, psychological indicators can provide valuable insights into market sentiment, and overlooking them might lead to missing critical signals, such as overly bullish investor sentiment that could precede a market top. Similarly, neglecting economic data could result in failing to recognize shifts in interest rate trends or other economic factors that can significantly impact investment performance. By monitoring a diverse set of indicators, you can develop a more comprehensive view of the market and reduce the risk associated with unforeseen developments.

MONITORING PSYCHOLOGICAL INDICATORS

Stock market investors must monitor psychological indicators, which are discussed in this section, as investor sentiment and market psychology play significant roles in shaping price movements.

Analyze Psychological Indicators

Analyzing psychological indicators is crucial because both economic fundamentals and investor sentiment jointly influence stock market performance. While economic factors drive a company's profitability and, in the long run, play a primary role in determining stock performance, investor psychology often comes into play in the short term. The level of optimism or pessimism among investors can significantly impact buying and selling decisions, leading to market fluctuations. Therefore, for investors seeking success in the stock market, understanding both economic fundamentals and investor psychology is essential.

To gauge investor sentiment and the levels of optimism and pessimism, psychological tools based on the principles of supply and demand can be valuable. These tools provide insights into market dynamics and the prevailing mood among investors, helping traders make more informed decisions. By incorporating psychological indicators into their analysis, investors can better navigate the stock market and make adjustments to their strategies as market sentiment evolves.

Learn to Recognize Sentiment Extremes

Recognizing sentiment extremes is essential because the stock market operates at the intersection of economics and psychology. It experiences shifts in sentiment, moving from fear and pessimism to greed and euphoria. These emotional cycles play a significant role in influencing stock prices. Investors must understand and identify the signs of sentiment extremes in the market to make well-informed decisions.

When you identify periods of excessive speculation, you can exercise caution to avoid potential market bubbles or unsustainable rallies. On the contrary, during times of panic and widespread pessimism, recognizing sentiment extremes can be an opportunity to find undervalued assets or stocks poised for recovery. By being attuned to the psychological aspects of the market, investors can adapt their strategies to different phases of the market cycle and make more profitable decisions.

Be a Contrarian

Being a contrarian investor involves the willingness to go against the crowd and the prevailing market sentiment. Many investors tend to follow popular trends or react emotionally to market movements, which can lead to herd behavior. Yet it's important to note that successful investing requires independent thinking and making decisions based on careful research and analysis rather than succumbing to prevailing emotions.

Contrarian investors recognize that market bottoms often coincide with widespread fear and panic. In these moments, they see opportunities to buy undervalued assets before a potential rebound. Conversely, they understand that market tops are often marked by euphoria and excessive optimism, which can be a signal to sell and take profits before a market correction. By being contrarian, investors aim to capitalize on market inefficiencies and make more informed, rational decisions that align with their long-term investment goals rather than short-term trends.

Buy on the Rumor—Sell on the News

The saying "Buy on the rumor—sell on the news" is a valuable reminder of the role that sentiment and expectations can play in the stock market.

When there is widespread anticipation of positive news about a stock, investors often rush to buy shares, driving up the price in the lead-up to the actual news release. This behavior is based on the belief that the anticipated news will have a positive impact on the stock's performance.

Once the news is officially released, the stock may not react as expected because the market had already priced in the good news during the anticipation phase. In such cases, selling on the news can be a prudent move. It is important to note that this strategy relies on market sentiment and psychology, rather than strict adherence to fundamental analysis. Therefore, investors should exercise caution when following this adage, as the actual impact of news on a stock can vary, and trading decisions should be based on a combination of factors, including fundamentals and technical analysis.

Do Not Get Overexcited by News Stories About a Company

The stock market often operates on the principle of anticipation, where smart investors try to forecast future events before they become widely known. Stocks tend to make their most significant moves while they are still under the radar and have yet to capture the attention of the general public and media. These early moves are often driven by institutional investors who accumulate positions before the broader market catches on. As a result, buying a stock before it becomes a popular topic in the media can be a strategic move.

When news stories about a company start appearing in widely read publications like Forbes or Barron's, it is a signal that the stock's story has already been disseminated to a broad audience. At this point, many market participants are aware of the positive news, and the stock may have already seen a significant price increase in anticipation of that news. As a result, there might be fewer buyers left to drive the stock higher, and investors should be cautious about chasing a stock after it becomes a media sensation. Instead, it is important to evaluate the potential impact of positive news stories and consider whether the stock has already benefited from the positive sentiment generated by media coverage.

Stock Price Relative to Its Moving Averages Influences Sentiment

The relative position of a stock's price in relation to its moving averages can provide valuable insights into both its past performance and future trend. In particular, comparing the current stock price to its 200-day moving average is a common practice among investors. When a stock's price is trading above its 200-day moving average, it is generally considered a positive sign. This suggests that the long-term trend for the stock is upward, and it also indicates that the majority of investors who purchased the stock in the past two hundred days are in a profitable position, which tends to contribute to positive sentiment.

Conversely, when a stock's price is trading below its 200-day moving average, it often indicates a more negative sentiment. This means that many investors who have bought the stock in the past two hundred days are experiencing losses, which can lead to pessimism and a bearish outlook on the stock. Monitoring the stock's position relative to its moving averages is a fundamental aspect of technical analysis, and it helps investors gauge the sentiment of the market participants, which can be influential in predicting future price movements.

USING PSYCHOLOGICAL INDICATORS

Psychological indicators enable investors to anticipate potential shifts in market trends, caused by fear and greed. This section discusses how to use and benefit from various psychological indicators.

Monitor Sentiment Indicators

Monitoring sentiment indicators is essential for understanding the psychological dynamics within the stock market. Two major groups whose sentiment significantly impacts the market are consumers and investment advisors. Consumer sentiment is typically measured using tools like The Conference Board's consumer confidence index and the University of Michigan's consumer sentiment index. When these indicators are on the rise, it signals an increasing level of consumer optimism, which, in turn, translates to greater spending, contributing to economic growth and ultimately benefiting companies' profitability. This positive sentiment tends to have a favorable effect on the stock market.

Alternatively, the sentiment of investment advisors is measured by the Investors' Intelligence Survey, which serves as a contrarian indicator. In this context, a high level of bullish sentiment (or a low bearish sentiment) is often considered a negative signal, indicating that there may be too much optimism in the market, potentially signaling an overheated market. Conversely, a high level of bearish sentiment (or a low bullish sentiment) is seen as a positive signal, suggesting that there might be more room for upside potential as the market is not overly optimistic. Monitoring these sentiment indicators provides investors with crucial insights into market psychology, helping them make informed decisions.

Consumer Confidence Index

The Consumer Confidence Index is a critical monthly indicator, reported by the Conference Board, and plays a significant role in shaping economic and market sentiment. This index measures the level of confidence among consumers, a group responsible for roughly two-thirds of the US economy through their spending habits. The Consumer Confidence Index serves as an invaluable gauge of future consumer spending trends. When consumers are feeling optimistic and have a positive outlook, they are more likely to increase their spending, which is beneficial for economic growth. Conversely, when consumer confidence is low or declining, it can signal economic trouble on the horizon.

The release of the Consumer Confidence Index is often a highly anticipated event because it has the potential to influence the stock market. An unexpected rise or fall in this index can trigger significant market reactions.

Consumer Sentiment Index

The University of Michigan's Consumer Sentiment Index is a vital report among the two major consumer sentiment indexes that Wall Street closely watches. These reports provide key insights into how consumers, who are the backbone of the US economy, perceive their current financial situation and their future expectations. A positive report with a rise in consumer sentiment is viewed as a bullish sign, suggesting that consumers are optimistic about their financial prospects and may increase their spending. Conversely, a negative report with a decline in consumer sentiment is considered bearish, as it implies that consumers may become more cautious about their spending habits, which can have broader implications for the overall economy and the stock market.

The University of Michigan's Consumer Sentiment Index is particularly significant for market observers because it can provide hints about future market movements. When consumer confidence reaches its nadir, it often indicates a potential bottom for the stock market. In other words, when consumer sentiment is at its lowest point, it may signify a turning point where investors become more confident and start entering the market again, which can be the initial phase of a market recovery. Therefore, this index is an important tool for investors and analysts to gauge the sentiment of the general public and its potential impact on economic activity and stock market trends.

Bullish Readings Are Bearish and Vice Versa

Understanding the dynamics of bullish and bearish readings is crucial in interpreting the sentiment indicators accurately. When there is an excessive level of bullish sentiment among investors, it often suggests that a large percentage of investors have already invested their available funds in the market. This leaves limited buying power available to continue driving stock prices higher. In such situations, high levels of bullishness can coincide with market tops, indicating that the market may be overextended and a reversal could be on the horizon. Therefore, when the bullishness number exceeds 55%, it is generally considered a bearish sign as it may imply that the market has reached a point of excess optimism and could be vulnerable to a correction.

Conversely, widespread bearish sentiment suggests that many investors are holding cash on the sidelines, potentially poised to enter the market when they perceive attractive opportunities. When this sidelined cash is deployed into stocks, it can drive significant upward momentum. Therefore, a bearish sentiment indicator reading below 20% signals that investors are overly optimistic. When bearish advisors exceed 55%, it is viewed as very bullish because it indicates that the market may be oversold and could be due for a rebound. In practice, analysts often consider both bullish and bearish sentiment indicators in conjunction to obtain a more comprehensive view of market sentiment. For instance, a combination of high bullish sentiment (above 55%) along with bearish sentiment dropping below 20% can be seen as a dangerous sign, suggesting that market sentiment is excessively skewed, which may have serious implications for market direction and potential risks.

Sentiment Is a Leading Indicator

Sentiment indicators are considered leading indicators because they often provide insights into future market behavior. When investor sentiment reaches an extreme level of optimism and speculation, it is a sign that the market may be approaching a top. This is because, at such points, the majority of potential buyers have already invested their available funds, leaving limited buying power to drive prices higher. In contrast, when pessimism prevails, and investors are overwhelmingly bearish, it suggests a market bottom could be near. This is because most potential sellers have already sold their positions in response to negative sentiment, creating conditions for a potential rebound.

Understanding how to interpret sentiment indicators, especially when they reach extreme levels, is crucial for investors. When these indicators signal excessive bullish sentiment, it serves as an early warning sign that the market might be vulnerable to a correction or reversal. Conversely, a very negative bearish reading can imply that the market is poised to rise in the future as sidelined cash enters the market. By effectively utilizing sentiment indicators, investors can gain valuable insights into the timing of potential market tops or bottoms.

Monitor the Put/Call Ratio

The put/call ratio is a valuable sentiment indicator, particularly for monitoring the sentiment of option investors in the market. This ratio is determined by analyzing the relative number of put and call options being traded. When investors are optimistic about the market's future and anticipate rising stock prices, they tend to buy call options, which provide the right to purchase the underlying stock at a predetermined exercise price. Conversely, when bearish sentiment prevails, and investors expect stock prices to decline, they are inclined to buy put options, which grant the right to sell the underlying stock at a specific exercise price.

A significant spike in the put/call ratio, particularly when it reaches a value of 1 or higher, indicates excessive put buying, which signals a heightened level of fear in the market. Contrary to common expectation, this fear-driven extreme suggests that the market might be at or near a bottom, presenting a potential opportunity for investors. By monitoring the put/call ratio, investors can gain insights into the prevailing sentiment and position themselves to make informed decisions in response to shifts in market sentiment.

Loss Through Short Selling Can Be Devastating

Short selling is a strategy that carries significant risks due to its asymmetric nature. When an investor shorts a stock, the potential for profit is capped at 100% if the stock's price falls to zero. Not surprising, the downside risk is virtually limitless. As stocks have no upper limit to their potential appreciation, short sellers can face substantial losses as stock prices rise. In some instances, particularly with technology stocks, certain equities have experienced price increases of 1,000% or more. When such substantial rallies occur, the losses incurred by short sellers can indeed be devastating.

Despite the potential for profit in short selling, the long-term statistical trends in the stock market are not in favor of short sellers. Historically, equity markets have tended to rise over time, with upward movements significantly outweighing declines. Therefore, the odds are generally against short sellers, making it a high-risk strategy that requires careful consideration and risk management to avoid substantial losses. Investors need to be aware of these risks and exercise caution when implementing short selling as a trading strategy.

Analyze Short Interest

Short interest is a key indicator that can provide insights into market sentiment and the valuation of individual stocks. When short sellers believe that a particular stock or the overall market is overvalued, they tend to increase their short positions. This results in a higher level of short interest. Monitoring the trends in short interest can be valuable for investors as it reflects the collective opinion of short sellers regarding the future performance of stocks or the market. If short interest is on the rise, it signals that a significant number of investors are adopting a bearish stance and anticipate lower prices. Conversely, when short interest declines, it suggests a more bullish sentiment among investors.

In the long run, rising short interest can be a bullish signal for the market. This is because, eventually, short positions will need to be covered by repurchasing shares, potentially driving up prices. It is important for investors to keep an eye on short interest trends as they can provide valuable information about market dynamics and investor sentiment, helping them make more informed investment decisions.

Mutual Funds' Cash Levels Provide Valuable Insight

The cash levels held by mutual funds can offer valuable insight into the overall sentiment and health of the stock market. When mutual funds begin to increase their cash reserves, it is often interpreted as a bullish sign in a contrarian manner. This is because a higher cash reserve indicates that these funds have money available to invest in the stock market. When this cash is eventually deployed into equities, it can potentially drive up stock prices, leading to a positive impact on the overall market.

Conversely, when mutual funds hold low cash reserves, it suggests that they have already invested a significant portion of their available capital. In this scenario, there is limited buying power left among these funds, which is typically viewed as a bearish sign. A scarcity of available cash can restrain the market's ability to move higher. Therefore, investors often monitor cash levels held by mutual funds as an indicator of potential market trends and to make more informed investment decisions.

Monitor Mutual Funds' Cash Levels

Monitoring the cash levels of mutual funds can provide valuable insights into the current sentiment of the market. Historically, a cash level of around 7% was considered a fully invested position for these funds. Therefore, when analyzing these cash levels, it is important to pay attention to whether they are increasing or decreasing over time, as the trend can be a more meaningful indicator than a specific percentage figure.

The significance of the percentage number itself may vary in different market conditions, so observing the direction of the trend is crucial. It is important to note that the historical reliability of cash levels as an indicator has been somewhat mixed in recent years due to changing market dynamics and fund management strategies. Therefore, while monitoring this indicator, investors should consider it alongside other relevant market signals and not rely solely on cash levels for their investment decisions.

Know What the Insiders Know

Monitoring insider buying and selling activities is a valuable practice for investors because it allows them to gain insights into the knowledge and sentiments of company executives and major shareholders. These insiders have access to critical information that is not readily available to the general public, including details about a company's strategic decisions, financial performance, competitive positioning, and internal developments. As a result, their investment decisions can be considered well-informed and timely.

When insiders buy or sell a company's stock, it serves as a signal that can provide valuable clues about the company's future prospects. Insider transactions, especially when significant in scale, can indicate confidence or concern among those who know the company best. Consequently, regularly monitoring insider activity in the stocks you own or are considering buying can help inform your investment decisions. This information is publicly available through sources like the SEC, the Vickers Weekly Insider Report, and various websites dedicated to tracking insider trading. By paying attention to insider transactions, investors can gain a better understanding of a company's health and potential investment opportunity or risk.

Understand Limitations of Psychological Indicators

Psychological indicators are valuable tools for gauging market sentiment and can provide essential insights for investors. When examined collectively, these indicators tend to be reliable and often serve as leading indicators of future market behavior. One must remember that it is essential for investors to recognize the potential limitations associated with psychological indicators for making informed investment decisions.

One limitation of psychological indicators is the time lag between data collection and reporting. This lag can reduce their effectiveness as leading indicators, as market conditions may have evolved significantly by the time the data becomes available. Additionally, while these indicators are widely used and can be instrumental for decision-making, they are often underutilized during market bottoms, which is precisely when they can be most valuable, as investors may be hesitant to buy when sentiment is overwhelmingly negative. Understanding these limitations while still incorporating psychological indicators into your analytical toolkit can help you make more effective investment choices.

CHAPTER 14

BUYING AND SELLING MISTAKES TO AVOID

BUYING

Investors make many mistakes when buying stocks, which can impact the overall profitability of their various investments. The common mistakes that they make are discussed in this section.

Do Not Buy a Stock Without a Profitable Track Record

Ensuring that a stock has a profitable track record is a fundamental criterion for many investors, as it provides a historical perspective on a company's financial health and its ability to generate consistent earnings. This long-term profitability history, ideally spanning three to five years, offers insight into a company's resilience and financial management. An occasional losing year may be acceptable if it was followed by a quick turnaround, but a consistent pattern of losses should raise red flags. Note that exceptions can be made for companies facing unique challenges, such as a severe economic recession, as long as there is a clear path to profitability in the near future.

Furthermore, the current profitability of a company is equally important. A company that is currently incurring losses should demonstrate a strong potential for a turnaround or have a clear strategy in place to regain profitability. Investing in a company that has never been profitable can be exceptionally risky, as it mirrors the cautionary tales of the dot.com bubble where many companies with soaring stock prices and no profits ultimately faced significant declines or even bankruptcy. As such, maintaining a focus on a stock's profitable track record, both past and present, is a sensible approach to mitigate risks and increase the chances of long-term success.

Do Not Ignore Leaders

Ignoring leaders and winning stocks due to concerns about overvaluation is a common mistake made by investors. These stocks often exhibit strong fundamentals, but they might appear expensive based on traditional valuation metrics like the P/E ratio. This can lead to missed opportunities when such stocks are on the cusp of significant upward moves. The oversight stems from a failure to recognize the exceptional growth potential these companies possess, which can eventually drive their valuations to more reasonable levels.

Leaders and winning stocks tend to have compelling growth stories, and their rapid appreciation is often a reflection of their strong earnings and revenue growth potential. By investing in these stocks, investors can benefit from the potential for substantial returns as they continue to grow and expand. Rather than being deterred by temporarily high P/E ratios or recent price spikes, astute investors recognize the value of growth-oriented investments and focus on their long-term prospects. As they execute their growth strategies and deliver on their potential, these stocks have the potential to become highly profitable investments over time. Therefore, investors should avoid the pitfall of disregarding leaders and winners simply because they appear overpriced by traditional valuation standards, as this can lead to missed opportunities for significant gains.

Do Not Favor Low-Growth Companies

As a growth investor, your primary focus should be on high-growth companies rather than settling for those with mediocre growth rates. The most significant price appreciation in the stock market typically occurs for companies whose earnings are growing at an above-average pace. Therefore, it is essential to identify and invest in companies with a solid track record of long-term growth, ideally in the range of 20% to 30%. This growth rate should be sustainable and consistent, spanning at least three to five years into the future, rather than being solely based on the current year's performance.

When targeting high-growth companies, it is also important to exercise caution with hypergrowth firms that might experience exceptionally rapid growth within a short time frame. While these companies can be tempting, they come with elevated risk. The potential for rapid burnout within a year or two means investors need to be mindful of their investments, especially as the market dynamics may change, affecting the prospects of these firms. Therefore, in your quest for growth investments, it is wise to strike a balance by focusing on companies with consistent, sustainable, and above-average growth rates while avoiding the excessive risks associated with hypergrowth companies.

Do Not Buy Mediocre Companies

Investors should avoid buying mediocre companies because, in most cases, they are likely to deliver lackluster performance. Mediocre companies typically exhibit lower earnings growth, slower price appreciation, and have limited potential for significant business expansion. It is important to understand that choosing to invest in a mediocre company simply because its stock price is low is not a winning strategy. In fact, opting for a mediocre company because it's inexpensive can result in subpar returns and underwhelming investment results.

In the world of investing, the concept of "cheap" is relative. While a mediocre company's stock price might seem attractive from a valuation standpoint, it is crucial to recognize that this apparent cheapness is often a reflection of the company's inferior prospects and limited growth potential. Therefore, as an investor, it is generally more advisable to pay a premium for shares of an outstanding company with a track record of success and robust growth potential than to settle for a subpar investment with limited prospects for long-term success.

Avoid Leaders Nearing the End of Their Run

When investing, it is essential to focus on sectors or industry groups that exhibit strong fundamentals and clear growth prospects. While it may be tempting to invest in sectors or groups that are currently in an uptrend or are experiencing many new highs, it is crucial to consider the underlying fundamentals and future prospects. It is a common mistake to chase after short-term trends without a solid foundation of fundamentals. Instead, investors should prioritize sectors with healthy and rapidly improving earnings, as these have the potential to exceed earnings expectations and offer more sustainable growth.

Furthermore, it is important to exercise caution when dealing with industry groups that have been leaders for an extended period. While these groups may have enjoyed a strong run, they might be nearing a point of correction or pullback. To make more informed investment decisions, consider selecting stocks with robust fundamentals from industry groups that are currently trending upward and displaying a significant percentage of new highs. This approach helps ensure that your investments are grounded in solid financial performance and positioned for long-term success.

Avoid Companies Embroiled in Serious Litigation

Investors should exercise caution when considering companies that are entangled in significant litigation issues. Such legal disputes introduce an elevated level of uncertainty and risk into the investment equation. The outcome of litigation is often uncertain, and if a company does not prevail or faces an adverse judgment, it can have severe financial repercussions. A negative judgment may lead to substantial financial penalties, damages, or other adverse consequences, jeopardizing the company's financial health and impacting its stock price.

Moreover, ongoing litigation tends to deter investors and keep them at bay, causing the stock's performance to suffer. The uncertainty and potential legal liabilities can overshadow any positive fundamental aspects of the company. As a result, investors are advised to be cautious and avoid investing in companies embroiled in serious litigation, particularly those heavily reliant on a single product or source of revenue, as the litigation's outcome can significantly impact their financial stability and stock performance.

Do Not Buy a Stock Just Because It Has a Low Price

Investors should exercise caution when considering stocks solely based on their low price. A low stock price does not necessarily equate to a good investment opportunity. In many cases, a low stock price is indicative of a company with an unproven or risky business model and often low earnings. A high-priced stock often corresponds to a company with a strong track record of earnings and growth. It is important to consider the relationship between a stock's price and its earnings, as this provides valuable insights into its valuation.

Instead of solely focusing on a stock's price, investors should conduct a comprehensive analysis that includes an assessment of the company's financial health, competitive position, industry outlook, and growth prospects. While an undervalued or oversold stock may appear attractive due to its low price, it is crucial to evaluate these factors alongside the stock's current valuation. The price should be just one of several selection criteria, and it should be considered in the context of the company's fundamentals, such as its earnings and future growth potential.

Do Not Buy Immediately After a Big Price Drop

It is generally advisable to exercise caution when considering a stock purchase immediately after a significant price drop. After a sharp decline, it is essential to allow the stock to stabilize and consolidate its price for a period. This stabilization period is often referred to as basing, during which the stock trades within a relatively narrow price range. During this time, it is crucial for investors to investigate the reasons behind the stock's decline, ensuring they understand the underlying causes.

Investors should also conduct a thorough analysis of the company's fundamentals to ascertain its financial health, competitive position, and future growth prospects. Once the stock has stabilized and investors have confidence in its fundamentals, it can be evaluated as a potential buy candidate. It is important to consider the stock's potential for price appreciation based on its newly stabilized price. In some cases, experienced investors with an in-depth knowledge of the company may choose to act quickly if they are confident that the stock will rebound soon. For most investors, it is advisable to take a more cautious approach and allow the stock to base and stabilize before making an investment decision, as this approach can help minimize risks associated with volatile price movements.

Do Not Buy Just Because Stock's Price Declined to a Lower Level

Purchasing a stock solely based on the fact that its price has declined to a lower level can be a risky and often counterproductive approach. While it is understandable that stock trading at a lower price may seem like an attractive opportunity, it is essential to recognize that price alone does not tell the full story. Stocks that have experienced significant declines may have underlying issues, and their price may continue to deteriorate. The history of the stock market is rife with examples of companies whose shares plummeted from high price levels to single-digit values, leaving investors with substantial losses.

Instead of focusing on the historical price of a stock, prudent investors should base their buying decisions on its future prospects. This approach involves a comprehensive analysis of the company's fundamentals. Assessing where the stock is headed in terms of future performance is more crucial than dwelling on where it has been. By considering the stock's prospects rather than fixating on its historical price, investors can make more informed and forward-looking decisions, reducing the risk of buying into a deteriorating investment.

Do Not Focus Only on the Buy Price

Focusing solely on the buy price, without considering the stock's future potential, can lead to missed opportunities and suboptimal investment decisions. Investors who fixate on buying at a specific price, such as waiting for a stock to drop from $41 to $40 before making a purchase, may overlook the broader picture. If a stock is poised for substantial growth and expected to reach the $60s in the near future due to strong fundamentals, projected earnings, and a competitive advantage, the difference between entering at $40 or $41 becomes less significant. In such cases, waiting for a minor price drop might result in missing out on the stock's upward momentum and potential profits.

This approach of focusing on the stock's future direction is particularly relevant for long-term investors who have a horizon extending beyond short-term price fluctuations. For traders with a shorter time frame, it may make sense to be more price-sensitive and wait for specific entry points, but investors with a longer investment horizon should prioritize the stock's growth potential over minor variations in the entry price. By considering the stock's expected trajectory and fundamental strength, investors can make more strategic and forward-thinking decisions, maximizing the potential for portfolio growth.

Do Not Avoid Buying Because the Stock Price Is at a New High

Buying stocks at new highs can be a successful strategy for momentum investors who recognize the advantages of such opportunities. One key benefit is the absence of overhead supply or resistance, which can allow the stock to move higher without facing significant obstacles. Despite these advantages, some investors following different approaches may hesitate to invest in stocks at new price highs, often perceiving them as overvalued or overpriced. It is essential, however, to adopt a more comprehensive perspective before disregarding a stock just because it is trading at a new high.

To make an informed decision, investors should conduct a thorough evaluation of the stock in question. Assess key factors such as estimated earnings, growth prospects, and other fundamental indicators that can influence the stock's future performance. By analyzing the potential price appreciation and growth prospects for the stock in the coming year, investors can make a well-informed decision about whether the stock is worth buying despite trading at new highs. This approach allows investors to capitalize on stocks with strong upward momentum and the potential for further gains, rather than missing out on opportunities due to preconceived notions about new highs.

Do Not Buy a Company Just Because It Has a Low P/E Ratio

It is common for investors, particularly those following a value-based investing strategy, to focus on stocks with a low P/E ratio. The rationale behind this approach is that stocks with low P/E ratios are seen as reasonably priced, with limited downside risk and the potential for significant upside gains. It should be noted, however, that investors who solely rely on a low P/E ratio as their primary buying criteria might find themselves in an unfavorable situation if they neglect to examine the underlying reasons for the low P/E.

In many instances, a company's low P/E ratio is justified by the fact that it has a poor business outlook or a bleak earnings forecast. Consequently, these stocks may not appreciate in price for an extended period or might even experience price declines. This highlights the importance of conducting a comprehensive analysis that goes beyond the P/E ratio and takes into account the company's overall financial health, growth prospects, and the reasons behind the low valuation. Such a holistic approach can help investors avoid making the mistake of investing in companies with low P/E ratios due to fundamental weaknesses that could hinder their long-term performance.

Do Not Buy Low Liquidity Stocks

Liquidity is a crucial factor for stock investors, and it directly impacts the ease and speed at which you can buy or sell a stock. One of the primary reasons people invest in the stock market is the ability to quickly liquidate their investments, either partially or in full, if the need arises. Most stocks can be sold within minutes on any of the stock exchanges, providing a high level of liquidity. Although for some stocks, this is not the case, and low liquidity can pose a significant issue.

Low liquidity typically pertains to stocks that have a limited daily trading volume, meaning only a small number of shares change hands each day. These stocks can be challenging to sell even during normal market conditions, but the real problem becomes apparent during turbulent periods. During market volatility or uncertainty, it can become extremely difficult to sell low-liquidity stocks, potentially leading to substantial losses. To mitigate this risk, it is advisable to focus on stocks with a higher level of liquidity, preferably those that trade at least 200,000 shares per day. This ensures that you have the flexibility to enter and exit positions swiftly, providing greater peace of mind and control over your investments.

Do Not Buy Defensive Stocks Near the End of a Recession

As a smart investor, it is essential to pay attention to the economic cycle and understand its impact on different types of stocks. Defensive stocks are typically favored by investors when they anticipate an economic recession because these companies tend to have more stable revenues and profits that are less sensitive to economic downturns. It is crucial to be strategic about the timing of your investments. As the economy begins to emerge from a recession and shows signs of recovery, the focus of investors shifts. They start anticipating that company profits will rebound, and they redirect their investments toward cyclical and growth stocks, which are positioned to benefit from the economic upturn. This shift in investor sentiment often leads to these stocks experiencing significant price appreciation.

To maximize your returns and participate in the broader market rebound, it is advisable not to invest heavily in defensive stocks near the end of a recession. Instead, consider reallocating your investments to sectors and stocks that are poised for growth as the economy improves. This approach allows you to capture the potential gains associated with the recovery phase of the economic cycle, taking advantage of the changing market dynamics.

Do Not Give Importance to Tips and Rumors

Receiving stock tips and rumors from various sources is a common occurrence in the world of investing. While it is acceptable to consider such information, it is crucial not to assign undue importance to these tips. The key to making informed and successful investment decisions is to separate the tip itself from the person or source providing it. Rather than blindly acting on a tip, it is essential to subject the recommended stock to the same rigorous fundamental analysis that you would apply to a stock identified through your usual investment research process. This approach ensures that you make decisions based on solid information and analysis rather than on hearsay, reducing the level of risk associated with your investments.

By conducting thorough due diligence and relying on fundamental analysis, you can make well-informed investment choices that align with your financial goals and risk tolerance. Avoiding knee-jerk reactions to tips and rumors helps you maintain a disciplined and strategic approach to investing, ultimately improving your chances of success in the stock market.

SELLING

Investors also make many mistakes when selling stocks, which can also impact the overall profitability of their various investments. The common selling mistakes that they make are discussed in this section.

Do Not Focus Too Much on the Buy Price

When evaluating a sell decision, investors often tend to focus too much on the buy price and the current "loss" or "profit" associated with their holdings. This approach may lead to suboptimal decisions because it does not take into account the stock's future price appreciation potential. A more rational and forward-looking strategy involves assessing whether the stock is expected to be a winner based on its forecasted price appreciation. If the analysis indicates that the stock is likely to deliver significant future gains, it should be retained, regardless of the current paper loss. If the stock's total holding period does not align with the expected returns and the fundamentals are sound, it might be time to consider selling. Confidence should not be eroded by a paper loss, but a sell decision becomes justified if the company's future prospects appear uncertain.

Investors must remember that the objective is not just to recover the initial investment or breakeven but to optimize returns. This means considering the stock's future potential rather than dwelling solely on the past. A disciplined approach to evaluating stocks based on their long-term outlook and fundamental strength can lead to more informed sell decisions and ultimately contribute to better investment outcomes.

Do Not Fail to Cut Your Losses and Let the Profits Run

One of the common mistakes investors make is failing to cut their losses when a stock turns into a loser. There is often an emotional attachment to the stock, leading to irrational hopes that it will rebound. This emotional bias can lead to paralysis, and the small loss initially incurred can snowball into a larger one. To mitigate this, it is crucial to adhere to your predefined selling rules. When you identify a stock as a loser, you should sell it immediately. This proactive approach ensures that you do not find yourself stuck in a situation where you are unable or unwilling to cut your losses.

Contrarily, successful investors adopt the strategy of letting their profits run. When a stock becomes a winner, it is tempting to cash in immediately to lock in gains. The key is to ride your winning stocks for as long as possible, selling only when their fundamentals deteriorate or when the price significantly outpaces earnings growth. By prioritizing the selling of underperforming stocks and holding on to the winners, you can maximize your investment returns and reduce potential losses in your portfolio.

Do Not Hold on to Mediocre Performers

It is crucial not to hold on to mediocre performers in your portfolio for an extended period. While patience is important in stock investing, you should also establish a regular review process, typically after twelve to eighteen months, to evaluate your holdings. When this review reveals that a stock is a mediocre performer with a lackluster outlook for the future, it is important not to delay in selling it. Instead, consider reallocating your capital to stocks with better performance expectations.

The decision to sell a mediocre performer isn't only about freeing up capital but also about optimizing your portfolio's performance potential. By actively managing your investments and replacing underperforming stocks with stronger opportunities, you can enhance your overall returns and ensure your portfolio remains aligned with your financial goals.

Do Not Delay Selling for Minor Gains

When you have made the decision to sell a stock, it is important to act promptly and not delay the sale for minor gains. Attempting to extract every last cent from a stock can backfire, especially when its fundamentals are deteriorating. In such situations, it is crucial to sell the stock immediately and not to hesitate. Delaying the sale in hopes of earning a few extra cents per share can expose you to significant losses, as the likelihood of a substantial price decline often outweighs the potential for slight upward movement in such cases.

Recognize that a swift and decisive approach to selling underperforming stocks is essential to minimize your exposure to risk and safeguard your investment capital. By avoiding unnecessary delays and making sell decisions based on the stock's fundamentals and market conditions, you can make more informed and effective choices in managing your portfolio.

Do Not Delay Selling Due to a Rebound Expectation

It is imperative not to delay selling a stock due to the expectation of a rebound that may yield only marginal gains. If your fundamental analysis indicates that a stock should be sold, it is essential to act on that information promptly. Waiting for a rebound can be risky, as it's difficult to predict the precise point at which a declining stock will find stability. Believing that a stock that has already experienced significant losses cannot decline further can lead to prolonged holding of losing positions; this can ultimately result in even greater losses. Moreover, holding onto a losing stock with the belief that stocks always recover is a misconception. In reality, many stocks never come close to reaching their all-time highs again.

Maintaining discipline in your selling decisions, guided by objective analysis rather than emotions or unrealistic expectations, is crucial to managing risk and protecting your investment capital. By avoiding the trap of waiting for rebounds that may not materialize and taking proactive steps to manage underperforming stocks, you can make more informed choices and better position your portfolio for success.

Do Not Sell Too Early

Selling winning stocks too early is a common mistake among investors, and it often occurs when they focus solely on the price appreciation that has already occurred. In order to maximize the returns on your portfolio, you should evaluate a stock's potential to rise even higher based on its fundamentals. If your analysis suggests that there is significant upside potential left, it is wise to let your profits run. A few successful winners can more than compensate for multiple small losses in your portfolio.

The key to successful investing is to identify and maintain positions in stocks that have strong growth prospects and the potential for substantial price appreciation. By avoiding the temptation to sell prematurely and holding onto your winning stocks as long as they align with your fundamental analysis, you can capture the full benefit of their upward momentum and achieve better overall portfolio performance.

Do Not Sell Your Slightly Overpriced Fast Growers

Selling your slightly overpriced fast-growing stocks can be a costly mistake. While conventional valuation criteria might suggest that these stocks are overvalued, it is essential to understand that high-growth winners and leaders often appear overpriced because of the strong demand they attract. This demand drives their prices and P/E ratios higher.

When fundamentals are sound and the stock is showing the potential for substantial growth, selling it solely based on valuation can result in a missed opportunity for a substantial profit.

In such cases, it is crucial to consider the long-term growth prospects of the stock, as well as the strength of its fundamentals, instead of focusing exclusively on the current price or P/E ratio. The market rewards high-growth stocks for a reason and holding onto them even when they seem slightly overpriced can often lead to significant returns in the future. By staying focused on the company's growth potential and fundamentals, you can make more informed decisions about when to sell such stocks.

Do Not Make Taxes an Important Factor

While tax considerations should be a part of your investment strategy, it is important not to make them the primary factor when deciding whether to retain or sell a stock. Many investors tend to hold onto a stock that has reached its peak, even when they are aware that it is time to sell, just to delay the associated tax liability. This delay can come at the cost of missing out on potential profits by not moving into a more promising stock. Taxes should be taken into account, but they should not overshadow the fundamental and price appreciation potential of the stocks in your portfolio.

In some cases, holding onto a stock just to avoid taxes can result in missed opportunities and potential losses that outweigh the tax benefits. It is crucial to strike a balance between managing your tax liability and making investment decisions based on a stock's growth potential and overall fundamentals. By keeping this perspective, you can make more informed choices when it comes to selling stocks.

CHAPTER 15

MISCELLANEOUS TIPS

GENERAL

The stock market is a complex environment where many variables are at play. This section provides additional tips that investors can use for making or monitoring stock investments.

Be an Informed Investor

Being an informed investor is the key to success in the stock market. Success is not a matter of luck but rather a result of careful preparation and diligent research. Those who invest with a well-thought-out plan and stay informed about their investments tend to be rewarded, while those who rely on gut feelings or chance often end up with losses. To be a successful investor, you must maintain a state of perpetual alertness and information-gathering.

This involves continuous monitoring of the companies in which you have invested, as well as the industry or group to which those companies belong. Understanding the competitive landscape and what factors can influence the fundamentals of your stock investments is crucial. Economic, financial, and political news can all impact your investments, so it is vital to stay informed about these developments and analyze how they might affect your stocks or their respective industries. A well-informed investor is better equipped to make sound decisions and adapt to changing market conditions, and, as such, should never stop monitoring their investments and the broader economic and political environment.

Learn to Filter Out the Noise

In the stock market, numerous factors and forces are at play, and their influence can vary significantly over time. Economic data, political developments, market sentiment, and other variables can all impact stock prices to varying degrees. As a result, the stock market can be a noisy and chaotic place, making it challenging for investors to discern the essential factors from the less significant ones. Typically, seasoned investors develop the skill of filtering out the noise and honing in on the critical variables that truly affect the stock market and their individual investments.

To become adept at filtering out the noise, investors must prioritize their focus on key factors like economic indicators, company financials, industry trends, and market sentiment. They need to discern which variables have the most significant impact on their investment strategies and concentrate their research and analysis on those aspects. This ability to sift through the noise and maintain a clear focus on what truly matters is a valuable skill in making informed investment decisions.

Never Stop Monitoring

In the world of investing, the concept of never-ending monitoring is an essential one. The stock market is a highly dynamic and ever-changing environment, where factors that influence stock prices, from economic shifts to corporate developments, constantly evolve. Even if you hold a stock with promising prospects, you cannot assume that its position will remain unaltered over time. Business conditions, competitive landscapes, growth rates, and various other fundamental aspects are subject to change. Therefore, the investor's vigilance and ongoing monitoring are crucial because complacency can lead to unpleasant surprises.

The stock market is known for its capacity to defy expectations and provide unforeseen developments, and investors must adapt to these changes. The economy, stock market, and individual stocks can all deliver unexpected events and challenges. As a result, staying alert and continuously monitoring your investments is a practice that should remain in place for as long as you are involved in the stock market, as it has a way of surprising even the most seasoned investors.

Avoid Excessive Monitoring

The frequency of monitoring your investments should align with the time frame in which the variables you are tracking can change significantly. Different factors are subject to distinct reporting schedules. Earnings reports, for example, are released on a quarterly basis, while employment data is published monthly, and GDP reports come out quarterly. Stock prices and news, however, fluctuate daily, and they might provide vital insights into your investments. As such, daily monitoring is often necessary for news that pertains to your specific company, as it can reflect major changes in the business environment or profitability. Monthly analysis is typically sufficient for reports such as inflation and employment data, while more infrequent checks, perhaps quarterly, may suffice for variables like GDP.

In general, dedicating approximately three to four hours per week to investment research and monitoring can be a reasonable commitment for most investors. The key is to strike a balance between staying informed and not letting monitoring consume an excessive amount of your time. By understanding the nature of the variables you are tracking and their significance to your investments, you can develop a monitoring schedule that effectively aligns with your investment strategy and goals.

Follow a Few Stocks but Monitor Them Closely

To be an effective investor, it is important to focus your attention on a select few stocks while monitoring them closely. In-depth understanding of a company's business, its stock's behavior, and its industry dynamics takes a considerable amount of time and effort. Therefore, it is essential to recognize the finite nature of the time available for stock investment research and make a conscious effort to limit the number of stocks you track closely. Trying to follow too many stocks can lead to a lack of depth in your analysis and can become overwhelming.

Monitoring should not be confused with daily tracking of stock prices. Instead, it involves staying well-informed about every aspect of the business and its broader environment that can impact the stock's performance. This could include understanding the company's financials, industry trends, competitive landscape, and any external factors like economic conditions or political developments that may influence the stock. By focusing on a manageable number of stocks, you can dedicate the necessary time and attention required to make well-informed investment decisions and avoid spreading yourself too thin across a large number of investments.

Learn How to Interpret Recommendations

Understanding analyst recommendations can be a challenging task due to the multitude of categories and ratings used by analysts. These categories can vary from "strong buy" to "sell," and the interpretation of these recommendations might differ between analysts. The terminology can become even more confusing when different analysts use the same categories but have slightly different criteria for assigning them. Some analysts may also avoid using the "sell" category altogether.

It is essential to grasp the specific categories and their meanings used by the analysts you follow to accurately interpret their recommendations. For instance, a rating such as "hold" from one analyst could imply a suggestion to sell the stock, while for another it may just mean they see no compelling reason to buy or sell at the moment. To avoid misinterpretation, it is important to understand the specific criteria and context behind each recommendation. Carefully researching the analyst's methodology and any accompanying research reports can provide valuable insights into the true meaning of their stock ratings, helping you make more informed investment decisions.

Ensure That Stock Being Considered Is Adequately Covered

The level of analyst coverage for a company is indeed quite variable, and it is essential for investors to take this into account when considering an investment. Newer or smaller companies may have limited analyst coverage, making it more challenging to obtain comprehensive and accurate information about their financial performance and prospects. Established and well-known companies often attract a larger number of analysts who track their performance, issue recommendations, and provide earnings forecasts.

Having at least four analysts covering a company is considered a minimum threshold, as this helps reduce the risk of significant inaccuracies in financial projections. When multiple analysts are tracking a company, there is a greater likelihood of balanced and accurate assessments. Investors often rely on the earnings estimates and recommendations provided by these analysts to make informed investment decisions. The more analysts covering a company, the more confidence investors can have in the accuracy of the information they rely on for their investment strategies.

Understand Stock Classifications

Understanding stock classifications is crucial for investors when building a diversified portfolio that aligns with their financial objectives and risk tolerance. Market capitalization is one of the key metrics used to classify stocks, and it provides insights into the size of a company. Large-cap companies typically have market capitalizations of $1 billion or more, and they are often considered more stable and established. Medium-cap stocks fall within the $100 million to $1 billion range and represent companies that are somewhat smaller but still significant in size. Small-cap stocks are typically defined as those with market capitalizations under $1 billion or sometimes by their stock price, such as being under $20.

Investors should consider their investment goals and risk tolerance when determining their preference for stock classifications. Large-cap stocks may be suitable for those seeking stability and more modest growth, while small-cap stocks can be attractive to investors who are willing to take on higher risk in exchange for the potential of significant growth. By carefully analyzing and selecting stocks based on their classification, investors can tailor their portfolios to align with their individual investment strategies and financial objectives.

Monitor Brokerage Asset Allocation Announcements

Monitoring asset allocation recommendations made by prominent brokerage houses like Goldman Sachs can provide investors with valuable insights into the overall sentiment and expectations of major financial institutions. These recommendations often involve adjustments in the suggested allocation of funds between stocks and bonds, and they are typically rooted in the brokerage house's outlook on market conditions. For instance, if a brokerage house increases its recommended stock allocation from 55% to 60%, it signifies a bullish view on the stock market. Conversely, a decrease in the recommended allocation may indicate a more bearish outlook.

These announcements hold significance because they reflect the collective wisdom and market influence of these brokerage firms, which manage substantial sums of money. When multiple brokerages are increasing their recommended stock allocations, it suggests a broader consensus that the stock market holds potential for growth. This information can be valuable for investors in understanding the current market sentiment and making informed decisions about their own asset allocation strategies.

MONITORING EXTERNAL FACTORS

Many external factors influence the stock market as well as individual stocks. The impact of the key external indicators, which can be significant, is discussed in this section.

Do Not Ignore Either Internal or External Factors

Internal and external factors play significant roles in influencing the performance of your stocks, and as an investor, it is crucial not to overlook either of these factors. Internal factors include elements related to the specific company you have invested in, such as its financial health, management team, competitive position, and growth prospects. External factors encompass broader economic, political, and industry-related elements that can affect the market and your stocks, including inflation rates, government policies, and global events. Neglecting any of these factors can have severe consequences for your stock investments.

While there are numerous internal and external factors at play, not all of them will impact your stocks in the same way or to the same extent. Therefore, it is essential to identify and closely monitor the specific factors that have the potential to significantly influence the performance of your stocks. Understanding the dynamics between these factors and your investments will allow you to make more informed decisions and better navigate the complexities of the stock market, ultimately helping you to protect and grow your portfolio.

Monitor Economic Indicators

Monitoring economic indicators is essential for investors because the performance of the stock market is closely tied to the broader economic conditions. A strong understanding of the economic cycle, fiscal and monetary policies, and other relevant indicators is crucial for evaluating the potential impact on individual companies and their profitability. Economic factors can significantly affect stock prices; for instance, during an economic boom, many companies tend to thrive, while in a recession, corporate profits may decline, resulting in negative stock price movements. Therefore, keeping an eye on key economic indicators is essential for assessing the economic environment that your stocks are operating within.

By staying informed about economic indicators, you can make more informed investment decisions. Whether it is monitoring employment data, inflation rates, interest rates, or government policies, these factors have the power to influence your portfolio's performance. By analyzing the economic landscape, you can better position your investments and be prepared to adjust your strategies in response to changes in the economic environment, ultimately helping you navigate the stock market more effectively.

Monitor Political Events

Political events can significantly influence the stock market, often driven by the market's aversion to uncertainty. When there is a crisis or political event with an unclear outcome, investors become cautious and prefer to stay on the sidelines. This hesitancy results in an absence or shortage of buyers, which can lead to market declines. As an informed investor, it is vital to monitor major political events closely and analyze their potential consequences for the economy and the stock market.

By keeping tabs on political developments and their potential impact on the economy, you can better prepare for different market scenarios and adjust your investment strategies accordingly. It is essential to understand how these external factors can create uncertainty and affect investor sentiment, as this knowledge will help you make more informed decisions in the ever-changing landscape of the stock market.

Learn How to Navigate Markets in Times of Uncertainty

Political and economic uncertainty can significantly impact the stock market. Wall Street generally dislikes uncertainty, and when political or economic crises create ambiguity, it tends to trigger poor stock market performance. While these impacts are typically transitory, and the underlying profitability of companies remains the ultimate driver of stock prices, investors need to grasp how such crises can sway the market and affect their individual stock holdings. Effective monitoring enables investors to assess how unfolding events may affect their stocks, their industry sectors, and industry groups. This knowledge empowers investors to make well-informed investment decisions and adapt their strategies based on the prevailing conditions.

Political and economic uncertainties introduce an element of risk and unpredictability into the stock market. When major events or crises create an atmosphere of uncertainty, investors often prefer to take a cautious approach and adopt a wait-and-see attitude. As a result, the market can experience a decline in buyer interest, leading to market downturns. While these effects are usually temporary, they underscore the importance of monitoring political and economic developments closely. By keeping a watchful eye on such events and understanding their potential implications for stocks, investors can better navigate the uncertainties and make strategic decisions that align with the prevailing political and economic conditions.

Check If Money Inflow Is Rising

Monitoring the flow of money into the stock market through mutual funds is a critical aspect of understanding market dynamics. The influx of new funds into the market can be a powerful driver of stock demand, potentially boosting stock prices. When investors channel more capital into stock funds, it signals positive sentiment and a preference for equities, which can have a favorable impact on stock prices. Conversely, if there is a substantial outflow of money due to investors redeeming their investments, it can lead to reduced demand for stocks and adversely affect stock prices. The timing of these flows is also significant, with January historically witnessing a surge in inflows, contributing to the market's robust performance during that month. Therefore, as an investor, monitoring money flows into stock funds is a crucial practice for assessing overall market sentiment and potential trends. This data can be obtained from various online investment websites.

Additionally, it is important to consider how the direction of money flows can provide insights into investor behavior and confidence. Increased inflows often signify a positive outlook for the market, while outflows may indicate apprehension or a desire to reallocate investments. As such, staying informed about these trends can assist investors in making more informed decisions and adapting their strategies based on the prevailing market conditions. This monitoring should be an integral part of an investor's routine, alongside other fundamental and technical analyses, to gain a comprehensive understanding of market dynamics.

Analyze Risk Due to Currency Fluctuations

Profits of a US company with foreign operations can be significantly influenced by currency fluctuations. These fluctuations stem from the varying exchange rates between the US dollar and foreign currencies, which affect the translation of foreign revenues into US dollars. Depending on the timing of currency conversion, a company may see its revenue appear higher or lower when reported in US dollars. Such fluctuations can have a direct and immediate impact on a company's profitability, as they affect the bottom-line results reported to shareholders and investors.

For investors evaluating a company, it is essential to take into account the geographical spread of the company's operations and the level of currency risk it is exposed to. The extent of this risk can vary significantly depending on the countries in which the company conducts business. For instance, if a company has a substantial portion of its operations in a country with a volatile currency, like the Russian ruble, this may be seen as a significant risk factor due to the potential impact on its profits when converting revenues back into US dollars. Therefore, in-depth scrutiny of a company's international exposure and currency risk is a crucial part of fundamental analysis, allowing investors to make more informed decisions and manage their portfolios effectively.

MONITORING INTEREST RATES AND THE FEDERAL RESERVE

Interest rates are among the most important external variables impacting the stock market. This section discusses how to monitor them, as well as the role and impact of the Federal Reserve on interest rates.

Monitor Interest Rate Trends

Monitoring and understanding interest rate trends are essential for investors as it directly impacts the profitability of companies. Many businesses rely on borrowing capital to fund their operations and expansion, making interest payments a significant part of their expenses. When interest rates decline, the cost of borrowing money decreases which, in turn, increases a company's profits. This boost in profitability often leads to higher stock prices as investors are more inclined to invest in companies with improving financial performance. Conversely, when interest rates rise, borrowing costs increase, potentially squeezing profit margins, and consequently leading to lower stock prices.

To be a successful investor, you should closely monitor interest rates and their trends to assess the potential impact on the financial performance of companies and the overall stock market. Understanding the relationship between interest rates and stock prices is crucial for making well-informed investment decisions and being prepared for market shifts driven by changes in borrowing costs. By doing so, you can position your portfolio to take advantage of market conditions related to interest rate trends and react accordingly to maximize your investment returns.

Learn How to Forecast Interest Rates

To forecast interest rates, investors can monitor the Dow Jones Utility Index, representing the performance of utility companies. Utilities heavily depend on borrowing for operations, making them sensitive to interest rate fluctuations. The utility index's strength or weakness can signal changes in interest rates. A strong utility index often suggests upcoming interest rate decreases. As the bond market usually precedes interest rate changes, the Dow Jones Utility average reflects shifts before impacting the broader stock market. The performance of utilities acts as a leading indicator for the overall market trend, providing insights into future interest rates and, consequently, stock market conditions.

Closely monitoring the Dow Jones Utility Index offers investors valuable information on potential interest rate movements impacting investment decisions. Recognizing the utility index as an early predictor of interest rate changes helps investors position themselves effectively in response to market shifts, enhancing their chances of making informed and profitable choices.

Monitor the Federal Reserve's Policies and Decisions

Understanding the role and impact of the Federal Reserve is crucial for investors, as it wields substantial influence over the stock market. The Federal Reserve's key responsibilities include managing inflation and determining short-term interest rates. To achieve these goals, it adjusts interest rates based on the prevailing economic conditions. When the economy shows signs of slowing down or enters a recession, the Federal Reserve tends to lower interest rates. This move encourages businesses to invest and consumers to spend, ultimately leading to increased corporate earnings and higher stock prices. Conversely, if the economy is expanding rapidly or facing inflationary pressures, the Federal Reserve raises interest rates to cool down economic activity. As a result, this tightening of monetary policy has the opposite effect on the economy and the stock market, potentially leading to a decline in stock prices.

Given the Federal Reserve's substantial impact on the stock market, investors must closely monitor the central bank's policies and decisions, as they can significantly influence market conditions. By staying informed about Federal Reserve actions and their potential effects on interest rates and the economy, investors can make more informed investment decisions and better position themselves in response to changing market dynamics.

Monitor Federal Reserve Meetings

Monitoring Federal Reserve meetings and their outcomes is essential for investors as it provides critical insights into the central bank's monetary policy decisions. The FOMC plays a pivotal role in controlling interest rates, specifically the discount rate and the federal funds rate. The discount rate is the interest rate at which member banks can borrow funds directly from the Federal Reserve. Alternatively, the federal funds rate represents the interest rate at which banks lend money to one another to meet their reserve requirements. The FOMC convenes approximately every six weeks to deliberate on monetary policy and interest rates. When it makes decisions regarding changes in the discount rate or the federal funds rate, they are conveyed through a statement that it issues.

Investors pay close attention to FOMC meetings and the resulting statements because they can profoundly impact financial markets. Changes in interest rates can influence borrowing costs for businesses and consumers, affecting investment decisions and spending patterns, which in turn have repercussions on corporate earnings and stock market performance. Thus, staying informed about the outcomes of these meetings is a fundamental aspect of monitoring the financial landscape and making well-informed investment decisions.

Monitor Federal Reserve Actions and Hints

Monitoring the Federal Reserve's policies, actions, and statements is crucial for investors seeking to gain insights into the central bank's stance and its potential impacts on the stock market. The Federal Reserve holds significant sway over the economy and financial markets due to its control over interest rates. A primary focus for investors is to ascertain whether the Federal Reserve is in an easing (bullish) or tightening (bearish) mode. Easing refers to a policy stance where the central bank lowers interest rates to stimulate economic growth, which can be favorable for the stock market. In contrast, tightening involves raising interest rates to curb inflation, which can be seen as a bearish signal for stocks as it increases borrowing costs for businesses and consumers.

To stay well-informed, investors should closely monitor the outcomes of FOMC meetings, particularly their statements. The content of these statements often holds critical information about the central bank's concerns and priorities. This information can be even more revealing than the decisions regarding interest rates. The statements may signal concerns about inflation threats, economic weakness, or other issues, and the market's interpretation of these concerns can significantly impact stock prices. Therefore, understanding and interpreting these statements are essential for stock market investors.

Monitor How the Federal Reserve's Tools Are Being Deployed

Observing how the Federal Reserve deploys its monetary policy tools provides valuable insights into its intentions and can help investors gauge the market's potential direction. The Federal Reserve wields three crucial tools to enact its policies and influence interest rates, inflation, and the broader economy. These tools are the discount rate, the federal funds rate, and the level of reserve requirements imposed on member banks. Among these, the discount rate holds significant power, and its adjustments can have substantial impacts on the economy and financial markets. When the Federal Reserve lowers the discount rate, it typically aims to stimulate economic growth by making it more attractive for banks to borrow from the central bank. This can result in lower interest rates in the broader financial system, making it more affordable for businesses and consumers to borrow, ultimately fostering economic expansion. Observing changes in the discount rate and its impact on borrowing costs is, therefore, an essential task for investors seeking to understand the Federal Reserve's economic stance and its effects on stock market trends.

Understanding the role and significance of each of these tools is pivotal for investors. By closely following the Federal Reserve's utilization of these tools, investors can interpret the central bank's policy direction and its implications for the stock market. The Federal Reserve's decisions regarding interest rates and reserve requirements are key determinants of market conditions, so tracking their deployment helps investors align their strategies accordingly.

Monitor Real Interest Rates

Real interest rates, as distinguished from nominal interest rates, hold vital significance for investors and economists. They represent the actual return or cost of borrowing after accounting for inflation in the economy. Investors closely monitor real interest rates to understand the true impact of monetary policy and economic conditions on borrowing and lending. This interest rate is determined by the difference between the nominal interest rate, such as the federal funds rate set by the central bank, and the prevailing inflation rate. For instance, if the federal funds rate stands at 5% and inflation is at 3%, the real interest rate would be 2%. This implies that lenders or investors are earning a real return of 2% after adjusting for the eroding effects of inflation. In cases where inflation is lower, say 2%, the real interest rate would increase to 3%, indicating a more significant interest rate return in real terms. Therefore, understanding real interest rates is essential as it provides insights into the actual return on investment or cost of borrowing when considering the impact of inflation.

Monitoring real interest rates is particularly valuable for investors seeking to evaluate the attractiveness of various investment options. Real interest rates reflect the true value of investing in different assets, helping investors make informed decisions about the allocation of their funds. When real interest rates rise, it signifies a more favorable climate for saving and investing, as it means that the returns on investment are greater than the rate of inflation. Conversely, when real interest rates decline, it suggests a less attractive environment for saving, investing, and borrowing. Investors pay close attention to fluctuations in real interest rates as they can significantly influence investment strategies and portfolio decisions, impacting the performance of various assets, including stocks and bonds.

Monitor Bond Yields

The dynamic relationship between bond yields and stock prices is a crucial factor that investors need to monitor closely. These two asset classes, stocks, and bonds, are in constant competition for investors' capital. The interplay between interest rates and bond yields significantly influences the allocation of investment funds. When bond yields are high, they tend to attract more capital from investors looking for secure income, which can result in capital flowing out of the stock market. Conversely, when bond yields are low, stocks become more appealing as they offer the potential for higher returns, attracting investment dollars away from bonds and into equities.

Moreover, there is a correlation between bond yields and the valuation of the stock market, often measured by metrics such as the P/E ratio of the S&P 500. When economic growth accelerates, long-term bond yields tend to decrease, leading to higher interest rates. In such a scenario, investors may shift their focus from stocks to bonds as the yields become more attractive. On the contrary, during economic slowdowns, bond yields may rise as interest rates decrease, making stocks a more appealing investment. Understanding this relationship and monitoring bond yields is essential for investors to gauge the potential effects on stock prices.

MONITORING YOUR PERFORMANCE AND PORTFOLIO

This section discusses how investors should monitor the performance of their individual stocks as well as portfolios to ensure that they are performing as expected, which will ensure their success in the stock market.

Analyze Your Strategy

Regularly reviewing and analyzing your investment strategy is crucial for long-term success in the stock market. This process allows you to assess the effectiveness of your strategy and make necessary adjustments to improve your approach. It is essential to have a flexible and adaptive mindset, as market conditions and your financial goals can change over time.

When conducting a strategy analysis, consider various factors such as your investment goals, risk tolerance, and time horizon. Reflect on the performance of your portfolio and whether it aligns with your objectives. Determine if your strategy is still relevant given the current economic and market conditions. Major paradigm shifts can occur in the financial land-scape, and you should be prepared to adapt when necessary. Notably, it is important to avoid making drastic changes based on short-term mistakes or market fluctuations. Instead, evaluate your strategy's performance over a reasonable time frame to make well-informed decisions about potential modifications. Ultimately, the key is to strike a balance between flexibility and consistency in your investment strategy.

Test and Evaluate Your Own Decisions

As an independent investor, it is important to recognize that making mistakes is a natural part of the learning process. No one can be right all the time in the stock market. In fact, some of the most successful investors have experienced their fair share of failures along the way. What distinguishes them is their ability to learn from those mistakes and adapt their approach.

Regularly evaluate your investment decisions, both the successful ones and the errors. Identify the factors that led to each outcome and use this analysis to refine your strategy and techniques. This self-assessment will help you understand your strengths and weaknesses as an investor, allowing you to make more informed and effective decisions in the future. It is crucial to maintain a steady mindset and view your mistakes as valuable learning opportunities on your path to becoming a successful investor. Remember the fundamental rule in investing: cut your losses and let your profits run. A few significant winning investments can more than compensate for smaller losses if you follow this principle.

Analyze Your Trades

Regularly analyzing your trades is a critical aspect of improving as an investor. It allows you to gain insights into your decision-making process and refine your approach. When reviewing your trades, focus on understanding what went well and what didn't. Examine your buying and selling decisions to identify what factors influenced your choices. Did you correctly assess the stock's potential? Were you too hasty or too slow to act? By analyzing your trades, you can pinpoint the moments when you made sound decisions and those moments when you faltered.

Furthermore, scrutinize your monitoring activities. Were there signals or indicators that you overlooked or misjudged? Identifying these missed opportunities can help you fine-tune your strategy to avoid repeating the same mistakes in the future. Remember that mistakes are a natural part of investing, but it is crucial to learn from them and not let them become recurring issues. Consistent self-analysis and improvement will lead to more informed and profitable decisions over time.

Evaluate Each Stock's Performance

When assessing the performance of individual stocks over time, it is imperative to define a specific time frame aligning with your investment objectives. The appropriate duration for evaluating stock performance may differ depending on factors like the company's nature and industry. Typically, allowing a stock six to eighteen months to meet your investment goals is considered reasonable, and maintaining flexibility within this time frame is crucial. The decision to hold or sell should hinge on a thorough examination of the stock's fundamentals and its performance concerning your initial expectations.

Flexibility becomes paramount as market conditions and company dynamics evolve. If a stock demonstrates solid fundamentals and exhibits positive trends relative to your expectations, holding onto it may be prudent, even if the initially set time frame has not fully elapsed. Contrastingly, if the stock underperforms or if there are shifts in the market or industry landscape that adversely impact its prospects, being flexible allows for timely adjustments to your investment strategy. The ability to adapt your approach based on ongoing evaluations is key to optimizing investment outcomes over time.

Periodically Evaluate Your Portfolio

Regularly evaluating your portfolio is an essential part of effective investment management. This periodic review allows you to assess various elements of your portfolio to ensure it aligns with your investment objectives. One critical aspect to consider is asset allocation, which involves analyzing how your assets are distributed among different types of investments, such as stocks, bonds, and cash. Rebalancing your portfolio may be necessary to maintain your desired level of risk and return. Another key component to review is the allocation among different industries and groups within your portfolio. This analysis helps you understand if your investments are well diversified and not overly concentrated in a single sector.

It is also essential to assess the risk associated with the individual stocks in your portfolio and make buy, sell, or hold decisions based on their performance. Finally, you should evaluate your portfolio's overall performance compared to relevant benchmarks, such as industry group averages or market indexes. This comparison can provide insights into whether your portfolio is meeting your financial goals and expectations. Periodic portfolio evaluations give you the opportunity to identify under-performing assets (laggards) that may need to be replaced with new invest-ments to improve the overall performance and health of your portfolio.

Select an Appropriate Benchmark

Comparing your portfolio's performance to a relevant benchmark is a cru-cial step in assessing its success. Choosing an appropriate benchmark is important as it allows you to gauge how well your investments are doing relative to a comparable group of assets. For example, if your portfolio primarily consists of technology stocks, it would make sense to compare its performance to a technology sector index, like the NASDAQ. By doing so, you can see if your portfolio is outperforming or underperforming its peers in the same sector.

Consistently underperforming the chosen benchmark should be a cause for concern, as it may indicate that your current investment strat-egy and techniques are not yielding the expected results. This can serve as a signal to reevaluate your approach and consider potential adjustments to your portfolio, such as revising your asset allocation, rethinking your stock selection criteria, or fine-tuning your risk management strategy. Regularly assessing your portfolio's performance relative to a benchmark helps ensure that your investments align with your financial goals and objectives.

16

COMMON MISTAKES TO AVOID

APPROACH AND STRATEGY

The numerous mistakes that investors make span many areas and functions. This section discusses the common mistakes pertaining to their investing approach and strategy.

Do Not Delay Investing in the Market

Delaying your entry into the stock market can have significant consequences on your financial goals, especially when it comes to saving for retirement. Starting early allows your investments more time to grow, benefiting from the power of compounding. For every year you delay investing, the monthly amount you will need to set aside for your retirement or other financial objectives will increase. This means that if you procrastinate, you will have to allocate a much larger portion of your income to reach the same retirement income target as someone who started investing earlier.

In addition to requiring a higher monthly investment to catch up, the need for a higher return on your investments also increases the level of risk. Seeking higher returns often means taking on riskier investments, which can lead to greater volatility and the potential for significant losses. By starting your investment journey early, you can build a diversified and balanced portfolio that offers long-term growth potential while minimizing unnecessary risks. This not only sets you on a more secure path toward achieving your financial goals but also allows you to weather market fluctuations with a longer time horizon for recovery.

Do Not Be a Follower

In the world of investing, being an independent thinker is a valuable trait that can set you apart from the crowd and lead to more successful outcomes. By not simply following the herd and making decisions based on your own thorough analysis and understanding of the market, you can increase your chances of achieving your investment goals. It is important to recognize that market sentiment can often swing from extreme pessimism to euphoria, and following the crowd during these emotional fluctuations can lead to poor investment decisions. Instead, making well-informed choices based on your own research can help you avoid buying stocks at peak prices and panic-selling during downturns.

One common pitfall is becoming enamored with stock picks promoted by TV commentators or investment advisors. While their insights can be valuable, they should be just one part of your decision-making process. By seeking out undiscovered opportunities and making independent investment decisions, you can identify assets that may have been overlooked by Wall Street. It is also essential to maintain an awareness of the overall market trend to ensure that your investments align with the broader economic conditions. This balanced approach allows you to leverage your independent thinking while staying attuned to market dynamics.

Do Not Invest Without Discipline

Investing without discipline can lead to emotional decision-making and erratic trading behaviors. To be a successful investor, it is crucial to have a well-defined plan and strategy and then adhere to them with unwavering discipline. Your strategy should be well-thought-out and aligned with your long-term objectives, allowing you to make decisions based on rational analysis rather than short-term fluctuations. It is natural to encounter occasional setbacks or periods of underperformance, but it is essential not to deviate from your plan too hastily in response to these challenges. Instead, give your strategy time to work and evaluate its effectiveness periodically.

Discipline also entails following your predetermined rules without exceptions. If your strategy includes selling rules, it is crucial to implement them when they are triggered, even if it is emotionally difficult to part with a stock that is not performing as expected. Deviating from your rules based on temporary sentiment or market noise can lead to poor outcomes. Discipline is a fundamental component of successful investing, as it ensures that your decisions are based on rational analysis and not swayed by emotional reactions or short-term market fluctuations. By sticking to your well-defined plan, you are better equipped to navigate the complexities of the stock market and achieve your long-term financial goals.

Do Not Be a Casual Investor

Being a casual investor is not conducive to success in the stock market. It is a place that requires a serious and dedicated approach, involving consistent study, research, and monitoring. Merely checking daily stock prices is not enough; it is only a surface-level observation. To make informed decisions, you need to dive deeper into the factors that drive a stock's behavior and understand the "why" behind price movements. This means conducting thorough research and monitoring.

For each stock you own, you should establish a routine of regularly monitoring developments and news related to the company. These external factors have the potential to influence a company's business prospects and fundamentals, which in turn impact the stock price. By staying vigilant and informed, you can make more proactive and informed investment decisions, minimizing the risks associated with a casual approach. Remember that in the stock market, dedication to research and vigilance in monitoring are essential for long-term success.

Do Not Invest Without a Strategy

Investing without a well-defined strategy is akin to navigating uncharted waters without a compass. It is crucial to take the time to review and evaluate different investment strategies and choose the one that aligns with your unique investment profile, risk tolerance, and financial goals. Each strategy has its own set of principles and approaches, such as value investing for conservative investors or momentum investing for those seeking higher risk and returns. Selecting the strategy that best suits your preferences is the first step in setting the foundation for a successful investment journey.

Once you have chosen your strategy, it is essential to stick with it for a reasonable period and let it work. Consistency is key when it comes to investing, and constantly changing strategies based on short-term results can lead to suboptimal outcomes. It is only after giving a strategy a fair chance that you should consider modifying it or exploring alternatives if the results do not align with your objectives. Having a clear investment strategy and adhering to it is the cornerstone of a disciplined and effective investment approach.

Do Not Invest Without Rules

Investing without a well-defined set of rules is akin to embarking on a journey without a map or compass. These rules provide you with a structured and methodical approach to navigate the complexities of the stock market. Having a clear set of rules for buying and selling stocks is especially important because it helps you remain disciplined and avoid emotional decision-making. Emotions, such as fear and greed, can cloud your judgment and lead to impulsive and often detrimental choices.

For example, if you have a predefined rule that dictates selling a stock if it declines by a certain percentage, say 10%, you are less likely to let emotions drive your decisions. This rule acts as a safeguard, ensuring that you make rational choices based on predetermined criteria. It can protect you from experiencing significant losses that might occur if you allow your emotions to take over. These rules are a crucial part of your investment strategy and serve as a guiding framework to keep you on track toward your financial goals.

Do Not Invest Without a Selection Criterion

Investing without a well-defined set of stock selection criteria is like attempting to find a needle in a haystack while blindfolded. You risk exposing yourself to a higher level of risk and making haphazard investment decisions that may not align with your financial goals. Sound and systematic stock selection criteria are essential to guide your investment choices and ensure they are in line with proven investment principles.

Your selection criteria should be based on indicators and methods that have demonstrated their effectiveness in identifying potential winners while weeding out underperforming stocks. For instance, incorporating indicators like earnings growth rate in your screening process is a smart move. Equally important is using the right values for these criteria. By setting reasonably high figures for your screening indicators, you increase the likelihood of selecting high-growth companies that have a better chance of delivering favorable returns. Developing and adhering to well-defined selection criteria can significantly enhance your stock-picking process and help you build a more robust and diversified investment portfolio.

Do Not Buy Before Performing Fundamental Analysis

Investing in stocks based solely on intuition or external recommendations is akin to navigating through a dense forest without a map, as it is risky and unpredictable. While the allure of quick gains or hot tips can be tempting, investing without conducting thorough fundamental analysis is a recipe for potential financial disaster. Fundamental analysis is a cornerstone of prudent investing and serves as a critical tool for evaluating the long-term prospects of a company.

Performing fundamental analysis involves delving deep into a company's financial health, examining its financial statements, assessing key performance indicators, and understanding its competitive position within the industry. By doing so, investors can make informed decisions and determine whether a stock aligns with their investment goals and risk tolerance. Before you invest in any stock, it is imperative to conduct comprehensive fundamental analysis to gain a clear understanding of the company's financial health, growth potential, and overall stability. This approach not only reduces the level of risk you expose yourself to but also enhances the probability of making sound, well-informed investment decisions.

Do Not Ignore a Stock's Sector or Industry Group

In the stock market, correlation within sectors and industry groups can have a significant impact on individual stock performance. Understanding this interconnectedness is crucial for investors. Stocks are not isolated entities but are part of a larger ecosystem where industry trends and sector performance play a pivotal role in their success or failure. Ignoring the influence of a stock's sector or industry group can be a costly mistake.

When you invest, you must assess not only the individual stock's financial health and prospects but also consider the broader context in which it operates. This means taking a close look at the performance and outlook of its industry and sector. A company may have strong fundamentals and be well-managed, but if its industry is facing challenges or in a decline, it can be dragged down along with the rest of the sector. A company in a healthy and growing industry might benefit even if its own fundamentals are not as strong. By evaluating a stock within the framework of its sector and industry group, you can make more informed investment decisions, anticipate trends, and position yourself strategically in the market.

TIMING

Stocks should be bought after thorough evaluation of their fundamentals. However, after a decision has been made, additional factors should be considered from a timing perspective, which are discussed in this section.

Do Not Wait for the Perfect Scenario

It is common for some investors to fall into the trap of waiting for the "perfect" scenario before making any investment decisions. They want to minimize every possible risk and uncertainty, which leads to a prolonged state of inaction. The quest for a flawless set of circumstances is essentially a futile one in the dynamic and unpredictable world of stock market investing. The perfect alignment of market conditions, individual stock prospects, and economic factors is more of a fantasy than a reality.

Recognizing that the ideal scenario will never manifest, it is crucial to understand that all investment decisions entail a degree of ambiguity and imperfection. It is the ability to make informed decisions under less-than-ideal conditions that sets successful investors apart. Waiting endlessly for the perfect moment can result in missed opportunities and capital that remains uninvested. Investors should learn to embrace a level of calculated risk and uncertainty while maintaining a strategic and well-researched approach to stock market investing. In essence, the key is to act with prudence and adaptability, not inactivity based on the elusive goal of perfection.

Do Not Try to Time the Market

Attempting to time the market is a challenging and often futile endeavor that investors should avoid. While some investors may achieve short-term success with market-timing strategies, it is exceptionally challenging to consistently time the market with a high degree of accuracy. Market dynamics are influenced by a multitude of factors, many of which can be unpredictable, and they change over time. A timing strategy that works effectively under specific market conditions may not perform as expected when market dynamics shift, which they inevitably do in the dynamic world of stock market investing.

Market timing based on perceived market "highs" and "lows" is a strategy fraught with risk and uncertainty. It is common for investors who engage in market-timing to fall into the trap of buying at market peaks and selling at market troughs, often resulting in poor returns. Instead of attempting to time the market, a more prudent approach is to focus on long-term investing, portfolio diversification, and sound fundamental analysis. These strategies are likely to lead to more consistent and successful outcomes over time, without the anxiety and pitfalls associated with market-timing efforts.

Do Not Avoid Averaging Up

Dollar-cost averaging is a strategy that can be employed in two directions, averaging up or down. While many investors are comfortable with averaging down, where they acquire more shares of a stock when its price declines, they are often reluctant to average up. The common belief is that a stock that has already appreciated is less likely to continue its upward trajectory, leading investors to wait for a price decline. This approach may cause investors to miss out on the potential for further gains in strong-performing stocks. Instead of dwelling on where the stock has been historically, it is essential to focus on its future potential. If sound fundamental analysis and market conditions support the belief that the stock is likely to continue rising, it may be a good decision to average up when the opportunity arises.

Averaging up should not be ruled out simply because a stock's price has already appreciated. Rather, investors should assess the stock's future growth prospects and investment potential. If the fundamentals remain strong and there's a reasonable expectation of continued growth, averaging up can be a strategic move that maximizes returns, allowing investors to capture further gains and participate in the success of a high-performing stock. This approach highlights the importance of making investment decisions based on a stock's potential for future price appreciation, rather than dwelling solely on past performance.

Do Not Ignore the Market's Seasonal Factors

The stock market, like many aspects of the economy and individual companies, is influenced by seasonal factors that can have a significant impact on investment decisions. Recognizing these seasonal patterns is essential for investors. For instance, understanding that summer tends to be a slower season for semiconductor companies or that January historically is a strong month for small stocks can help investors make informed decisions. In addition, it is crucial to be aware of events like window dressing at the end of each quarter, which can lead to increased volatility as portfolio managers adjust their holdings. This practice can affect stock prices as managers sell underperforming stocks and invest in recently outperforming ones. Investors should take these seasonal factors into consideration when managing their portfolios and be cautious about making major changes during strong seasonal periods.

While it is important not to overemphasize the significance of seasonal factors, ignoring them can be equally detrimental. Seasonal patterns can offer valuable insights into potential market trends and economic conditions, helping investors make more informed choices about buying or selling stocks. By staying informed about how the market responds to different seasons and understanding the impact on various sectors, investors can develop more effective strategies and avoid making impulsive decisions based on seasonal fluctuations.

Take Advantage of Cyclical Stocks' Movements

Cyclical stocks, which are highly sensitive to economic cycles, can offer significant opportunities for investors who understand their movements and can time their investments strategically. These companies, like Caterpillar and International Paper, tend to thrive during economic expansions, as increased economic activity leads to higher earnings. On the flip side, during economic contractions, these stocks often experience a sharp decline in earnings. Therefore, it is important for investors to recognize the cyclical nature of these companies and adjust their portfolios accordingly.

During periods of economic slowdown or recession, investors should consider reducing their exposure to cyclical stocks to minimize risk. When the economy begins to rebound, cyclical stocks tend to outperform, making them attractive investment opportunities. Timing is crucial when dealing with cyclical stocks, and astute investors can take advantage of their potential for growth during periods of economic expansion while being cautious during downturns. By carefully monitoring the economic cycle and the performance of cyclical stocks, investors can optimize their portfolios.

PSYCHOLOGY

Along with fundamentals, emotions drive the behavior of stocks. However, many investors make some common mistakes because they do not understand the role of psychology in the stock market, which is discussed in this section.

Do Not Be Overawed by Wall Street Professionals

Overcoming the perception that Wall Street professionals hold an insurmountable advantage in the stock market is crucial for individual investors. While it is true that professionals have access to extensive resources and research tools, individual investors can still achieve success by following fundamental investment principles. Confidence in your own abilities and a commitment to learning can be powerful assets in the stock market. Additionally, it is important to recognize that many individual investors have outperformed professional money managers, highlighting the potential for individual success.

Investors should focus on conducting their own research, selecting stocks based on thorough analysis, and approaching stock recommendations from professionals with caution. While it can be informative to consider expert opinions, it is essential to make investment decisions independently, guided by your own strategy and analysis. With the right approach, individual investors can successfully navigate the stock market and achieve their financial goals without being overawed by Wall Street professionals.

Do Not Confuse the Company With the Stock

A critical distinction in stock market investing is understanding that a good company does not automatically equate to a good stock. Investors frequently fall into the trap of assuming that well-known, reputable companies are surefire investments, regardless of the stock's current conditions. They often make the mistake of buying stocks from these companies based on their reputation or familiarity, disregarding the possibility that even a great company's stock can underperform or decline if it's overvalued or if the business prospects take a negative turn due to unpublicized factors.

To be a successful investor, it is essential to base your investment decisions on clear criteria and focus on evaluating the current and potential value of a company's shares, rather than solely relying on its historical performance or brand recognition. By keeping the distinction between the company and the stock in mind, investors can make more informed decisions and avoid falling into the trap of assuming that all strong companies will necessarily result in strong stock investments.

Never Get Attached to a Stock

Your primary goal as an investor is to generate profits, and it is important to remember that investing in stocks is not a long-term relationship; it is a financial transaction with the objective of achieving gains. Whether you hold a stock for a few months or several years, your connection with it should always be analytical and goal-oriented. When investing in stocks, you must establish clear objectives, and your decision to keep or sell a stock should be based on those objectives. It is crucial to approach each stock investment with an analytical and clinical mindset, devoid of emotional attachment, which can cloud your judgment and hinder your ability to make rational decisions.

Getting emotionally attached to a stock is a common pitfall for investors. This attachment can lead to biases, poor decision-making, and a reluctance to let go when it is in your best financial interest to do so. To succeed in stock market investing, it is vital to remain disciplined, follow your predetermined criteria and objectives, and not let emotions get in the way of making logical investment decisions.

Do Not Be Impatient

Investing in the stock market is fundamentally a long-term endeavor. The idea is to select strong and profitable businesses that have the potential for long-term growth and appreciate over a period of several years. During this investment horizon, it is inevitable that you will encounter challenges, market fluctuations, and obstacles along the way. Successful investing requires patience and a long-term perspective to allow your investments to flourish and grow. Nevertheless, many investors seek quick and immediate returns, making them more reactive to short-term events. This impatience can lead to hasty decisions and may prevent investors from fully capitalizing on the wealth-building potential of the stock market. Therefore, it is essential to recognize that stock market investing demands patience, and you should only engage in it if you have the temperament and mindset to endure the necessary time horizon.

As an investor, it is crucial to acknowledge that the stock market, like any other investment, has its cycles and fluctuations. Instead of reacting emotionally to these short-term changes, patient investors maintain a long-term focus and understand that the overall growth and performance of their investments will outweigh short-term volatility. Being patient not only allows your investments to ride out market volatility but also provides the opportunity to benefit from the compounding effect, which can lead to significant wealth accumulation over time. If you do not possess the necessary patience for stock market investing, it is important to reevaluate your investment approach and possibly consider alternatives that better align with your financial goals and time horizon.

Do Not Get Carried Away By Stock Splits

It is essential for ordinary investors not to be overly influenced by stock splits. While stock splits can generate excitement, their long-term impact on a stock's performance remains a subject of debate. What a stock split essentially accomplishes is an increase in the number of shares and a reduction in the stock's price, which may attract investors who prefer lower-priced shares. For instance, a two-for-one stock split of a $100 stock with four hundred shares will lead to the stock's price being halved to $50, while the number of shares doubles to eight hundred. Regardless of these numbers, the total investment remains at $40,000. It is important to recognize that the true driver of a stock's performance is its fundamental strength and growth prospects, not the number of shares or the stock's price.

Investors should understand that stock splits do not fundamentally alter the intrinsic value or financial health of a company. The same company with the same assets, earnings, and growth potential exists both before and after a split. Stock splits are merely a cosmetic adjustment, and while they can make shares appear more accessible to some investors, they do not change the underlying economic realities of the business. Therefore, investors should focus on the company's fundamentals, its competitive position, and its growth prospects when considering an investment, rather than getting carried away by the superficial appeal of stock splits.

SPECULATION

At times, speculation drives the stock market and/or individual stocks, which can lead to unpredictable and unsustainable stock price action. However, many investors do not know how to avoid the mistakes due to speculation, which are discussed in this section.

Do Not Speculate

Engaging in speculation poses a considerable risk for investors, as it entails making bets on price movements without a solid foundation of research and analysis. This lack of a robust strategy can lead to substantial financial losses, especially when market movements don't align with speculative predictions. To navigate these risks successfully, investors are advised to adhere to a disciplined approach rooted in fundamental analysis and long-term investing principles. This involves carefully evaluating a company's financial health, industry trends, and other relevant factors before making investment decisions.

Relying on speculation can be likened to gambling in the financial markets, introducing a high level of uncertainty and unpredictability.

Investors seeking consistent and reasonable profits are better served by adopting a more strategic and informed approach. By focusing on fundamental analysis, which involves assessing a company's intrinsic value and growth prospects, and adopting a long-term investment horizon, individuals can build a more resilient and sustainable investment portfolio. This approach provides a solid foundation for weathering market fluctuations and achieving financial goals over the long run.

Do Not Buy Penny Stocks

Penny stocks are typically not a suitable choice for the majority of investors due to their inherent risks and speculative nature. High-quality stocks from established companies are more transparent and well-researched, making them a safer investment. Penny stocks often lack adequate research materials and information, making it challenging for investors to conduct thorough due diligence. This limited information can increase the uncertainty associated with penny stocks, making them a riskier option.

Penny stocks also tend to have lower liquidity and higher trading commissions as a percentage of the total buying cost, which can erode potential gains and increase transaction costs. These factors make them less attractive from a trading perspective, particularly for investors seeking consistent and reliable long-term returns. Therefore, for most investors, focusing on stocks from reputable, well-established companies with share prices above $20 is a more prudent and less risky approach to building a diversified and balanced investment portfolio.

Do Not Believe Message Boards

Online message boards can be a double-edged sword for investors, and it is essential to approach them with caution. While there may be a few valuable insights and informed discussions on these platforms, the vast majority of posts are often filled with misinformation, rumors, uninformed, and biased opinions. Message boards attract a wide range of participants, including novices, speculators, and those with personal agendas, and it's often challenging to distinguish between credible information and baseless claims. This can make them a less reliable source of investment advice and decision-making.

One common issue with message boards is that many contributors may have hidden agendas. Some may aim to manipulate stock prices or promote certain stocks for personal gain, while others may simply vent their frustrations or share unsubstantiated rumors. For these reasons, investors should approach online message boards with skepticism and rely on thorough research and analysis from credible sources when making their investment decisions.

MISCELLANEOUS

There are additional common mistakes that many investors tend to make. These mistakes, which can impact their portfolios in a significant way and cause avoidable losses, are discussed in this section.

Do Not Fight the Trend

The old saying "the trend is your friend" underscores the importance of aligning your investment strategy with the prevailing market trend. Attempting to swim against the current can be a perilous endeavor in the stock market. It is essential to recognize that market trends are driven by the collective sentiment and actions of countless investors, and these trends often persist for extended periods. Instead of trying to predict or counteract these trends, prudent investors acknowledge their presence and seek to capitalize on them.

For instance, when you identify a strong and sustained market uptrend, it is generally a favorable time to invest in equities. Conversely, during a prolonged downtrend, it is wise to exercise caution and potentially reduce your equity exposure. Being attuned to market trends and adjusting your investment strategy accordingly can significantly enhance your prospects for success in the stock market, and it aligns with the fundamental principle of "going with the flow" to make profitable investment decisions.

Never Fight the Fed

The Federal Reserve's influence on the stock market, particularly through its management of short-term interest rates, is significant. As the central bank of the United States, the Federal Reserve plays a pivotal role in maintaining economic stability and controlling inflation. Changes in short-term interest rates, particularly the federal funds rate, have a ripple effect throughout the financial markets and the broader economy. It is critical for investors to understand that the level and direction of interest rates can significantly impact the stock market's performance.

When the Federal Reserve raises interest rates to combat inflation, it tends to put downward pressure on stock prices, as borrowing costs increase for businesses and consumers. Conversely, when the Fed lowers interest rates to stimulate economic growth or address financial crises, stocks often respond positively, as lower interest rates can boost corporate profits and investor sentiment. Investors who closely monitor the Federal Reserve's policies and the associated interest rate trends are better equipped to position their portfolios in alignment with these influential market dynamics, allowing them to make more informed investment decisions that complement, rather than oppose, the Fed's actions.

Do Not Focus on the Number of Shares

Focusing solely on the number of shares rather than the dollar amount invested is a common psychological bias that investors should be aware of and overcome. When investors favor low-priced, cheap stocks with the aim of acquiring more shares or round lots (usually in multiples of 100 shares), they often overlook the more important aspect of investment: the potential return on their capital. The reality is that the percentage price appreciation or depreciation of a stock is not determined by the number of shares one owns, but rather by the performance of the stock based on the total amount invested.

Investors should think in terms of the dollar amount they are committing to a particular investment. In essence, the goal is not to maximize the number of shares but to optimize the return on investment. A high-priced quality stock may have a higher potential for growth, and by focusing on the dollar amount invested, investors can benefit from the capital appreciation of such stocks, which could result in substantial gains. Instead of chasing cheap stocks with lower prices, investors should prioritize the quality of the investment and the potential for positive returns on their capital. By considering the dollar amount and the quality of the investment, investors can position themselves to capture opportunities for significant growth and financial success.

Do Not Use Flawed Logic

Investors often use flawed logic when justifying their decisions to buy beaten-down stocks that have declined into the single-digit price range. Two common points are frequently cited in defense of this approach. First, they assert that the stock has hit its bottom, suggesting that it is an opportune time to buy. With that said, it's important to remember that determining the precise bottom of a stock is highly uncertain, and it is only truly known when a stock reaches a value of zero, which may not be the case for every struggling company. Second, they make the claim that buying a $5 stock limits their potential loss to a maximum of $5, implying a small risk. A more accurate perspective considers such a decline as a 100% loss rather than a minor one, as the initial investment has been entirely eroded.

It is crucial for investors to avoid such flawed logic and take a more rational approach when evaluating investment opportunities. Rather than relying on uncertain bottom-picking strategies, it is advisable to conduct thorough research and analysis to assess whether a stock represents a sound investment with the potential for positive returns. Making investment decisions based on solid fundamentals, future prospects, and risk management strategies will lead to more informed and responsible choices, ultimately enhancing the potential for long-term success in the stock market.

Do Not Make Dividends the Primary Objective

Investors should not become overly fixated on dividends as the primary objective in stock investing. The key focus should be on achieving price appreciation, rather than solely seeking a high yield. While dividends can provide a steady income stream, it is crucial to avoid buying a stock solely because it pays dividends. It is important to recognize that, while you may receive dividend payments, a struggling stock may potentially experience a significant decline, in percentage terms, that outweighs the dividend income. In this context, a 5% dividend yield cannot adequately compensate for a 10% price decline.

Furthermore, investors should be cautious of stocks with cloudy future prospects, even if they provide a consistent dividend. The risk of dividend reduction or elimination should not be ignored. Sound investment decisions should prioritize a thorough assessment of a stock's overall health and future potential, rather than being solely influenced by dividend income. In the end, price appreciation and the overall performance of the stock remain the primary objectives for successful investing.

Do Not Favor Timing Over Selection

In the realm of stock market activities, one must make a fundamental choice between adopting an investor's perspective or embracing the role of a trader. For the majority of individuals seeking to build wealth through the stock market, the path to success is rooted in long-term investing, where the focus is on acquiring and holding investments over an extended period. Long-term investors prioritize the process of selection, as it plays a pivotal role in determining the quality of their portfolio. The key is to identify and acquire high-quality assets with the potential for long-term growth.

Alternately, traders operate with a distinct mindset and a shorter investment horizon. Their approach places greater emphasis on timing, as quick and strategic entry and exit points are crucial for short-term trading success. Timing is a paramount concern for traders, who need to be precise in their execution to maximize profits within their defined time frame. Therefore, it is important to recognize that the approach to timing and selection varies based on whether one assumes the role of an investor or a trader, and this choice will significantly impact the investment strategy employed.

Do Not Let the Spread Eat Into Your Profits

Understanding and managing the spread, the difference between the bid and ask prices for a stock, is crucial for any investor or trader. Spreads can vary significantly among different stocks and are especially pronounced for small-capitalized and thinly traded companies. These large spreads can negatively impact the stock's overall price, liquidity, and trading pattern. It is essential for both buyers and sellers, particularly for traders who seek to capitalize on short-term price movements, to take into consideration the spread and its potential impact on their profits.

To mitigate the effect of a large spread on your trades, one strategy is to use limit orders rather than market orders. A limit order allows you to specify the price at which you are willing to buy or sell a stock, ensuring you get the desired price if the order is executed. While this approach can help you secure a better price, it may reduce the likelihood of your order being filled. It is a valuable tool for investors who want to be more precise in their trading and avoid having the spread eat into their profits.

Do Not Be Over Leveraged

Leveraging stocks by using them as collateral with a broker to magnify potential gains can be tempting for investors looking to amplify their returns. While this strategy can indeed double profits if the stock price rises, it is essential to be aware of the significant risks involved. One of the key drawbacks of leveraging is that it can lead to amplified losses in the event the stock price declines. This downside is especially relevant in a volatile market where price fluctuations can be substantial.

Furthermore, when an investor uses margin to leverage their investments, they are essentially borrowing money from the broker. This borrowed capital incurs interest, which can erode the potential gains or exacerbate the losses. Additionally, brokers can issue margin calls during a down market, demanding that the investor deposit more capital to cover potential losses or face the liquidation of their positions. For most investors, especially those looking for a relatively lower level of risk, it Is advisable to avoid using margin and remain cautious of overleveraging, as it can significantly increase the risk in the stock market.

17

Risk Management

RISKS

Investors should be aware that mistakes in the stock market, which are discussed in this section, can pose significant risks to their financial portfolios.

Be Aware of Risks Facing Stocks

Stock market investing carries a variety of risks that can affect investments in different ways. Understanding and assessing these risks is a crucial part of formulating a sound investment strategy. The various sources of risk in the stock market include market risk, inflation risk, interest rate risk, business risk, liquidity risk, currency risk, and specific risks.

Market risk, also known as systematic risk, stems from broad economic and market conditions and can impact the entire market or a particular sector. Investors need to consider how their investments will fare in various market scenarios, including bull markets and bear markets. Inflation risk pertains to the erosion of the purchasing power of money over time due to rising prices. Investments that fail to keep pace with inflation may not provide real returns for investors. Interest rate risk arises from changes in interest rates, which can affect bond and interest-sensitive stocks.

Business risk is associated with a company's internal operations and industry-specific factors, such as competition and regulatory changes. Liquidity risk relates to an investor's ability to buy or sell assets in the market without significantly affecting the asset's price. Currency risk is prevalent in international investing and can result from fluctuations in exchange rates. Specific risks are unique to individual stocks and can include events such as management changes, product recalls, or legal issues. Understanding and managing these risks is essential for making informed investment decisions.

Determine Your Risk Tolerance

Evaluating your risk tolerance is a fundamental step in the investment process. It involves a careful examination of your financial situation, investment goals, and psychological disposition toward risk. Your risk tolerance is influenced by factors such as your age, financial resources, investment time horizon, and personal comfort with market volatility. Younger investors with a longer investment horizon may typically have a higher risk tolerance, as they have more time to recover from potential losses. Conversely, older investors nearing retirement may have a lower risk tolerance as they prioritize capital preservation and income generation.

To determine your risk tolerance, you should consider your financial objectives, including your desired rate of return and acceptable level of risk. For example, if you have a specific goal of achieving a 10% annualized return and are comfortable with the associated level of risk, you can select investments that align with this objective. It is essential to be realistic about your tolerance for potential losses and select investments that align with your long-term financial goals while also ensuring that you can sleep well at night without excessive worry about market fluctuations. By defining your risk tolerance, you can create an investment strategy that matches your personal and financial objectives.

Market Risk

Market risk, often referred to as systematic risk, is a fundamental consideration when investing in stocks. The broader market's behavior can significantly impact individual stocks, and this risk can manifest in various ways. During market corrections or bear markets, the risk to stocks, even those with strong fundamentals, increases substantially. In such conditions, the sentiment of market participants, macroeconomic factors, and global events can overshadow a company's performance. As a result, even the best-performing stocks can suffer substantial declines in a bearish market environment. It is crucial to recognize that no stock is entirely immune to the market's influence, making it essential for investors to closely monitor market conditions and their potential impact on their stock holdings.

Being vigilant about market risk involves keeping a watchful eye on market indicators, economic trends, and geopolitical events that could affect overall market sentiment. Understanding the broader market's behavior and potential trends can help investors make more informed decisions and adjust their portfolio strategy when necessary. By assessing market risk, you can position your investments to align with your risk tolerance and financial objectives, mitigating the impact of market downturns on your stock holdings.

Risk Due to Inflation

Inflation risk is a critical factor that investors should consider when participating in the stock market. Rising inflation leads to an increase in the prices of goods and services, eroding the purchasing power of consumers. This reduction in real income can have adverse effects on stock investments, as investors may perceive stocks as less attractive when inflation erodes their returns. Inflation can lead to higher costs of living and can negatively affect stock investments, which are often considered a hedge against inflation. During times of high inflation, the real return on investments may decrease, and stocks may face competition from alternative investments, such as bonds, which can put downward pressure on the stock market. Therefore, investors must remain vigilant about the impact of inflation on their stock investments, as rising inflation levels can increase the risks associated with stocks. During periods of low or manageable inflation, stock investments may carry lower risk, potentially leading to higher returns.

To address inflation risk, investors can explore different strategies such as diversification or investing in assets that historically perform well during inflationary periods, like certain commodities or inflation-protected securities. By proactively considering and managing inflation risk, investors can make more informed decisions about their stock investments and align their portfolio strategy with their financial goals and risk tolerance.

Risk Due to Unfavorable Interest Rates

Unfavorable interest rates can exert a significant influence on the stock market and individual stock performances. When interest rates are on the rise, they can make alternative investments, particularly bonds, more appealing than stocks. This change in investor preferences can have a negative impact on the stock market's overall performance. Furthermore, rising interest rates can also affect the profitability of companies because their borrowing costs increase, leading to potential earnings declines and subsequent stock market declines.

Specific sectors within the stock market may be more sensitive to interest rate fluctuations due to their borrowing needs. For example, sectors with higher borrowing requirements, such as banks and utilities, are more directly influenced by interest rate changes, causing their stock prices to move in tandem with shifts in interest rates. In contrast, growth stocks or companies with lower borrowing needs tend to be less sensitive to interest rate changes. It is important for investors to remain vigilant and monitor interest rates as well as the factors driving them. Assessing interest rate risk on a sector and individual stock level is crucial to making informed investment decisions, adjusting portfolios, and managing exposure to interest rate-related risks.

Risk From the Business

Business risks are an inherent part of the stock market and are contingent upon the performance and stability of individual companies. These risks can stem from various sources, both external and internal, and can manifest as obsolescence of products and services, competitive pressures, ineffective strategies or execution, unresponsiveness to customer needs, poor management, and more. It is essential for investors to carefully evaluate and understand these business risks, as they can significantly impact the performance and stability of an investment.

One way to mitigate business risks is to invest in companies and sectors that you are knowledgeable about and understand well. Having a strong grasp of the companies you are investing in enables you to better assess and manage associated risks. For instance, if you prefer a more hands-off approach to your investments, it is advisable to avoid investing in companies with a single product and a short product cycle, as these businesses are susceptible to rapid changes in fortunes, leading to elevated levels of risk exposure. By aligning your investments with your expertise and risk tolerance, you can make more informed decisions and navigate the stock market with greater confidence.

Risk From Company Performance

Stock performance is subject to a complex interplay of factors, encompassing the broader stock market, the specific industry or sector it belongs to, and the company's own performance. As an investor, you can diligently choose solid companies operating within robust sectors. The inherent risk is that even a well-researched investment may underperform due to the company's failure to meet expectations.

To mitigate this risk, diversification is a key strategy. By spreading your investments across a broad spectrum of companies, sectors, and industries, you create a protective buffer. This diversification ensures that a subpar performance by one or two companies will not jeopardize your entire portfolio. This risk management strategy allows you to weather the volatility of individual stock performances while benefiting from the potential growth of a well-diversified portfolio.

Risk of Growth Stocks

Investing in growth stocks carries a distinct set of risks. Growth companies, often in their early stages, lack the extensive performance history that established firms have, making their evaluation more challenging. Smaller companies, known for their higher-than-average growth rates relative to the broader market, are inherently riskier. In the event of failing to meet investor expectations, they are vulnerable to severe market reactions, with the potential to lose a substantial portion of their value in a single day. Due to these inherent risks, it is crucial to exercise caution and thorough assessment when considering investments in growth stocks. Moreover, investors should limit their allocations to these companies to avoid excessive exposure.

Selecting growth stocks requires careful analysis and research, including a comprehensive evaluation of the company's fundamentals, competitive positioning, growth potential, and management quality. Additionally, diversification within your portfolio can help manage the inherent volatility associated with growth stocks. By investing only a portion of your funds in these high-risk, high-reward opportunities, you can strike a balance between potential returns and risk mitigation.

Other Risks

Investors should be aware of a variety of other risks that can impact their investments. Liquidity risk is one such concern, where a stock may lack sufficient trading volume or float, leading to erratic price swings or difficulties in selling the stock during a market downturn. Mitigating this risk can be achieved by selecting stocks that are highly liquid and have substantial trading volumes, ensuring smoother market participation.

Currency risk is another important consideration for investors. Fluctuations in exchange rates can significantly affect the value of your investments, especially if a stock derives a substantial portion of its business revenue from overseas operations. While currency risk is difficult to control, investors can limit their exposure to it by favoring stocks that are less dependent on international revenues or by using hedging strategies to offset potential currency fluctuations. By assessing these risks and implementing appropriate strategies, investors can make more informed decisions and manage their investments more effectively.

Managing Risk

Managing stock market risk is a critical part of successful investing. While risk cannot be completely eliminated, there are strategies to mitigate it. One key approach is investing for the long term, as time tends to have a moderating effect on stock market risk. Short-term market fluctuations can be volatile, but long-term investors have historically seen more stable returns.

Diversification is another important risk management technique. Spreading investments across a range of stocks, sectors, and industries can reduce the impact of any single stock's poor performance on your overall portfolio. Overdiversification should be avoided, as it can lead to subpar returns. Investing in companies based on thorough fundamental research and analysis is also essential for reducing risk. By focusing on companies with strong financials and promising growth prospects, investors can make more informed decisions. Last, staying informed and making calculated moves based on research, rather than reacting impulsively to market events, can help reduce risk and improve your chances of success in the stock market.

VOLATILITY AND RISK

The stock market is characterized by volatility and many risks, which are discussed in this section. To avoid losses, investors should be aware of these factors which can impact their individual stocks as well as the market.

Understanding Price Fluctuations

Price fluctuations in the stock market are a common and inherent part of its dynamic nature. These fluctuations occur at various time scales, ranging from daily, hourly, and even on a minute-by-minute basis. They are influenced by a multitude of factors, with changes in investor perceptions playing a central role. Positive news, such as strong corporate earnings or favorable economic indicators, tends to drive stock prices higher, while negative news can have the opposite effect.

Investors and traders use the term volatility to describe the degree of these price fluctuations. High volatility indicates that stock prices are experiencing rapid and significant changes, whether upward or downward. While short-term traders often thrive on volatility, long-term investors may not be as concerned with short-term price swings. Understanding the reasons behind these fluctuations and the role of investor sentiment can help investors make more informed decisions, whether they are actively trading or taking a long-term approach.

Do Not Confuse Volatility With Risk

It is important for investors to distinguish between volatility and risk. While these terms are often used interchangeably, they have distinct meanings in the context of investing. Risk refers to the potential danger that an investment may lose its value, posing a threat to an investor's capital. Volatility, however, pertains to the short-term price fluctuations of an investment, which can sometimes be quite substantial.

Many investors equate volatility with risk, believing that if a stock experiences significant short-term price swings, it must be risky. This is not always the case. Growth stocks, for instance, tend to have above average volatility because of their potential for rapid growth and market sentiment shifts. While some volatile stocks can be risky, it is essential to focus on the long-term prospects of a company. Volatility can provide opportunities for investors, and stocks that experience short-term price fluctuations might still have strong fundamentals and growth potential in the long run. If an investor's temperament is not suited to handling volatility, they may choose to avoid highly volatile stocks and focus on more stable investments.

Assess Risk Tolerance

The level of risk associated with an investment can vary significantly based on the type of investment and the specific stock in question. Generally, bonds and fixed-income securities are considered to be less risky compared to stocks. Within the stock market, there is a risk spectrum, with large capitalization and blue-chip companies typically being more stable and less risky than smaller, less established companies. Investors generally expect a higher rate of return when they take on higher levels of risk. This expected return, often referred to as the risk premium, can vary from one investor to another based on their individual risk tolerance, investment goals, and market conditions. For stock investments, investors typically demand a higher return to compensate for the risk associated with the potential volatility in earnings compared to government-backed instruments like bonds. This premium is often estimated to be approximately 4%, although it may fluctuate over time.

Investors need to carefully assess their risk tolerance, understanding how much risk they are willing to accept to achieve their financial objectives. It is essential to align one's investment strategy with their risk tolerance, as investing too conservatively may result in insufficient returns, while taking on too much risk can lead to substantial losses. Diversifying a portfolio by including different types of assets and investments can help mitigate risk and provide a more balanced approach to achieving long-term financial goals.

Measuring Volatility

Measuring volatility is a critical step in assessing investment risk, especially for stocks. The level of risk associated with a particular stock can vary significantly based on its characteristics and market conditions. To quantify this risk and understand the expected price fluctuations, investors often rely on a financial metric known as beta. Beta measures the price volatility of a specific stock in comparison to a broad market benchmark, such as the S&P 500 index. It provides valuable insights into how much a stock's price can be expected to move, either upward or downward, in relation to the overall market.

When evaluating stocks, a higher beta suggests that the stock has a higher degree of price volatility and risk, making it suitable for investors who are comfortable with large price swings and are willing to take on more risk. Conversely, stocks with lower beta values are characterized by less price volatility and risk, making them a preferred choice for conservative investors who seek more stability in their investments. By considering a stock's beta, investors can align their investment choices with their risk tolerance and overall financial goals, ensuring that their portfolio is well-suited to their individual preferences and circumstances.

Which Beta to Use

When using beta to assess investment risk, it is essential to consider your individual risk profile and investment objectives. The S&P 500 index serves as the benchmark with a beta value of 1, representing a baseline level of price volatility and risk. Stocks are compared to this index, and their beta values indicate how much more or less volatile they are compared to the S&P 500. For instance, a stock with a beta of 1.5 is anticipated to be 50% more volatile than the S&P 500. So, if the S&P 500 moves up or down by 15%, this stock would be expected to move by 30% in the same direction.

Conversely, a stock with a beta of 0.5 is considered to be half as volatile as the S&P 500, resulting in a more stable price performance. When selecting stocks, it is important to align the stock's beta with your personal risk tolerance and investment goals. If you are risk averse, you may prefer to invest in low beta stocks, which offer greater stability. If you are comfortable with taking on higher risk, you may opt for technology or growth stocks with high beta values, knowing they have the potential for greater price volatility and returns. Your choice of beta should be in line with your overall investment strategy and risk appetite.

Do Not Use Beta for Timing

Using beta for timing can be a risky strategy. It relies on the assumption that the market's direction can be accurately predicted, which is a challenging and uncertain endeavor. Attempting to time the market based on beta values involves switching between high and low beta stocks in response to market conditions. For example, during a rising market, investors might favor high beta stocks to potentially outperform the market, and during a declining market, they may opt for low beta stocks. This approach is not only based on the unpredictable movement of the market but also requires timely and accurate decision-making, which can be difficult to achieve.

Instead of using beta for market timing, it is generally advisable for long-term investors to focus on their overall investment strategy and objectives. Trying to time the market can result in missed opportunities, higher transaction costs, and increased risk. It is often more prudent to invest in a diversified portfolio that aligns with your risk tolerance and long-term financial goals rather than constantly adjusting your investments based on market timing strategies.

Favor Volatility Over Margin

Investing in high volatility stocks can indeed offer the potential for above average returns while still maintaining control over your investment risk. When compared to using margin, high volatility stocks may provide a more prudent way to take on higher risk. One crucial advantage of investing in high volatility stocks is that it allows you to maintain direct ownership of the shares without borrowing money or incurring interest charges, as is the case with margin investing. This means that even if the stock experiences significant fluctuations, your losses are limited to your initial investment.

Contrastingly, using margin to amplify your positions exposes you to the risk of significant losses that can go beyond your initial investment. With margin trading, you are effectively borrowing funds from your broker, and you will be responsible for paying back those borrowed funds, along with any associated interest charges. If the market moves against you, the losses can accumulate rapidly, potentially resulting in financial distress or a margin call. In this sense, high volatility stocks may offer a more controlled approach to taking on additional risk in your portfolio without the added complexity and potential financial burden of margin trading. Always keep in mind that it is crucial to carefully research and understand the high volatility stocks you choose to invest in, as they can still carry substantial risks.

MINIMIZING TRADING RISKS

There are many risks associated with trading stocks, discussed in this section, which can be avoided or minimized by knowledgeable investors.

Limit Your Losses

Setting a predetermined threshold for selling your stocks is a crucial part of effective risk management and capital preservation. By implementing a stop-loss rule, such as a 10% decline limit, you create a disciplined approach to limiting losses in your portfolio. This practice helps prevent emotions from clouding your judgment, allowing you to make rational decisions based on your predetermined criteria. The psychological aspect of selling is often a significant challenge for investors, as they may become emotionally attached to their investments or hope that the stock will rebound. A stop-loss rule provides an objective guideline, reducing the risk of incurring larger losses due to delayed decision-making.

Additionally, employing a stop-loss strategy can help protect your overall portfolio and minimize the impact of a significant decline in any single stock. By adhering to this rule, you can swiftly exit losing positions, freeing up capital that can be reallocated to better investment opportunities. In this way, you maintain flexibility in managing your portfolio, allowing you to adjust your holdings and take advantage of more promising investments. Overall, having a clear-cut stop-loss strategy is a valuable tool for maintaining discipline, controlling risk, and preserving your investment capital.

Make Use of Stops

Utilizing stop sell orders is an essential practice for risk management and protecting your investment capital. These orders act as a safety net to automatically trigger a sell when the stock's price declines to a predefined level. By placing a stop sell order below your purchase price, such as at $90 when the stock is trading at $100, you create a safeguard against significant losses. This proactive approach ensures that if the stock experiences a decline, you can limit your losses by selling your position at the predetermined stop price. It allows you to set a threshold based on your risk tolerance at approximately 8%–15% below the purchase price, although the exact level may vary based on the stock's volatility and your investment strategy.

One significant advantage of using moving averages, such as the 200-day or 50-day moving average lines, as stop-loss limits is that they offer a dynamic approach to managing risk. These indicators help you align your stop-loss levels with the stock's price movements over time. This means that as the stock's performance evolves, your stop loss adapts accordingly. This flexibility can be particularly useful in different market conditions and with stocks that exhibit varying degrees of volatility. Overall, incorporating stop sell orders in your investment strategy is a prudent way to control risk, safeguard your capital, and ensure you have an exit plan in place to protect your investments.

Keep Cash Reserves

Maintaining cash reserves in your investment portfolio is a smart strategy that provides you with financial flexibility and risk mitigation. While it is essential to participate in the stock market to achieve your financial goals, having some funds on the sidelines can be advantageous, particularly during specific market conditions. The specific allocation of cash reserves varies according to factors like the market's current state, the volatility of your stocks, and the sector or industry conditions. Investors often set aside 5%–10% of their funds as cash reserves to be ready for opportunities when they arise.

These reserves act as a financial cushion, allowing you to capitalize on market corrections or individual stock opportunities. When the market or a specific stock experiences a downturn, you can utilize these funds to take advantage of discounted prices, thereby enhancing your long-term returns. While maintaining cash reserves might temporarily affect the overall portfolio return, the risk mitigation and strategic benefits they offer can significantly outweigh the drawbacks, providing you with the confidence to navigate various market conditions effectively.

Limit Exposure to Thinly Traded Stocks

Investors should exercise caution when considering stocks with limited liquidity, typically characterized by a small float or low daily trading volume, especially those with less than 200,000 shares. These thinly traded stocks pose higher risks, making them a less attractive option. There are two primary drawbacks associated with these stocks. First, they tend to exhibit higher volatility, resulting in more significant price swings and fluctuations that can lead to unexpected and potentially substantial losses. Secondly, the limited trading volume can make these stocks challenging to sell, particularly during market downturns.

In times of market panic or extreme volatility, it may be extremely difficult to execute sell orders for thinly traded stocks. In some cases, even regular or routine selling can be problematic, as there may not be sufficient demand or liquidity to accommodate your trade. This illiquidity risk highlights the importance of opting for stocks with more substantial trading volumes and greater market participation, ensuring that you have the flexibility to enter or exit positions as needed, thereby reducing your exposure to potential losses.

Avoid Short Selling

Short selling is a high-risk strategy where investors borrow and sell shares, speculating on a stock's decline to repurchase them later at a lower price for a profit. This approach, potentially lucrative but laden with risks, demands careful monitoring, strict risk management, and thorough analysis, making it challenging even for experienced investors. Theoretically, losses in short selling are unlimited if the stock's price rises unexpectedly, making it less suitable for those not well-versed in the stock market intricacies. Successful short selling requires a profound understanding of market dynamics and is often best left to seasoned professionals.

Despite potential profitability in a declining market, this strategy poses significant risks, particularly the potential for theoretically unlimited losses. Unlike traditional investing, where a stock's value can only drop to zero, short selling exposes investors to the risk of the stock's price rising without an upper limit. In such cases, short sellers may be compelled to buy back shares at a considerably higher cost, resulting in substantial financial losses.

Investigate Before Acting on Any Hot Tip

Hot tips can be tempting, but they should be approached with caution. It is essential to maintain a critical and analytical mindset when evaluating such tips. First and foremost, it is crucial to separate the source of the tip from the information itself. Sometimes, individuals sharing these tips might have ulterior motives or lack sufficient expertise. Once you've disassociated the tip from the tipster, you should conduct thorough research. Begin by examining the story or news that is said to make the stock "hot."

Your analysis should delve into the company's business operations, competitive positioning, financial fundamentals, earnings potential, industry conditions, and other pertinent factors. Apply the same rigorous screening and selection criteria that you would to any other investment opportunity. Only after conducting a comprehensive evaluation and concluding that the stock has genuine potential for future appreciation should you consider taking action. This approach helps you make informed decisions based on your investment criteria rather than blindly following hot tips that can often be unreliable or driven by short-term hype.

Learn How to Identify a Weakening Stock

Identifying a weakening stock is crucial for investors, as it allows them to proactively manage their portfolio and avoid potential losses. Several warning signs can help you recognize when a stock is weakening. One common sign is distribution, which occurs when a stock is heavily traded on days when its price declines and lightly traded on days when it rises. This asymmetrical trading pattern indicates a lack of buying interest and can be a red flag. Another indication of a weakening stock is when it experiences a rally back on below-average volume after a decline. This suggests that there might not be sufficient buying support for the stock to sustain its recovery.

Additionally, pay attention to a stock that does not move in sync with the broader market, especially on days when the market is rising. A stock that fails to participate in a market rally or even moves in the opposite direction may be signaling weakness. Watch out for signs like breakout failures, where a stock attempts to move higher after a consolidation phase but repeatedly fails to do so. This can be a clear signal of underlying weakness. To avoid getting caught in such situations, it is essential to closely monitor your stock for these warning signs. Keep an eye on the leaders in your stock's industry group, as their behavior can often serve as a leading indicator of your stock's future performance. Lastly, stay informed and vigilant about any early signs of weakening fundamentals, as they are often reflected in a stock's behavior and can help you make timely decisions to protect your investments.

Handle Red-Hot Stocks With the Greatest Care

Red-hot stocks that defy expectations by soaring to new heights can be a double-edged sword for investors. While they may seem like enticing opportunities, they come with substantial reward and risk. It is crucial to approach such stocks with great care and caution. The potential for both significant gains and significant losses is much higher than with typical stocks. Investing in these stocks requires a thoughtful and informed approach. Before considering an investment in a red-hot stock, it is essential to conduct a thorough analysis. Understand the underlying reasons for the stock's exceptional performance and determine whether the surge is sustainable or if it is merely a speculative bubble.

Unfortunately, many investors let their emotions drive their decisions and dive into such stocks without conducting proper due diligence. This impulsive behavior often leads to unfavorable outcomes. To avoid being burned by a red-hot stock, make sure you maintain a disciplined and analytical approach when evaluating these opportunities. Remember, when dealing with these exceptional cases the stakes are higher, and careful consideration is paramount.

Protect Yourself During a Blow-Off Move

During a blow-off move, a stock can exhibit remarkable price surges that seem unstoppable, often defying conventional expectations. These extraordinary rallies can propel a stock upward by 25%–50% within a very short time, or they may take it significantly above its 200-day moving average. While the potential for substantial profits is undeniable, these meteoric rises also carry a high level of risk. It is crucial to exercise extra caution if you hold such stocks in your portfolio, as they have a propensity to run out of momentum suddenly and undergo a rapid descent. These stocks typically offer warning signs that they are about to reverse course, such as closing near their daily lows, experiencing their largest price gain of the rally, failing to appreciate despite heavy trading volume, presenting an exhaustion gap, or reaching a new price high on substantially lower trading volume.

To protect yourself during a blow-off move, you can employ various strategies. One option is to sell a portion of your position to lock in profits, reducing your exposure to any potential downturn. Another approach is to use stop orders that are based on the stock's chart pattern. This way, you can establish predetermined exit points at which your stock will automatically be sold if it starts to decline. These measures help safeguard your investments and allow you to capitalize on the exceptional gains while managing the increased risk associated with stocks experiencing blow-off moves.

USE OPTIONS

This section discusses how options can be used to generate income, reduce the cost basis, and also the risks and rewards associated with call and put options.

Sell Call Options to Decrease the Cost Basis

When you own a stock that you intend to hold for an extended period, implementing a covered call strategy can be a useful technique to generate income while effectively reducing your overall cost basis in the stock. Covered call writing involves selling a call option, granting the option buyer the right, though not the obligation, to purchase the underlying stock from you at a pre-established price known as the strike price. As the seller of the call, you receive a premium from the option buyer, thereby enhancing your returns. The primary risk you face in this strategy is that the stock may appreciate significantly above the strike price, potentially forcing you to sell the stock.

By employing covered calls, you effectively decrease your cost basis in the stock, enabling you to acquire shares at a lower net cost compared to the initial purchase price. This strategy allows you to benefit from generating extra income from the premium received while still participating in the stock's potential price appreciation, all within a longer-term investment horizon. It is always important to consider your overall investment objectives and risk tolerance when implementing this approach to ensure it aligns with your financial goals.

Risks and Rewards of Call Options

Understanding the risks and rewards of call options is crucial for effective investment decision-making. When it comes to buying call options, it is essential to acknowledge the inherent risk involved. As an option buyer, you pay a premium for the right, but not the obligation, to purchase the underlying asset at a predetermined strike price before the option's expiration. The main risk is that if the price of the underlying asset does not reach the strike price by the option's expiration, you may lose your entire premium investment. Therefore, buying call options is speculative in nature and carries the potential for significant losses.

Contrarily, selling call options, particularly when you already own the underlying stock, involves different risks and rewards. The primary risk for call sellers is the opportunity cost of potentially missing out on additional profit if the stock's price appreciates beyond the strike price. Keep in mind you retain the premium received from the option buyer, which can act as a hedge against potential losses. By consistently selling call options over time, you can enhance your overall investment returns, particularly in markets with limited price movements. It is important to understand the trade-off between the potential opportunity cost of capping gains and the income generated from selling calls when implementing this strategy.

Risks and Rewards of Put Options

Understanding the risks and rewards of put options is essential for effective risk management in your investment strategy. When you buy a put option, you are essentially purchasing insurance against a potential decline in the stock's price. The put option provides you with the right, but not the obligation, to sell the underlying asset (in this case, a stock) at the predetermined strike price. This strategy is suitable for investors who anticipate a significant decline in the stock's value and want to protect their investment. The downside of buying put options is that it reduces the overall portfolio return because you are essentially paying for this insurance, which can be costly if the stock does not decline as expected.

Alternatively, if you are pessimistic about a stock's future and believe it may experience a substantial decline, an alternative to buying put options is to consider selling the stock. Selling the stock can be a more straightforward approach and may eliminate the need to pay premiums for put options. The choice between buying puts and selling the stock depends on your risk tolerance, your confidence in the stock's performance, and your overall investment objectives. It is crucial to carefully evaluate these factors and understand the trade-offs associated with each strategy to make an informed decision.

CHAPTER 18

AI IN STOCK INVESTING

AI EVOLUTION IN THE STOCK MARKET

The use of artificial intelligence (AI) in the stock market has revolutionized financial markets, from early algorithmic trading to advanced machine learning models. This section discusses its evolution and recent developments, which have influenced how the stock market operates.

History

The history of AI in the stock market is a narrative of continuous innovation and transformation, reshaping the landscape of financial markets and influencing the way investors approach trading and decision-making. This evolution spans several decades, witnessing key milestones in the application of AI technologies.

The initial forays into AI for finance emerged in the mid-twentieth century, marked by attempts to implement rule-based systems and algorithms for automated trading. It's important to note that computational limitations and the intricate nature of financial markets constrained the practicality of these early AI models. The 1980s saw the rise of expert systems, designed to emulate human decision-making processes in financial analysis. Despite providing some automation, these systems faced challenges due to their static rule-based nature and struggled to capture the dynamic complexities of financial markets.

A pivotal shift occurred in the late 1990s and early 2000s with the adoption of machine learning, particularly neural networks. These systems, capable of learning from data, brought a more dynamic and flexible approach to financial modeling. Neural networks were applied to tasks such as pattern recognition, stock price prediction, and risk management. The 2000s marked the era of algorithmic trading, with AI-driven algorithms playing a central role. High-frequency trading (HFT) algorithms emerged, executing trades at speeds beyond human capability and reacting to market changes in fractions of a second. This period witnessed a transition toward more sophisticated AI-driven trading strategies.

Recent Developments

The advent of big data technologies and increased computational power in the 2010s further propelled AI applications in finance. Machine learning models, fueled by vast datasets, became adept at analyzing market trends, identifying patterns, and making predictions. Sentiment analysis through natural language processing (NLP) gained prominence, extracting insights from news articles, social media, and financial reports. Robo-advisors, another significant development, characterized the latter part of the 2010s. These platforms leveraged AI algorithms to provide personalized investment advice based on individual preferences, risk tolerance, and financial goals. This marked a shift toward more accessible and automated portfolio management.

In the current decade, AI in the stock market continues to evolve with advancements in deep learning, reinforcement learning, and the integration of alternative data sources such as satellite imagery and social media trends. AI is now employed for market surveillance, fraud detection, and dynamic pricing strategies.

The history of AI in the stock market reflects a journey of continuous adaptation and innovation. From early attempts at rule-based systems to the current era of sophisticated machine learning models, AI has reshaped how financial markets operate and how investment decisions are made. The ongoing evolution underscores the transformative impact of AI on the financial industry, with implications for the future of stock market dynamics.

TRADING AND ANALYSIS

This section discusses how AI has significantly influenced stock market trading and analysis by introducing sophisticated algorithms that analyze vast datasets, identify patterns, and execute trades at remarkable speeds.

Algorithmic Trading

Algorithmic trading is a prominent facet of modern financial markets, where AI-driven algorithms play a pivotal role in executing transactions with unparalleled speed and frequency, surpassing human capabilities. The application of artificial intelligence enables algorithms to swiftly respond to market fluctuations, capitalize on opportunities, and manage risks at a scale and pace that would be unattainable through manual trading. High-frequency trading, a subset of algorithmic trading, leverages AI to execute a large number of orders within fractions of a second, capitalizing on small price differentials across various securities.

In this dynamic landscape, machine learning models form the backbone of algorithmic trading strategies. These models meticulously analyze vast volumes of market data, ranging from historical prices and trading volumes to macroeconomic indicators. Through pattern recognition and trend identification, machine learning algorithms discern subtle signals within the data, unveiling potential market movements and opportunities. This data-driven approach not only enhances the efficiency of automated trading decisions, but also allows for adaptability as models continuously learn and evolve based on new information. The synthesis of AI and algorithmic trading has reshaped the financial landscape, ushering in an era of sophisticated, data-driven strategies that seek to optimize trading outcomes in today's fast-paced and complex markets.

Predictive Analytics

AI has become a formidable force in predicting stock price movements and market trends by harnessing the power of historical and real-time data. Machine learning models, equipped with advanced algorithms, meticulously analyze extensive datasets that encompass historical stock prices, trading volumes, and a myriad of market indicators. These models sift through vast amounts of information, discerning patterns and relationships that may elude human analysis. By identifying correlations and leveraging statistical techniques, AI models generate predictions about potential future price movements. The ability to process and interpret both historical and real-time data empowers these models to make informed forecasts, offering investors valuable insights into market dynamics.

Sentiment analysis, another facet of AI's impact on stock market prediction, involves the evaluation of market sentiment through the analysis of news articles, social media, and financial reports. Natural language processing algorithms dissect textual content, gauging the tone and context of information disseminated across various platforms. By assessing the sentiment expressed in news articles, tweets, or financial reports, AI models can infer the collective mood of market participants. Positive or negative sentiment can be indicative of market trends or potential shifts in investor sentiment, influencing stock prices. Integrating sentiment analysis into stock market predictions adds a layer of qualitative data to quantitative models, providing a more comprehensive understanding of market dynamics and contributing to more nuanced and informed decision-making.

Quantitative Analysis

AI's impact on quantitative analysis in stock market investing is transformative, primarily due to its unparalleled ability to process vast datasets swiftly and efficiently. Quantitative analysis relies on crunching numbers, identifying trends, and extracting meaningful insights from a plethora of financial data. Traditional methods often struggle to handle the sheer volume and complexity of this data, leading to time-consuming processes and potential oversights. AI, however, excels in this domain by leveraging advanced algorithms and computing power.

Machine learning models, a subset of AI, play a crucial role in quantitative analysis. These models are designed to identify statistical patterns and correlations within the datasets, providing quantitative analysts with valuable insights. By analyzing historical market data and real-time information, these models can uncover hidden relationships and trends that may not be apparent through traditional analytical methods. The ability to recognize intricate patterns in financial data empowers investors to make data-driven and informed decisions. In essence, AI-driven quantitative analysis contributes to more robust investment strategies, enabling market participants to navigate the complexities of the stock market with greater precision and efficiency.

Pattern Recognition

AI algorithms have revolutionized the way investors analyze and interpret financial data by leveraging advanced pattern recognition capabilities. These algorithms excel at identifying intricate patterns and trends within vast datasets, providing investors with valuable insights that may not be apparent through traditional analytical methods. Through machine learning models, AI can discern subtle relationships and correlations in financial data, unveiling hidden opportunities or potential risks.

One of the key advantages of AI in this context is its ability to handle large volumes of data in real-time. These algorithms process information swiftly, allowing investors to stay ahead of market movements and make timely decisions. Whether it is recognizing market trends, identifying potential investment opportunities, or assessing risk factors, AI algorithms offer a sophisticated and data-driven approach to financial analysis. By employing these tools, investors can gain a more comprehensive understanding of the dynamics influencing financial markets, empowering them to make more informed and strategic investment decisions.

Market Forecasting

AI algorithms have revolutionized the way investors approach market analysis by leveraging advanced techniques to process a vast array of data sources. These algorithms go beyond traditional analysis methods, incorporating various economic indicators, geopolitical events, and global trends into their models. By examining a broad spectrum of data, AI algorithms can identify complex patterns and correlations that might elude human analysts. This comprehensive approach allows for a more nuanced understanding of the factors influencing overall market conditions.

The ability of AI algorithms to forecast market conditions is grounded in their capacity to adapt and learn from historical and real-time data. Machine learning models continuously refine their predictions based on new information, ensuring that the analysis remains dynamic and responsive to evolving market dynamics. Investors benefit from these forecasts as they provide valuable insights into potential market trends, helping them make informed decisions on asset allocation, risk management, and overall investment strategy. The integration of AI-driven market forecasting has become an essential component for investors seeking a data-driven and forward-looking perspective on the complex and ever-changing landscape of financial markets.

Alternative Data Sources

Artificial intelligence plays a transformative role in financial analysis by harnessing alternative data sources to provide unique and nuanced insights into specific industries or companies. Traditionally, financial analysts relied on conventional datasets, but AI expands the horizons by incorporating nontraditional sources like satellite imagery, social media trends, and consumer behavior. The integration of these diverse datasets allows AI algorithms to uncover hidden correlations and trends that might not be evident through traditional analysis methods.

Satellite imagery, for example, can offer a real-time view of activities such as shipping traffic, crop growth, or infrastructure development, providing valuable indicators for industries like logistics, agriculture, or construction. Alternatively, social media trends and consumer behavior data can offer sentiment analysis and early signals of public perception, influencing stock movements. By processing and interpreting these different types of data sources, AI enhances the depth and accuracy of financial analysis, enabling investors to make more informed decisions. This sophisticated approach to data analysis positions AI as a powerful tool in gaining a competitive edge in financial markets.

OPERATIONS AND MARKET OVERSIGHT

AI has transformed stock market operations by automating processes, enhancing efficiency, and providing real-time insights for better decision-making. It also plays a crucial role in market oversight by enabling regulators to monitor trading activities, detect anomalies, and ensure compliance with regulations.

Market Surveillance

Artificial intelligence plays a pivotal role in market surveillance, significantly enhancing the capabilities of monitoring trading activities, identifying irregularities, and ensuring compliance with regulations. Traditional market surveillance methods faced challenges in processing the vast and complex datasets generated by modern financial markets. AI algorithms address these challenges by rapidly analyzing large volumes of data to detect patterns and anomalies that might indicate market manipulation, insider trading, or other illicit activities.

One of the key strengths of AI in market surveillance is its ability to adapt and learn from evolving market conditions. Machine learning models can continuously refine their understanding of normal market behavior, allowing them to identify abnormal activities more accurately over time. This adaptability is crucial in an environment where new trading strategies and technologies continually emerge. Additionally, AI-powered surveillance systems can provide real-time alerts and insights, enabling regulatory authorities to respond swiftly to potential violations. By leveraging AI in market surveillance, financial institutions and regulatory bodies can enhance the integrity and transparency of financial markets, fostering a more secure and trustworthy trading environment.

Dynamic Pricing

Artificial intelligence is a transformative force in the realm of dynamic pricing strategies, particularly in the context of adjusting stock prices in real-time based on market demand and supply dynamics. Traditional pricing models often struggle to keep pace with the rapid and complex fluctuations inherent in financial markets. AI algorithms, however, excel at processing vast datasets and identifying patterns, enabling them to swiftly analyze market conditions and adjust stock prices dynamically.

Machine learning models play a crucial role in dynamic pricing by learning from historical market data and adapting to changing circumstances. These models can recognize trends, correlations, and anomalies, providing a more nuanced understanding of market dynamics. By continuously updating pricing strategies based on real-time information, businesses and investors can optimize their pricing decisions to align with market demand, maximize profitability, and respond promptly to changing economic conditions. The use of AI in dynamic pricing not only enhances the efficiency of pricing mechanisms but also enables organizations to stay competitive in fast-paced and volatile financial environments.

Portfolio Management

AI algorithms play a pivotal role in optimizing investment portfolios, incorporating factors such as risk tolerance, investment goals, and market conditions. Machine learning models, armed with vast datasets, identify optimal asset allocations tailored to an investor's financial profile. Historical performance, market trends, and economic indicators are analyzed, allowing these algorithms to craft portfolios aligned with investor objectives amid the dynamic nature of financial markets.

Automated portfolio rebalancing is a key application, adapting strategies to changing market dynamics. As conditions evolve, AI-driven systems monitor and realign portfolio allocations with predefined objectives. By automating this process, AI enhances portfolio resilience and performance. Additionally, AI-driven robo-advisors provide personalized, data-driven investment advice. These platforms leverage algorithms to analyze individual preferences, risk tolerance, and financial goals, democratizing financial planning and investment management by swiftly processing large datasets and executing unbiased investment decisions.

Risk Management

AI tools have revolutionized the assessment and management of risks in the realm of stock market investing. These tools leverage advanced algorithms to analyze a multitude of factors contributing to market dynamics. Market volatility, macroeconomic indicators, and geopolitical events are scrutinized in real-time, allowing AI systems to gauge potential risks and their potential impact on investment portfolios. By processing vast amounts of data at speeds beyond human capacity, AI tools can swiftly identify patterns and correlations that may signify elevated risk levels. This proactive risk analysis enables investors to stay ahead of potential threats to their portfolios and take timely measures to mitigate adverse effects.

Predictive models, powered by machine learning, represent a cornerstone of AI-driven risk management. These models use historical and real-time data to forecast potential risks and their likelihood of occurrence. By identifying patterns indicative of risk, AI tools empower investors to make informed decisions and implement risk-mitigation strategies. Whether it is anticipating market downturns, responding to economic shifts, or navigating geopolitical uncertainties, these predictive models provide investors with a comprehensive understanding of potential risks. In doing so, AI tools contribute to a more proactive and adaptive approach to risk management in stock market investing.

Fraud Detection

AI plays a pivotal role in safeguarding the integrity of the stock market by actively detecting and preventing fraudulent activities. One key area where AI excels is in identifying insider trading and market manipulation. Machine learning models are trained on vast datasets containing historical instances of fraudulent activities, enabling them to learn intricate patterns and characteristics associated with such behaviors. This training empowers AI systems to distinguish between normal market activities and suspicious transactions that may indicate fraudulent practices.

Pattern recognition and anomaly detection algorithms are at the forefront of AI's capabilities in this domain. These algorithms continuously analyze market data, transaction histories, and other relevant information to identify irregularities or deviations from expected patterns. Unusual trading volumes, rapid price movements, or abnormal order placements can be flagged as potential indicators of fraudulent activities. By leveraging these AI-driven tools, regulatory bodies, financial institutions, and market participants can stay vigilant against illicit activities, fostering a fair and transparent stock market environment. The proactive nature of AI in recognizing patterns associated with fraud contributes significantly to maintaining the integrity of financial markets.

INTERACTIVE AI APPLICATIONS

AI interactive applications have revolutionized the stock market by offering investors advanced tools for analysis, prediction, and decision-making. These applications leverage machine learning algorithms to provide personalized insights, helping traders navigate the complexities of the market with greater precision and speed.

Natural Language Processing

NLP has become a pivotal technology in the financial sector, particularly in the realm of extracting actionable insights from a vast sea of textual data. Financial news, reports, and earnings calls are rich sources of information, but their sheer volume makes manual analysis impractical. NLP algorithms are designed to understand and interpret human language, enabling them to sift through extensive textual data quickly and efficiently. By processing financial news articles, reports, and transcripts of earnings calls, NLP systems can identify key information, market sentiments, and emerging trends.

One of the primary applications of NLP in finance is sentiment analysis, where algorithms gauge the overall sentiment expressed in textual content. This sentiment analysis plays a crucial role in decision-making, helping investors and financial professionals assess the market's mood and sentiment toward specific stocks or sectors. Additionally, NLP is used to extract relevant information about financial events, market-moving news, and company performance from unstructured textual data. As a result, NLP contributes significantly to informed decision-making in the financial industry, offering a more efficient and data-driven approach to extracting valuable insights from the vast ocean of financial information available.

Customer Service and Chatbots

AI-powered chatbots have become invaluable tools in the realm of stock market investing, offering investors real-time assistance and enhancing their overall experience. These chatbots are designed to understand natural language queries and provide accurate and up-to-date information on stocks and market conditions. Investors can interact with these bots through various channels, including websites, messaging platforms, and dedicated applications. The immediate accessibility of information is particularly beneficial for investors who need quick insights or have specific questions about their investments.

The capabilities of AI-powered chatbots extend beyond basic information retrieval. They can analyze vast datasets and market trends, offering personalized recommendations based on individual investment profiles and preferences. For instance, a chatbot might provide tailored insights on potential investment opportunities, portfolio diversification, or risk management strategies. The real-time nature of these interactions enables investors to make more informed decisions promptly. Additionally, AI chatbots contribute to democratizing access to financial information, leveling the playing field by providing retail investors with sophisticated tools that were once exclusive to institutional players. In this way, AI-powered chatbots play a pivotal role in making stock market information more accessible, understandable, and actionable for a broader audience.

19

AI Risks and How to Mitigate Them

Artificial intelligence in the stock market presents a plethora of opportunities, revolutionizing the way investors make decisions and navigate the complexities of financial markets. It's widely known that this transformative technology is not without its challenges and risks. As we delve into the realm of AI-driven stock market activities, it becomes crucial to recognize and understand the potential pitfalls that may arise. These risks range from algorithmic errors and biased decision-making to the lack of transpasrency in complex AI models.

Acknowledging these challenges is essential for developing robust mitigation strategies, ensuring that the deployment of AI in the stock market aligns with ethical standards, fairness, and investor confidence. In the following sections, we delve into each risk, offering insights into their nature, impact, and strategies to mitigate their adverse effects on stock market dynamics.

RISKS

The integration of artificial intelligence into the stock market introduces many risks, such as algorithmic errors, cybersecurity threats, and market manipulation, which are discussed in this section.

Algorithmic Bias and Opacity

The integration of AI in stock market investing brings forth the potential challenge of algorithmic bias and opacity. AI algorithms, crucial components in decision-making processes, operate based on historical data which can be biased. When AI algorithms are trained on biased historical data, there is a real concern that these biases can be perpetuated and, in some cases, even amplified. This phenomenon becomes particularly problematic when dealing with sensitive issues such as gender or racial disparities within the market. For instance, if historical data reflects existing inequalities, AI algorithms may inadvertently incorporate and perpetuate these biases, resulting in unfair and discriminatory outcomes.

The ramifications of algorithmic bias and opacity extend beyond mere technical intricacies, influencing the very fabric of market practices. The unintentional reinforcement of historical biases through AI decision-making processes raises questions about the fairness and equity of market outcomes, necessitating careful consideration and evaluation of the role of AI in stock market investing.

Overreliance on Historical Data

In the realm of stock market investing, AI models play a pivotal role by leveraging historical data to discern patterns and trends, facilitating predictive analytics. This reliance on historical data introduces a significant risk—the potential inadequacy of such data to capture unforeseen events or sudden market shifts. Financial markets are inherently dynamic, susceptible to external shocks, geopolitical events, or economic changes that may not have clear parallels in historical datasets. Therefore, while AI models excel at processing and learning from historical information, their adaptability in navigating uncharted territory or responding to unprecedented events is of critical concern.

The risk associated with overreliance on historical trends is not merely theoretical; it has practical implications for the effectiveness of AI models in real-world scenarios. Market conditions can evolve rapidly, and unforeseen events, such as global crises or technological breakthroughs, can disrupt established patterns. Investors and financial institutions need to be cognizant of this limitation and work toward enhancing the resilience of AI models by incorporating mechanisms that allow them to adapt to changing dynamics, beyond the scope of historical data. Balancing the utilization of historical trends with a forward-looking and adaptive approach is key to ensuring the robustness of AI-driven strategies in the face of unpredictable market developments.

Transparency

The lack of transparency in artificial intelligence systems presents a significant risk, as it undermines the accountability and trustworthiness of these technologies. Many advanced AI algorithms, particularly those based on complex machine learning models, often operate as "black boxes," making it challenging for users and stakeholders to comprehend the decision-making processes behind their outputs. This opacity can lead to a lack of insight into how AI systems arrive at specific conclusions, raising concerns about bias, fairness, and ethical considerations.

In contexts where AI influences critical decisions, such as healthcare diagnostics or financial transactions, the absence of transparency can result in unintended consequences and hinder the identification and rectification of errors or biases. Striking a balance between protecting proprietary information and providing sufficient transparency is essential to address these risks and ensure that AI systems are deployed responsibly and ethically.

Lack of Interpretability

One significant risk associated with artificial intelligence is the lack of interpretability, which refers to the challenge of understanding and explaining the decision-making processes of complex AI algorithms. As AI systems, particularly machine learning models, become more intricate and sophisticated, their internal workings often become opaque, making it difficult for users to comprehend how specific decisions are reached. This lack of interpretability not only raises concerns about accountability and transparency but also poses potential dangers in critical domains such as finance, healthcare, and criminal justice.

In situations where AI algorithms influence consequential decisions, the inability to interpret their reasoning can lead to a loss of trust and confidence. Moreover, it can hinder the identification and mitigation of biases, exacerbating the risk of unintended and unjust consequences. Addressing the challenge of interpretability is crucial for fostering responsible and ethical AI deployment, ensuring that AI systems are not only powerful but also understandable and accountable.

Data Bias

The risk associated with biased data in AI models poses a substantial challenge in the domain of stock market investing. As AI algorithms heavily rely on historical datasets for training, the inherent biases within these datasets can lead to distorted predictions and, consequently, biased investment decisions. These biases often originate from historical data that mirrors societal or systemic biases prevalent in financial markets, introducing a layer of complexity to the decision-making processes of AI models.

In practical terms, if historical data exhibits disparities in the treatment of specific demographic groups, industries, or regions, AI models trained on such datasets may inadvertently perpetuate and magnify these biases in their decision-making. This risk underscores the importance of critically examining and addressing biases within training data to enhance the fairness and reliability of AI applications in stock market contexts. Investors and developers alike must be cognizant of these challenges to foster a more equitable and unbiased landscape in stock market AI, ensuring that decision-making processes align with ethical and inclusive principles.

Cybersecurity Threats

The susceptibility of AI systems to cyberattacks introduces a significant risk, especially in the context of stock market activities. The interconnected nature of financial systems and the reliance on AI-driven technologies make them attractive targets for malicious actors. Cyberattacks targeting AI systems in stock market settings can take various forms, ranging from hacking attempts to more sophisticated methods such as data breaches and manipulation of AI-driven trading strategies.

Hacking incidents can compromise the integrity and confidentiality of sensitive financial data, posing severe consequences for both investors and financial institutions. Data breaches, another facet of this risk, can lead to the unauthorized access and dissemination of valuable market information, potentially influencing trading decisions. Additionally, the manipulation of AI-driven trading strategies introduces a layer of complexity, as attackers may exploit vulnerabilities in the algorithms to execute unauthorized trades or manipulate market conditions for their gain. As the financial industry continues to embrace AI technologies, safeguarding against cyberthreats becomes paramount to ensure the stability and integrity of stock market operations.

Market Manipulation

The risk associated with malicious actors exploiting vulnerabilities in AI systems poses a significant threat to the integrity of stock market operations. These actors may target weaknesses in the algorithms, data processing pipelines, or communication channels within AI systems to manipulate market conditions for their gain. Market manipulation could take various forms, such as spreading false information, executing unauthorized trades, or influencing trading patterns to create artificial fluctuations. The potential impact of such manipulations can extend beyond financial losses, affecting market stability, investor confidence, and the overall credibility of the financial system.

Malicious activities by external actors also include engaging in fraudulent schemes that leverage vulnerabilities in AI-driven processes. This could involve unauthorized access to sensitive financial data, identity theft, or fraudulent transactions. By exploiting weaknesses in AI models or their implementation, attackers may compromise the accuracy and reliability of financial information, leading to deceptive market behaviors. The risk of such malicious activities underscores the importance of implementing robust security measures to protect AI systems from unauthorized access and manipulation, ensuring the trustworthiness and resilience of stock market operations.

Systematic Risks

The widespread adoption of similar AI strategies in the stock market introduces a notable risk: the potential amplification of market volatility and the contribution to systemic risks. As more market participants incorporate similar AI-driven algorithms and models, there is an increased likelihood of synchronized behavior in response to market events. This homogeneity in strategies can lead to cascading effects, where a large number of automated trading systems respond in a similar fashion to specific triggers, such as economic indicators or unexpected news.

The risk of amplified market volatility is particularly heightened during periods of uncertainty or rapid market changes. If a substantial portion of market participants employs comparable AI strategies, the simultaneous execution of trades based on similar algorithms can exacerbate price movements. This interconnectedness and the rapid pace at which AI-driven systems operate may contribute to market fluctuations, creating challenges for traditional risk management mechanisms. As a result, the potential for systemic risks emerges, where the actions of AI-driven algorithms, if not well-coordinated or diversified, could lead to unintended consequences for the broader financial system.

Ethical Concerns

The integration of AI applications in the stock market introduces ethical considerations that extend beyond the realm of technological risk. One of the foremost concerns is the issue of fairness in algorithmic decision-making. AI models, when trained on historical data that may contain biases, can perpetuate and even exacerbate existing inequalities. This introduces the risk of discrimination, as AI systems may unintentionally favor or disadvantage certain demographic groups, industries, or regions based on historical data patterns.

Another ethical concern associated with AI in the stock market is accountability. As these systems operate on complex algorithms and vast datasets, understanding the exact rationale behind their decisions can be challenging. The opacity of AI decision-making poses difficulties in holding entities accountable for the consequences of their actions. The lack of transparency can erode trust among investors, regulatory bodies, and the general public, raising questions about who bears responsibility for unfavorable outcomes or unintended consequences resulting from AI-driven strategies. Additionally, there are concerns about the potential impact on employment within the financial sector, as the automation of certain tasks through AI applications may lead to workforce displacement and necessitate adaptations in skillsets for industry professionals.

Lack of Human Oversight

The risk of excessive reliance on AI without adequate human oversight poses a significant concern in the stock market. As AI systems become more sophisticated, there is a potential for these systems to autonomously make trading decisions without proper checks and balances. The absence of human oversight may lead to unchecked algorithmic trading, where AI-driven models execute decisions without considering the broader market context or unforeseen events. This lack of human intervention raises the risk of unintended consequences, as AI systems may struggle to adapt to rapidly changing market conditions or unforeseen events that were not accounted for in their training data.

Furthermore, the risk of unchecked trading decisions becomes more pronounced when AI systems encounter scenarios that deviate from their training data or face unprecedented market dynamics. Human oversight is essential in such situations to assess the appropriateness of AI-generated decisions and intervene if necessary. The challenge lies in finding the right balance between leveraging AI for its efficiency and incorporating human judgment to ensure prudence and adaptability in response to evolving market conditions. Striking this balance is crucial to prevent the potential negative impacts of excessive reliance on AI and to foster a symbiotic relationship between AI and human decision-making in the stock market.

Legal and Regulatory Challenges

The rapid advancements in AI within the stock market pose a notable risk, as the pace of innovation may outstrip the development of regulatory frameworks. This misalignment can result in legal uncertainties and potential regulatory gaps, creating challenges for oversight and enforcement. The dynamic and complex nature of AI technologies may present difficulties for regulators in keeping pace with emerging capabilities, making it challenging to establish clear guidelines and rules to govern AI-driven activities in the financial sector.

The risk of regulatory lag becomes more pronounced as AI applications evolve and become integral to various aspects of stock market operations. Issues such as algorithmic trading, robo-advisory services, and other AI-driven functions may not be adequately addressed by existing regulatory structures, leaving room for ambiguity and potential loopholes. As a consequence, this regulatory lag could impede the industry's ability to maintain a fair, transparent, and secure financial environment. Addressing this risk requires a proactive and collaborative approach between industry stakeholders, policymakers, and regulatory bodies to ensure that regulatory frameworks evolve in tandem with the rapid advancements in AI technologies, fostering an environment that balances innovation with effective oversight.

HOW TO MITIGATE RISKS

It is essential that the risks associated with the integration of AI in the stock market be mitigated, without which trust in the market can be seriously eroded. This section discusses the key mitigation steps that can be taken to reduce the AI-related risks.

Algorithmic Bias

Recognizing the potential for bias in AI algorithms, techniques like fairness-aware machine learning and continuous monitoring are being employed to identify and rectify discriminatory patterns in decision-making. The challenge of opacity in AI models, particularly complex ones like neural networks, is being addressed through the development of explainable AI (XAI) techniques. XAI aims to enhance transparency by providing insights into the decision-making process, allowing stakeholders to scrutinize and understand AI-driven decisions. This dual focus on fairness and transparency underscores the ethical considerations in deploying AI technologies in stock market contexts.

To address algorithmic error risks in the stock market, a comprehensive approach is adopted, involving meticulous testing, fail-safe mechanisms, and continuous monitoring. Rigorous testing procedures during development identify and rectify potential vulnerabilities, using simulations and backtesting to assess algorithm performance under diverse market conditions. Fail-safe mechanisms and circuit breakers play a critical role in risk mitigation, automatically halting trading activities in the presence of anomalies or errors to prevent losses and market disruptions. Continuous monitoring ensures prompt identification and resolution of any issues, striking a balance between the efficiency of AI-driven algorithmic trading and the need to mitigate inherent risks in the dynamic stock market environment.

Overreliance on Historical Data

The risk associated with overreliance on historical data in AI models is a pertinent concern in the stock market. Relying solely on past trends may limit the adaptability of AI algorithms, especially in dynamic market conditions where unforeseen events and shifts can significantly impact stock movements. To address this risk, financial institutions adopt proactive measures centered on the integration of real-time data. By incorporating up-to-the-minute information into AI models, these institutions aim to ensure that algorithms remain responsive to current market dynamics, allowing them to identify and react to events that may deviate from historical patterns.

Furthermore, machine learning models play a crucial role in mitigating the risk of overreliance on historical data. These models are designed with the capability to continuously learn and evolve based on new information. By updating their understanding of market trends and dynamics in real time, machine learning algorithms reduce the potential drawbacks of relying solely on historical data. This adaptive learning approach enhances the overall flexibility and resilience of AI systems, enabling them to navigate the intricacies of the stock market with a more nuanced and informed perspective.

Transparency

Mitigating AI transparency risks in the stock market is paramount to ensure fair and accountable financial practices. Employing XAI techniques is a crucial strategy in this context. By enhancing the interpretability of complex AI algorithms used in stock market activities, XAI provides stakeholders, including regulators and investors, with insights into the decision-making processes. This transparency not only helps in identifying and addressing potential biases but also enables a better understanding of how AI models operate in the dynamic and fast-paced stock market environment. Moreover, ongoing R&D in XAI contributes to the establishment of standardized practices for transparency, fostering consistent evaluation and scrutiny of AI models in financial contexts.

Regulatory frameworks also play a pivotal role in mitigating transparency risks associated with AI in the stock market. Governments and financial regulatory bodies are increasingly recognizing the importance of clear guidelines and standards for transparency in algorithmic trading and investment strategies. Implementing regulations that mandate disclosure of AI decision-making processes, especially in sectors with significant financial impact, serves as a safeguard against opacity and unethical practices. Striking the right balance between safeguarding proprietary information and providing sufficient transparency ensures that the integration of AI in the stock market aligns with ethical and regulatory standards, promoting trust and confidence in financial markets.

Lack of Interpretability

Addressing the intricacies of AI models and enhancing transparency requires a multifaceted approach. First, there is a critical need to develop AI models with interpretability features, allowing for a clearer understanding of the decision-making process. This involves designing algorithms that provide insights into the key variables and considerations influencing specific investment decisions. By making the inner workings of AI models more accessible, investors and stakeholders can gain a better understanding of how these models arrive at their conclusions.

Additionally, fostering transparency in the overall decision-making processes of AI models is paramount. Regulatory frameworks play a crucial role in achieving this goal by mandating the disclosure of key aspects of AI-driven strategies. This regulatory intervention empowers investors with essential information needed to make informed decisions, contributing to a more informed and accountable financial ecosystem. Emphasizing these aspects not only helps address the challenges associated with reduced transparency in AI models but also promotes the responsible and ethical deployment of AI in stock market activities. This approach aligns with the broader industry goals of ensuring that AI technologies are leveraged in a manner that enhances trust, accountability, and the overall integrity of financial markets.

Data Bias

Mitigating the risk associated with biased data in AI models necessitates a multifaceted approach. First and foremost, there is a critical need for diligent and ethical data curation during the model development phase. This involves identifying and addressing biases present in the training data, actively working to ensure that the data used to train AI models is representative and free from systemic prejudices. Rigorous scrutiny of the dataset helps to eliminate or minimize biases that could impact the model's decision-making processes.

Moreover, ongoing monitoring and auditing of AI algorithms are essential to identify and rectify biases that may emerge during their deployment. The financial industry must embrace a commitment to ethical AI practices, promoting transparency and fairness in data selection and model development. By actively engaging in continuous evaluation and improvement processes, financial institutions can ensure that their AI systems evolve responsibly, minimizing the risk of biased predictions in stock market activities. This commitment to ethical data practices not only aligns with industry standards but also serves to enhance the integrity and trustworthiness of AI applications in the financial sector.

Cybersecurity Threats

To mitigate the risk of cyberattacks on AI systems in the stock market, implementing comprehensive cybersecurity measures is essential. Robust cybersecurity protocols involve the adoption of encryption techniques to secure sensitive financial data and transactions processed by AI systems. Encryption plays a crucial role in safeguarding information, ensuring that even if unauthorized access occurs, the intercepted data remains unreadable and protected. This measure adds a layer of defense against potential breaches that could compromise the confidentiality and integrity of financial information.

Regular security audits represent another vital component of mitigation strategies. These audits involve systematic assessments of the AI systems' security infrastructure, identifying potential vulnerabilities, and weaknesses. Conducting routine security audits allows for the detection and remediation of any emerging threats or vulnerabilities before they can be exploited. By staying proactive in assessing and fortifying the security posture of AI systems, financial institutions and organizations can significantly reduce the likelihood of successful cyberattacks and enhance the overall resilience of their AI-driven stock market operations.

Market Manipulation

To mitigate the risk of malicious actors exploiting vulnerabilities in AI systems for market manipulation, robust market surveillance mechanisms, and regulatory oversight are essential. Implementing advanced surveillance technologies enables the continuous monitoring of market activities, allowing for the detection of irregularities and suspicious patterns indicative of manipulation. Automated surveillance systems, often powered by AI themselves, can analyze vast amounts of trading data in real time, identifying anomalies that may suggest fraudulent activities.

Regulatory oversight plays a crucial role in establishing and enforcing rules and standards that govern the use of AI in financial markets. Regulatory bodies collaborate with industry participants to develop guidelines that address potential vulnerabilities and risks associated with AI-driven systems. By establishing clear regulatory frameworks, authorities can ensure that financial institutions adhere to best practices, implement necessary security measures, and promptly report any incidents of market manipulation. Regular audits and inspections contribute to maintaining the integrity of the financial ecosystem, instilling confidence in market participants, and reinforcing the stability of AI-driven processes in stock market operations.

Systematic Risks

Diversifying AI strategies is a crucial element in mitigating the risk associated with the widespread adoption of similar AI approaches in the stock market. By encouraging market participants to employ a variety of AI-driven algorithms and models, the financial ecosystem can reduce the likelihood of synchronized behavior and herd mentality among automated trading systems. Diversification introduces heterogeneity in trading strategies, making it less likely that a significant portion of the market will react in the same way to specific events, thereby mitigating the risk of amplified market volatility.

In addition to diversification, regulatory oversight plays a pivotal role in managing the potential systemic risks arising from AI-driven strategies. Regulatory bodies can establish frameworks and guidelines that promote responsible and transparent use of AI in financial markets. Close monitoring of market participants using AI, periodic audits, and the enforcement of standards can help ensure that AI systems are aligned with market integrity and stability. By fostering a regulatory environment that addresses the unique challenges posed by AI in the financial sector, authorities can contribute to the overall resilience and soundness of the market.

Ethical Concerns

Mitigating the ethical concerns associated with AI applications in the stock market involves a multifaceted approach. One key aspect is the establishment of clear ethical guidelines that govern the development, deployment, and use of AI systems. These guidelines should emphasize fairness, transparency, and accountability, setting a framework for responsible AI practices within the financial industry. Additionally, ensuring accountability in AI decision-making is crucial. This involves implementing mechanisms that allow for the traceability of decisions back to their underlying algorithms and datasets. Accountability measures can include documentation of model development processes, transparent reporting, and external audits to assess compliance with ethical guidelines.

Addressing societal concerns regarding the ethical implications of AI in the stock market also requires regulatory frameworks. Regulatory bodies play a vital role in overseeing the adoption and impact of AI technologies, ensuring that they align with ethical standards and do not harm public interests. The development of regulations that encompass fairness, transparency, and accountability principles can provide a legal framework to govern the ethical use of AI in financial markets. Striking a balance between fostering innovation and safeguarding ethical considerations is essential, and regulatory bodies need to adapt and evolve alongside advancements in AI technology to effectively address emerging ethical challenges.

Lack of Human Oversight

The integration of human oversight in decision-making processes involving AI is imperative to ensure responsible and accountable practices. While AI systems offer remarkable efficiency and automation, they may lack the nuanced judgment and ethical considerations that humans bring to complex decision-making scenarios. Human oversight allows for the evaluation of AI-generated decisions within a broader context, considering factors such as ethical implications, societal impacts, and unforeseen circumstances that might not be explicitly encoded in the algorithms.

Setting predefined limits and maintaining control over AI systems further enhances risk management. Establishing clear boundaries for AI algorithms helps mitigate the risk of unchecked actions or decisions that may lead to unintended consequences. By defining parameters and limits within which AI operates, organizations can prevent undesirable outcomes and ensure that AI aligns with ethical standards and regulatory requirements. Additionally, maintaining control over AI systems involves continuous monitoring, updating, and refining algorithms to adapt to changing market conditions and evolving ethical considerations. The combination of human oversight, predefined limits, and ongoing control mechanisms is essential for harnessing the benefits of AI while responsibly managing the associated risks in decision-making processes.

Legal and Regulatory Challenges

Effectively addressing the risk associated with regulatory uncertainties in AI applications within the stock market involves proactive collaboration with regulatory bodies and a commitment to staying informed about legal developments. Engaging in a collaborative dialogue with regulators allows financial institutions and AI developers to provide insights into the technology's intricacies and potential risks, fostering a mutual understanding that can lead to more informed and targeted regulatory frameworks. Regular consultations and feedback mechanisms between industry experts and regulatory authorities can contribute to the formulation of rules that strike a balance between encouraging innovation and safeguarding the integrity of the financial system.

Staying abreast of legal developments is paramount for organizations leveraging AI in the stock market. This involves establishing robust mechanisms to monitor changes in laws and regulations related to AI applications, ensuring that the implemented technologies align with evolving legal requirements. Proactive adaptation to regulatory changes involves a continuous assessment of AI systems to ensure compliance with the latest standards. Companies can invest in legal expertise or collaborate with legal professionals specializing in AI and finance to navigate the complex regulatory landscape effectively. By embracing a proactive and collaborative approach, market participants can contribute to the development of regulatory frameworks that foster innovation while maintaining the necessary safeguards in the dynamic landscape of AI-driven stock market activities.

AI Risk Mitigation in the Stock Market

Navigating the intricate landscape of AI risks in the stock market necessitates a multifaceted and vigilant approach. As the financial industry continues to harness the power of artificial intelligence, understanding and mitigating these risks are imperative for fostering a resilient, and trustworthy financial ecosystem. Robust mitigation strategies, including transparency initiatives, ethical considerations, and proactive regulatory collaboration, form the cornerstone of a comprehensive risk management framework. By embracing these strategies, market participants can not only harness the potential benefits of AI but also contribute to the establishment of a secure and sustainable foundation for the future of AI-driven stock market activities. In this ever-evolving landscape, the symbiotic relationship between technological innovation and risk management will play a pivotal role in shaping the future of financial markets, ensuring their integrity, resilience, and adherence to ethical standards. The ongoing commitment to diligence and adaptability will be essential as the financial industry progresses into a future where AI is an integral part of stock market operations.

INDEX

www.ingramcontent.com/pod-product-compliance
Lightning Source LLC
Chambersburg PA
CBHW060808220326
41598CB00022B/2566